Dynamics of Virtual Work

Series Editors
Ursula Huws, Analytica Social and Economic Research,
London, UK
Rosalind Gill, Department of Sociology, City, University of
London, London, UK

Technological change has transformed where people work, when and how. Digitisation of information has altered labour processes out of all recognition whilst telecommunications have enabled jobs to be relocated globally. ICTs have also enabled the creation of entirely new types of 'digital' or 'virtual' labour, both paid and unpaid, shifting the borderline between 'play' and 'work' and creating new types of unpaid labour connected with the consumption and co-creation of goods and services. This affects private life as well as transforming the nature of work and people experience the impacts differently depending on their gender, their age, where they live and what work they do. Aspects of these changes have been studied separately by many different academic experts however up till now a cohesive overarching analytical framework has been lacking. Drawing on a major, high-profile COST Action (European Cooperation in Science and Technology) Dynamics of Virtual Work, this series will bring together leading international experts from a wide range of disciplines including political economy, labour sociology, economic geography, communications studies, technology, gender studies, social psychology, organisation studies, industrial relations and development studies to explore the transformation of work and labour in the Internet Age. The series will allow researchers to speak across disciplinary boundaries, national borders, theoretical and political vocabularies, and different languages to understand and make sense of contemporary transformations in work and social life more broadly. The book series will build on and extend this, offering a new, important and intellectually exciting intervention into debates about work and labour, social theory, digital culture, gender, class, globalisation and economic, social and political change.

More information about this series at
https://link.springer.com/bookseries/14954

Mascha Will-Zocholl · Caroline Roth-Ebner
Editors

Topologies of Digital Work

How Digitalisation and Virtualisation Shape Working Spaces and Places

Editors
Mascha Will-Zocholl
Darmstadt, Hessen, Germany

Caroline Roth-Ebner
University of Klagenfurt
Klagenfurt, Austria

Dynamics of Virtual Work
ISBN 978-3-030-80326-1   ISBN 978-3-030-80327-8   (eBook)
https://doi.org/10.1007/978-3-030-80327-8

© The Editor(s) (if applicable) and The Author(s), under exclusive license to Springer Nature Switzerland AG 2021
Chapters 1, 4 and 11 are licensed under the terms of the Creative Commons Attribution 4.0 International License (http://creativecommons.org/licenses/by/4.0/). For further details see license information in the chapters.
This work is subject to copyright. All rights are solely and exclusively licensed by the Publisher, whether the whole or part of the material is concerned, specifically the rights of translation, reprinting, reuse of illustrations, recitation, broadcasting, reproduction on microfilms or in any other physical way, and transmission or information storage and retrieval, electronic adaptation, computer software, or by similar or dissimilar methodology now known or hereafter developed.
The use of general descriptive names, registered names, trademarks, service marks, etc. in this publication does not imply, even in the absence of a specific statement, that such names are exempt from the relevant protective laws and regulations and therefore free for general use.
The publisher, the authors and the editors are safe to assume that the advice and information in this book are believed to be true and accurate at the date of publication. Neither the publisher nor the authors or the editors give a warranty, expressed or implied, with respect to the material contained herein or for any errors or omissions that may have been made. The publisher remains neutral with regard to jurisdictional claims in published maps and institutional affiliations.

Cover illustration: © oxygen Getty Images

This Palgrave Macmillan imprint is published by the registered company Springer Nature Switzerland AG
The registered company address is: Gewerbestrasse 11, 6330 Cham, Switzerland

Acknowledgements

Published with the support of research funding provided by the Hessian University of Police and Administration and the Faculty of Humanities at the University of Klagenfurt.

Editing and formatting of the volume according to the publisher's specifications by Ina Tuttelberg, the editorial office Lektorat Tuttelberg (https://www.tuttelberg.de).

English proofreading by Karen Meehan.

Contents

1	**Introduction to Topologies of Digital Work** *Mascha Will-Zocholl and Caroline Roth-Ebner*	1
Part I	**Geographies of Digital Work**	
2	**The Geography of the Digital Freelance Economy in Russia and Beyond** *Andrey Shevchuk, Denis Strebkov, and Alexey Tyulyupo*	19
3	**Supporting the Global Digital Games Industry: Outsourcing Games Production in Poland and Estonia** *Anna Ozimek*	51
4	**Automating Labour and the Spatial Politics of Data Centre Technologies** *Brett Neilson and Ned Rossiter*	77

Part II Places of Work

5 Doing Homework Again: Places of Work from a Historical Perspective   105
Christian Oggolder

6 The Spatial Production of Wanghong: Political Economy, Labour Mobility and the "Unlikely" Creativity   121
Jian Lin

7 Reconfiguring Workplaces in Urban and Rural Areas: A Case Study of Shibuya and Shirahama, Japan   149
Keita Matsushita

Part III Virtual Working Spaces

8 ICT Enforced Boundary Work: Availability as a Sociomaterial Practice   173
Calle Rosengren, Ann Bergman, and Kristina Palm

9 Virtual Spaces, Intermediate Places: Doing Identity in ICT-Enabled Work   197
Dominik Klaus and Jörg Flecker

10 The Duality of the Physical and Virtual Worlds of Work   225
Ingrid Nappi and Gisele de Campos Ribeiro

Part IV Synopsis

11 Synopsis: How Space and Place Matter in the Context of Digital Work   263
Caroline Roth-Ebner and Mascha Will-Zocholl

Index   285

Notes on Contributors

Ann Bergman was professor of Working Life Science at Karlstad University, Sweden. Tragically, she passed away from an aggressive brain tumour during the process of finalising her chapter to this anthology. Her research interests were within the fields of gender, work and family, segregation and inequality, working conditions and well-being, and future studies. Bergman was involved in several national and international research projects in the field of critical working life studies. Her most recent research focused on the digitalisation of work, working conditions, and work–life boundaries. Together with Jan Ch. Karlsson she wrote the book *Methods for Social Theory: Analytical Tools for Theorizing and Writing* (2017, Routledge).

Gisele de Campos Ribeiro works as an Associate Professor at Paris School of Business, France. She graduated in Statistics from UFPR in Brazil, and she has a master's degree and a Ph.D. in Management Sciences, both from Paris-Dauphine University in France. Her research interests are in marketing and consumer behaviour, workplace management, employee well-being and productivity, the Internet of Things (IoT) applications in the workplace, and the psychological process linking office employees and their workplaces. Her research has been published in the *Journal of Business Ethics, Journal of Business Research,* and the *Journal of Corporate Real Estate*, among others.

Jörg Flecker has been a full professor of Sociology at the Department of Sociology, University of Vienna, Austria, since 2013. He was the scientific director of the Working Life Research Centre (FORBA) in Vienna from 1991 to 2013. His main research areas are labour process analysis, information technology, industrial relations, the labour market, as well as social change and the political far right. He is the editor of *Space, Place and Global Digital Work* (2016, Palgrave Macmillan), the author of *Arbeit und Beschäftigung* (2017, UTB) and the co-author of *The Class Origin of Young Blue-Collar Workers and Their Commitment to Work* (2020, Sage).

Dominik Klaus is a Ph.D. researcher at the Department of Sociology, University of Vienna, Austria, and a lecturer at the Vienna University of Business and Economics. In his Ph.D. project, he focuses on the blurring boundaries of work, new technologies, and aspects of recognition. His research interests include new forms of employment, virtual work, knowledge work, and sustainable work.

Jian Lin is assistant professor at the Centre for Media and Journalism Studies at the University of Groningen, The Netherlands. His research interests include cultural industries, social media culture, platform studies, and Chinese contemporary culture.

Keita Matsushita is a professor at the Faculty of Sociology at Kansai University, Japan. He received his Ph.D. from Kyoto University for his study of the impact of new media technology on school education. His main research interests are workstyle, workplace, and media communication. He has conducted many research projects and workshops for workplace design and social innovation in urban or local areas with major Japanese companies. His publications include *Workstyles in Mobile Media Society* (Keisoshobo, 2019), *Various Phases of Internet Society* (Gakubunsya, 2015), *Digital Natives and Social Media* (Kyoiku Hyoronsya, 2012).

Ingrid Nappi FRICS, has been a tenured research professor at ESSEC Business School, France, since 1995 and is holder of both the Real Estate and Sustainable Development Chair and the Workplace Management Research Chair. She concentrates her research mainly on sustainable cities and sustainable real estate as well as workspaces in organisations. She holds a doctorate in Economics from the University of Paris and completed her post-doctorate in the Real Estate Department of the Wharton School in Philadelphia. She holds two HDRs (Habilitation to Conduct Research) in Management and in Urban Design. She is CNU qualified for the university professor function. Currently, she serves as the President of the European Real Estate Society (ERES) for 2020/2021.

Brett Neilson is professor at the Institute for Culture and Society, Western Sydney University, Australia. Together with Sandro Mezzadra, he is author of *Border as Method, or, the Multiplication of Labor* (2013, Duke University Press) and *The Politics of Operations: Excavating Contemporary Capitalism* (2019, Duke University Press). With Ned Rossiter, he edits *Low Latencies*, a book series with Open Humanities Press.

Christian Oggolder is senior scientist at the Institute for Comparative Media and Communication Studies of the Austrian Academy of Sciences and the University of Klagenfurt (CMC), Vienna, Austria. His research focuses on media development and media change, media history, memory studies, and media literacy.

Anna M. Ozimek is a research associate at the Department of Theatre, Film, Television and Interactive Media at the University of York, United Kingdom. In 2018 she defended her Ph.D. thesis on Polish game workers at the University of Leeds, School of Media and Communication. Between 2019 and 2020 she carried out a research project on working conditions in the Estonian digital games industries (Tallinn University). Her research interests include the political economy of cultural industries, creative labour, and digital media industries.

Kristina Palm is an associate professor (docent) at the Department of Sustainable Production Development, KTH Royal Institute of Technology, researcher at the Department of Medical Management Center, Karolinska Institutet, and at the Department of Working Life Science at Karlstad University, Sweden. She has an interest in understanding different aspects of working life, from the working conditions of the individual worker to leadership and HRM. In recent years she has specialised within the area of work and digitalisation.

Calle Rosengren is associate professor (docent) at the Faculty of Engineering, Lund University, Sweden. His main area of research interest is ongoing relations among new technologies, organising structures, cultural norms, and work practices. More specifically, threats and possibilities in the transition of working time from the standard work week in which employees work in one location to an increasingly fluid situation where working time has become more diverse and flexible.

Ned Rossiter is director of Research at the Institute for Culture and Society and Professor of Communication at the School of Humanities and Communication Arts, Western Sydney University, Australia. He is the author of *Organized Networks: Media Theory, Creative Labor, New Institutions* (2006, NAi Publishers), *Software, Infrastructure, Labor: A Media Theory of Logistical Nightmares* (2016, Routledge) and (with Geert Lovink) *Organization After Social Media* (2018, Minor Compositions).

Caroline Roth-Ebner is associate professor at the University of Klagenfurt, Austria. Her main fields of research are mediatisation processes, above all in the area of work, and with a focus on the transformations of space and time. Moreover, she works on children and youth media use, questions of media pedagogy and media literacy, and the commercialisation and mediatisation of childhood. She has authored contributions, e.g. on *Spatial Phenomena of Mediatised Work* (2016, Palgrave Macmillan).

Andrey Shevchuk is associate professor and senior researcher at the Laboratory for Studies in Economic Sociology at the National Research University Higher School of Economics (HSE University), Moscow, Russia. His work primarily examines the development of freelance contracting and online labour markets in Russia. He also has an interest in economic sociology and comparative political economy.

Denis Strebkov is associate professor and deputy head at the School of Sociology and senior researcher at the Laboratory for Studies in

Economic Sociology at the National Research University Higher School of Economics (HSE University), Moscow, Russia. His work primarily examines the development of freelance contracting and online labour markets in Russia. He also has an interest in the sociology of cyberspace and the sociology of financial behaviour.

Alexey Tyulyupo is intern researcher at the Laboratory for Studies in Economic Sociology at the National Research University Higher School of Economics (HSE University), Moscow, Russia. He has an interest in economic sociology and focuses on using big data in labour market research.

Mascha Will-Zocholl is full professor of Sociology with a specialty in digitalisation of work and organisation at the Hessian University of Police and Administration (Wiesbaden), Germany. Her research focuses on relations of work, technology and organisation with an emphasis on spatial implications of digital work and employees' perspectives on changes in work. She has authored contributions, for example in *New Topologies of Work: Informatisation, Virtualisation and Globalisation in Automotive Engineering* (2016, Palgrave Macmillan). Currently she is board member of the Sociology of Work and Industry Section in Germany and the TWR Network.

List of Figures

Chapter 2

Fig. 1	The density of freelancers in Russian cities depending on their whole population in 2018	33
Fig. 2	Number of clients per 100 freelancers in different countries in 2018	35
Fig. 3	Share of reviews left for freelancers by clients from different countries from 2005 to 2018 (percentages)	36
Fig. 4	Share of reviews left for freelancers by clients from main Russian cities and different federal districts from 2005 to 2018 (percentages)	37
Fig. 5	The share of freelancers from different countries on FL.ru from 2005 to 2018 (percentages)	40
Fig. 6	The share of clients from different countries on FL.ru in 2005 to 2018 (percentages)	41
Fig. 7	The share of freelancers from Russian regions on FL.ru from 2005 to 2018 (percentages)	42
Fig. 8	The share of clients from Russian regions on FL.ru from 2005 to 2018 (percentages)	43

Chapter 10

Fig. 1 The telework practice. n = 2,643 — 248
Fig. 2 The frequency of teleworking practices. n = 2,643 — 248

List of Tables

Chapter 2

Table 1	Geographical distribution of Russian-language freelancers by different occupations from 2005 to 2018 (percentages)	38
Table 2	Connections of clients with freelancers from Russia and other countries by different occupations from 2005 to 2018 (percentages)	39

Chapter 7

Table 1	Comparison of community of practice and community of style in co-working spaces	157

Chapter 10

Table 1	Cross-tab between the type of space or NWOW used most before the lockdown and the most adequate to needs in terms of work activities and physical space in the post-lockdown period (percentages)	250

1

Introduction to Topologies of Digital Work

Mascha Will-Zocholl and Caroline Roth-Ebner

At the turn of the millennium, a "spatial turn" (Crang & Thrift, 2000; Gunn, 2001) appeared, first in cultural studies and then increasingly in the social sciences, which triggered a controversial discussion, especially in the exchange with geography. The debate focused on whether the reflection about space as a category of analysis was really a new phenomenon or whether the previous historical development had hitherto been neglected in scientific debates: from oblivion of space to obsession of space. Progressive globalisation has also contributed to the spatial turn, and new concepts have increasingly been sought to describe new spatial relations and their consequences (Warf & Arias,

M. Will-Zocholl (✉)
Hessian University of Police and Administration, Wiesbaden, Germany
e-mail: Mascha.Will-Zocholl@hfpv-hessen.de

C. Roth-Ebner
University of Klagenfurt, Klagenfurt, Austria
e-mail: Caroline.Roth@aau.at

© The Author(s) 2021
M. Will-Zocholl and C. Roth-Ebner (eds.), *Topologies of Digital Work*, Dynamics of Virtual Work,
https://doi.org/10.1007/978-3-030-80327-8_1

2009, pp. 5f.). From today's perspective, it can be said that the reinvention of space as a category of analysis has led to a renewed focus on spatial issues. On this basis, we pursue spatial constellations, references and structures using the concept of "topologies". The term *topology*[1] refers to a rethinking of space as a relational phenomenon that emerges and can be changed through social practice. Spatial references are always created, shapeable and artificial in this sense. They are produced and experienced (Brenneis et al., 2018; Lefebvre 1974/1991; Massey, 2005).

Technological innovations have always had an impact on the perception of space. Wolfgang Schivelbusch (1977), for example, describes how the invention of the railroad and its establishment as a means of transport in the early nineteenth century led to a shrinking of the natural world (Schivelbusch, 1977, p. 16), because distances could be covered in a much shorter time by rail and the spaces between two places seemed to disappear (ibid., p. 39). During the past decades, the increasing spread and use of modern information and communication technologies (ICTs) in tandem with the general neoliberal capitalist paradigm have enabled a new dimension of "time–space compression", as diagnosed by Harvey as early as 1989. With the spread of the Internet, it became possible to communicate and cooperate worldwide in real time from different locations. And this to a much greater extent than telephony or telephony-based services such as teletext had made possible. ICTs include traditional communication technologies such as telephone, radio and TV, but most often refer to more recent communication technologies like computer soft- and hardware, mobile devices and the Internet. The use of ICTs has led to a multiplication of possibilities in our everyday lives, affecting the way people communicate, connect to each other, spend their leisure time, and work. In this anthology, the term *digital media* is used as well. It reflects the development of the past decades which entails that ever more of those ICTs are digital communication technologies which provide machine-readable communication in the form of videos, audio files, text and graphic messages.

1 Digitalisation, Informatisation and Mediatisation

Digital media are at the centre of the current *digitalisation* discourse. While the term *digitisation* refers to the computer-based transformation of communication and information into a digital mode, *digitalisation* is understood as the social transformation wrought by the establishment and ubiquitous use of ICTs respectively digital media (Brennen & Kreiss, 2016, n.p.). Digitalisation is a comprehensive social process that can be theoretically grasped in sociology as a new phase in "informatisation" (Boes & Kämpf, 2007; Schmiede, 2006) or in media and communications as a new push in "mediatisation" (Krotz, 2003, p. 173). The theory of informatisation describes the implementation of an information layer to manage and control working processes based on a "conscious, systematic handling of information, especially including the generation and use of information and information systems" (Boes & Kämpf, 2007, p. 197). The concept of mediatisation places emphasis on how the use of media changes the way we communicate, the way we construct our realities and hence, our culture, our social life and our work (Krotz, 2009, pp. 24, 31). Yet, this is not a unidirectional process, but a complex reciprocal relationship between societal and technological transformations.

Digitalisation is acting as a pivotal moment of profound change in workforce and labour, realigning value creation processes, business models, customer relations, work processes and—as taken up in this anthology—spatial relations of and in work.

Digitalisation processes are closely linked to those of virtualisation and the question of constructing reality. Manuel Castells identifies the emergence of "real virtuality" (Castells, 1996, pp. 367ff.) on the basis of electronic communication. These virtualities are not real in appearance, but real in their consequences. This notion can also be transferred to digitised and virtual work. We understand digitised work as work that is based on digital data and that processes them in some way. The core elements of digitised work are digital work tools (software applications), digital work objects (such as plans, graphics, text, calculations, videos, etc.), but also corresponding hardware that serves as an intermediary. Digitised work enables cooperation and monitoring as well as the storage, provision, integration or delivery of the work using digital ICTs. This also includes simulations of physical properties or complex scenarios of future developments. The term *virtual work* is often used synonymously with digital work or very broadly to describe a bundle of new developments of work, for example platform work or invisible labour (for an overview see Holts, 2018, p. 6f.). In this volume, virtual work refers to work and collaboration in virtual spaces from distributed places, that is, the disjunction of presence in a physical location and workspace. It has the form of information and communication streams which are processed and transported in computer networks (mostly Internet and Intranet; Roth-Ebner, 2015, p. 48).

Digitalisation and a worldwide ICT infrastructure in the form of the Internet also affect the perception of spatial references as well as the significance of places and can be seen as a basis for the emergence of "information space" (Baukrowitz & Boes, 1996). This information space is a space of opportunities, a "new sphere of social action" that enables the saving, handling or exchanging of information and information objects and furthermore interacting with others and building relationships based on the Internet (Boes et al., 2017, p. 156). The latter marks a difference from earlier information systems, which were prestructured and limited to human–machine action. In contrast to this, the information space is vivid, open for all kinds of topics and spheres of life and for interaction between human beings (ibid., p. 156f.). With regard to work, it offers new possibilities for the organisation and division of labour, for collaboration and a "new degree of use of mental productive forces" (ibid., p. 158) leading to innovations promoting transparency, but also to new forms of control.

Information space theory further refers to the changing materiality of workplaces in the course of digitalisation and the advancing use of technologies and especially to the emergence of new working spaces. This approach emphasises the matter of space as well as the challenges of the parallel existence of virtual spaces and of places where people work (Will-Zocholl, 2021). Over the past decades, the topologies of work have changed substantially. This manifests in an internationalisation of the division of labour no longer limited to the production sector, the creation of new value chains and business models in terms of outsourcing, near- and offshoring as well as in new labour markets (crowd sourcing, cloud working, platform work). Work is organised more flexibly and can be delocalised. Cooperation over distance with locally and globally distributed (team) mates has become normal. This counts particularly for the fields of knowledge and creative work. In these areas, and for a long time, work was considered to be embedded in local milieus of (creative) knowledge exchange. Further, this kind of work was able to escape the logic of reorganisation and rationalisation. Nowadays, even creative and knowledge workers are affected by consequences of those new topologies of work (e.g., Boes et al., 2017; Gill et al., 2019; Pfeiffer et al., 2016; Pitts, 2016; Schmiede & Will-Zocholl, 2011; Schörpf et al., 2017). During the time when the contributions to this anthology were being written, the relevance of virtual work increased dramatically. Due to the Covid-19 pandemic, people from all over the world had to stay at home and work from there in order to avoid infection, being connected via video conferencing and other computer-supported collaborative work tools. While before the Covid-19 pandemic, working from one's home was practised by only a small group of employees, around one in ten occasionally in 2019 (Sostero et al., 2020, p. 8), the share of workers performing their tasks at home at least some of the time increased to nearly half of the employees in Europe during the pandemic (Eurofound, 2020, p. 31). Assuming that most of this work was performed using ICTs, this is evidence for the thesis mentioned before, namely that social and technological changes are in constant interaction.

2   Rethinking Places and Spaces of Work

While the term *place* refers to clearly definable, geographically physical places, the concept of space is broader and also includes constructions that have no concrete reference to measurable points (Rothe & Schade, 2009, p. 195). This includes workspaces that emerge through the interaction and cooperation of people working together based on the Internet. They can be located in one place, for example, in the office, but also at different places, meeting virtually in the so-called information space. Along with the use of ICTs respectively digital media, workplaces change.

They extend to virtual spaces, they multiply (e.g., when working while commuting or travelling, in co-working spaces, in the home office, etc.) and even overlap, in the case of acting in different virtual spaces simultaneously and being co-present in a physical surrounding.

The term *topologies of work* focuses on those spatial reconfiguration processes. It refers to the importance of places and takes into account our thesis that places themselves change and multiply, but do not become meaningless. Hence the detachment of social spatial references from geographical spatial references for example, by no longer requiring the co-presence of team mates in one place for working activities, cannot be equated with the irrelevance of geographies (Will-Zocholl et al., 2019). Moreover, "placelessness" must be actively produced if a delocalisation of work is intended, as Jörg Flecker and Annika Schönauer (2016) showed with their study on digital service work in global value chains.

The debate about topologies of work emphasises that the changes of spatial references also extend beyond new geographical orders. This includes the reorganisation of the division of labour and the relocation of work to other places or regions as well as the emergence of virtual structures that are linked to the emergence of the information space.

This gives rise to a lively debate on the relationship and role of places and spaces, which is also reflected in the increasing number of publications on this topic. Some focus on the individual level of workplaces and their conditions as well as on employee identity (e.g., Anandarajan et al., 2006; Huws & Dahlmann, 2010; Lehdonvirta, 2016; Roth-Ebner, 2016; von Streit, 2011; Webster & Randle, 2016), others on the organisation and the design of new workplaces (e.g., Coles Levine & Johnson Sanquist, 2016; Miller & Marsh, 2014; Schittich, 2012). At a meso level, spatial reconfigurations in organisations are taken into account, especially in connection with questions of materiality (e.g., Carlile et al., 2013; Dale & Burell 2007; Leonardi et al., 2012; van Marrewijk & Yanow, 2010). On a macro level, the spatial reorganisation of work in a larger context is at the centre of scholarly focus: changing value chains, the information space and the international division of labour (e.g., contributions in Briken et al., 2017; Flecker, 2016; Newsome et al., 2015; further Holtgrewe, 2014; Huws, 2006). Only a few negotiate the triangle of space, place and work on a conceptual level (Boes & Kämpf,

2007; Boes et al., 2017; Flecker & Schönauer, 2016; Gill et al., 2019; Roth-Ebner, 2016; Will-Zocholl, 2016).

The *Dynamics of Virtual Work* series has been and still is an appropriate place to address the relationship of work, digitalisation and space. Hence, this volume aims at broadening the basis of topological research, taking into account the current developments of the digital transformation, theoretical considerations and empirical evidence. It investigates the topologies of digital work by addressing the following questions:

1. How relevant is the local embeddedness of work? To what extent does place matter in the context of a digitised world of work and what does this mean for the division of labour (national–international, but also urban–rural)?
2. What are the consequences of the digitalisation of work for previous concepts of geographical places, workplaces and workspaces?
3. How are those who work located in the digitised world of work? What subjective capacities do they need to cope with these changing working conditions?

These questions are reflected in three book Parts, taking into account different spatial scales: from the geographies of work to places of work (and their conditions) to virtual workspaces.

3 Brief Introduction to the Contributions

This book developed from the session "Digital Working Spaces. New Geographies Evolving Shaped by Digitalization and Virtualization of Work," a session at the ISA World Forum 2016 held in Vienna, as well as from a call for papers for the anthology.[2] The outcome is an international and interdisciplinary composition on the topologies of digital work. Country perspectives are taken into account, starting from Northern and Central Europe (Scandinavia, Austria), via Eastern Europe (Poland, Estonia, Russia) to Asia (China, Japan, Singapore). This promises particularly exciting insights, as different topics are considered from very different cultural, national and linguistic perspectives.

As Brenneis et al., (2018, p. 11) emphasise, the analysis of topologies requires the participation of different disciplines. Thus, the contributions present interdisciplinary perspectives, above all from sociology, media and communications, political economy, working life science, management sciences, environmental psychology and communication history. The issues and questions addressed in the contributions are distributed across all levels of human life: the micro level of the individual, the meso level of organisations and the macro level of society and culture, representing the fact that questions of technological and spatial transformation involve our social reality at all levels of scale.

The three Parts of the book discuss different aspects of the above-mentioned questions and along with this, working processes, conditions and the working environment. Taking a broader perspective, the development of new geographical arrangements in the division of labour, like the localisation, de- and relocalisation of work are addressed. In a narrow sense, light is shed on the way workplaces change from relatively stable local and physical environments ("office") to mobile and interchangeable places (café, beach, car, etc.). The physical offices themselves are expanded by means of the information space in the form of chat rooms or ticketing systems supporting team work (OneNote or Basecamp for example), with spatial consequences for the people working. In fact, the categorisation into three Parts does not represent a clear distinction of issues and phenomena, since they overlap. Yet, they might serve as a useful structuring aid for the readers of this volume. It should be noted that addressing "work" in this volume mainly refers to gainful employment or professional work. The only exception is the contribution of Jian Lin with its focus on social media work, which may be paid or unpaid. Yet, the boundaries between the two poles are blurring in times of "prosumer" culture (Thakur Varma & Devi Mishra, 2020), where consumers of media simultaneously act as producers thereof.

3.1 Part I: Geographies of Digital Work

Part I deals with the geographies of digital work, focusing on shifts and new formations of economic spatial relations in different areas of the globalised world. In their contribution, Andrey Shevchuk, Denis Strebkov and Alexey Tyulyupo shed light on the geography of the digital freelance economy in Russia and beyond that on a global scale. Using data from a Russian-language online labour platform (reaching fourteen years into the past), they determine a distinct online labour market based on the Russian language, which functions across the territory of the former Soviet Union and goes even further to extend around the globe. They observe the creation of a new spatial division of labour through virtual migration, leading to the decentralisation of the labour market, while showing that place still matters in times of the digitised world of work.

A concrete form of digital labour is dealt with in Anna Ozimek's contribution, where she investigates the global digital games industry and its outsourcing practices in the Central and Eastern Europe (CEE) region. Drawing on data from two research projects, involving an interview study with people engaged in the digital games industry, as well as analyses of secondary sources, she demonstrates that, on the one hand, games can be understood as a "global medium" that can be produced "everywhere". On the other hand, reasons stated for outsourcing software development to Poland and Estonia document the continuing significance of the local embeddedness of the digital games workforce.

The contribution by Brett Neilson and Ned Rossiter refers to Asia, but describes an extremely globalised issue. The authors analyse automating labour and the spatial politics of data centre technologies. Focusing on Singapore, a growth hub for data infrastructure, they depict data centres as automated environments that foster automation in workplaces across regional and global scales. In a project entitled "Data Farms: Circuits, Labor, Territory", they established that data centres act not just as technical infrastructures, but also as political institutions, which imply power shifts across vast territories and transform geopolitical patterns, hence they contribute to a transformation of digital capitalism.

3.2 Part II: Places of Work

Part II focuses on the places where work is done, as place does matter and has to be taken into consideration. In the first contribution in this section, Christian Oggolder applies a historical perspective to workplaces and production environments and contrasts work in the current digitalised environment with modern as well as premodern forms of work. By introducing typical places for each period—the house for the premodern era, the city for the modern and the network for late modern times—the author maintains that the modern separation of work and private life is a construction based on societal and economic demands. He interprets the digitally enabled flexible time and spatial arrangements of the current world of work as a reference back to premodern patterns of work.

Jian Lin's contribution explores the spatial production of China's entertaining social media industry, called "wanghong". Conducting a political-economic analysis and based on interviews with wanghong creators, Multi-Channel Network entrepreneurs and managers of platform companies as well as the study of secondary media reports, he observes networking effects that transform the local place into a *space of flows*. Individuals, participating in these communities both as creators and audience, gather together in the virtual space or in the cloud from disparate locations. The author describes this development as a transformation of various local places into mediaspaces by the economy's dissolving and expanding beyond spatial segregation and the urban-moulded popular culture.

Remaining in the Asian region, Keita Matsushita explores the transformations in the perception of workplaces and styles by examining working in co-working spaces as well as the phenomenon of *workationing* (working while on vacation). Based on fieldwork in Japan, which included interviews with managers and users of co-working spaces as well as *workationers*, he observes a transformation from place-based workstyles to style-based workplaces, in both urban and rural areas. While co-working in the urban area reflects the trend of deofficisation and localisation, workationing in the rural area can be described as officisation and delocalisation.

3.3 Part III: Virtual Working Spaces

Part III discusses emerging working spaces that are no longer connected to specific places and explores changes in work practices within the information space. Calle Rosengren, Ann Bergman, and Kristina Palm launch the section with their contribution on ICT-enforced boundary work, where they consider the weakening boundaries between work and private life due to the access to and use of ICT on the level of the individual. Applying a practice-based approach including time diaries and qualitative interviews, they explore the question of how ICT is used by employees to manage their availability for both private and professional life spheres. The data shows that rather than the question of being available or not, what is actually relevant for the individual's well-being is the feeling of being in control of one's boundary practices.

Delving deeper into the subject of blurring boundaries between work and private life, Dominik Klaus and Jörg Flecker address the interrelation of ICT-enabled boundaryless work and identity work drawing on the results of two case studies, where qualitative interviews were conducted in knowledge-intense business services. They ask for the ways in which the workers handle the blurring boundaries, deal with changing spatial resources, and the requisites for identity work. Continuing the argumentation of Calle Rosengren, Ann Bergman and Kristina Palm, to a certain extent, they emphasise that place, space and physical aspects of workplaces are important resources for the workers' identities, and when these spatial ties loosen in the course of teleworking, this poses both pillars for and threats to identity work.

The final contribution written by Ingrid Nappi and Gisele de Campos Ribeiro pays attention to the duality of the employee's interaction with physical and virtual worlds of work. Addressing the 2020 Covid-19 crisis as a trigger for teleworking, they conducted two online surveys with white-collar employees in France to find out more about the employees' attitude towards the virtual office. The first survey was run during a phase of lockdown, at a time when companies adopted virtual office practices as a crisis management tool. The second survey was conducted post-lockdown. Their results reveal (among others) that the participants missed their work routines, and face-to-face interaction with co-workers during the lockdown. Nevertheless, they would also like to continue their teleworking to varying degrees in the future.

Notes

1. Drawn from Greek *tópos* (place/location), topology literally means the "study of places" (Naylor and Sell 1982, p. 44). In various scientific disciplines, it is used to describe relationships between places of spatial structures (e.g., in biology, mathematics, but also in philosophy, linguistics and literature).
2. The entire proposal was reviewed by the series editors Ursula Huws and Rosalind Gill as well as the publisher. Moreover, the contributions of the book were subjected to a multistage peer review.

References

Anandarajan, M., Teo, T. S. H., & Simmers, C. A. (Eds.). (2006). *The internet and workplace transformation*. Routledge.

Baukrowitz, A., & Boes, A. (1996). Arbeit in der „Informationsgesellschaft": Einige Überlegungen aus einer (fast schon) ungewohnten Perspektive. In R. Schmiede (Ed.), *Virtuelle Arbeitswelten. Arbeit, Produktion und Subjekt in der „Informationsgesellschaft"* (pp. 129–158). edition sigma.

Boes, A., & Kämpf, T. (2007). The nexus of informatisation and internationalisation: A new stage in the internationalisation of labour in globalised working environments. *Work Organisation, Labour & Globalisation, 1*(2), 193–208.

Boes, A., Kämpf, T., Langes, B., & Lühr, T. (2017). The disruptive power of digital transformation. In K. Briken, S. Chillas, M. Krzywdzinski, & A. Marks (Eds.), *The new digital workplace: How new technologies revolutionise work*. Critical Perspectives on Work and Employment (pp. 53–175). Palgrave Macmillan.

Brenneis, A., Honer, O., Keesser, S., Ripper, A., & Vetter-Schultheiß, S. (2018). Topologie der Technik: Manifestation eines interdisziplinären Forschungsprogramms. In A. Brenneis, O. Honer, S. Keesser, A. Ripper,

& S. Vetter-Schultheiß (Eds.), *Technik – Macht – Raum: Das Topologische Manifest im Kontext interdisziplinärer Studien* (pp. 1–35). Springer VS.

Brennen, J. S., & Kreiss, D. (2016). *Digitalization*. Wiley Online Library. https://doi.org/10.1002/9781118766804.wbiect111. Accessed 17 February 2021.

Briken, K., Chillas, S., Krzywdzinski, M., & Marks, A. (Eds.). (2017). *The new digital workplace: How new technologies revolutionise work*. Critical Perspectives on Work and Employment. Palgrave Macmillan.

Carlile, P. R., Nicolini, D., Langley, A., & Tsoukas, H. (Eds.). (2013). *How matter matters: Objects, artifacts, and materiality in organization studies*. Oxford University Press.

Castells, M. (1996). *The rise of the network society: The information age: Economy, society and culture*. Blackwell.

Coles Levine, D., & Johnson Sanquist, N. (Eds.) (2016). *Work on the move 2: How social, leadership and technology innovations are transforming the workplace in the digital economy*. IFMA Foundation.

Crang, M., & Thrift, N. (Eds.). (2000). *Thinking space*. Routledge.

Dale, K., & Burrell, G. (2007). *The spaces of organisation and the organisation of space: Power, identity and materiality at work*. Palgrave Macmillan.

Eurofound. (2020). *Living, working and COVID-19* (COVID-19 series). Publications Office of the European Union.

Flecker, J. (Ed.). (2016). *Space, place and global digital work*. Palgrave Macmillan.

Flecker, J., & Schönauer, A. (2016). The production of 'placelessness': Digital service work in global value chains. In J. Flecker (Ed.), *Space, place and global digital work* (pp. 11–30). Palgrave Macmillan.

Gill, R., Pratt, A. C., & Virani, T. E. (Eds.). (2019). *Creative hubs in question: Place, space and work in the creative economy*. Palgrave Macmillan.

Gunn, S. (2001). The spatial turn: Changing histories of space and place. In S. Gunn & R. J. Morris (Eds.), *Identities in space: Contested terrains in the Western city since 1850* (pp. 1–14). Ashgate.

Harvey, D. (1989). *The condition of postmodernity: An enquiry into the origins of cultural change*. Blackwell.

Holtgrewe, U. (2014). New new technologies: The future and present of work in information and communication technology. *New Technology, Work and Employment, 29*, 9–24.

Holts, K. (2018). *Understanding virtual work: Prospects for Estonia in the digital economy* (Resource document). Riigikogu. https://www.riigikogu.ee/

wpcms/wp-content/uploads/2017/09/Virtual-work-size-and-trends_final1. pdf. Accessed 21 February 2021.

Huws, U. (2006). The restructuring of global value chains and the creation of a cybertariat. In C. May (Ed.), *Global corporate power*. International Political Economy Yearbook (pp. 65–82). Lynne Rienner.

Huws, U., & Dahlmann, S. (2010). Global restructuring of value chains and class issues. In N. J. Pupo & M. P. Thomas (Eds.), *Interrogation the new economy: Restructuring work in the 21st century* (pp. 65–92). UTP.

Krotz, F. (2003). Die Mediatisierung der Lebensräume von Jugendlichen. Perspektiven für die Forschung. In J. Bug & M. Karmasin (Eds.), *Telekommunikation und Jugendkultur: Eine Einführung* (pp. 167–183). Westdeutscher.

Krotz, F. (2009). Mediatization: A concept with which to grasp media and societal change. In K. Lundby (Ed.), *Mediatization: Concept, changes, consequences* (pp. 21–40). Peter Lang.

Lefebrve, H. (1974). *La production de l'espace*. Anthropos. English edition: Lefebrve, H. (1991). *The production of space* (D. Nicholson-Smith, Trans.). Blackwell.

Lehdonvirta, V. (2016). Algorithms that divide and unite: Delocalisation, identity and collective action in 'microwork.' In J. Flecker (Ed.), *Space, place and global digital work* (pp. 53–80). Palgrave Macmillan.

Leonardi, P. M., Nardi, B. A., & Kallinikos, J. (Eds.). (2012). *Materiality and organizing: Social interaction in a technological world*. Oxford University Press.

Massey, D. (2005). *For space*. Sage.

Miller, P., & Marsh, E. (2014). *The renaissance of work: Delivering digital workplaces fit for the future*. Gower.

Naylor, A. W., & Sell, G. R. (1982). Linear operator theory in engineering and science. *Applied Mathematical Sciences, 40*. https://doi.org/10.1007/978-1-4612-5773-8_3

Newsome, K., Taylor, P., Bair, J., & Rainnie, A. (Eds.). (2015). *Putting labour in its place: Labour process analysis and global value chains*. Critical Perspectives on Work and Employment. Palgrave Macmillan.

Pfeiffer, S., Wühr, D., & Schütt, P. (2016). Virtual innovation work: Labour, creativity, and standardisation. In J. Webster & K. Randle (Eds.), *Virtual workers and the global labour market* (pp. 77–93). Palgrave Macmillan.

Pitts, F. H. (2016). Rhythms of creativity and power in freelance creative work. In J. Webster & K. Randle (Eds.), *Virtual workers and the global labour market* (pp. 139–159). Palgrave Macmillan.

Roth-Ebner, C. (2015). *Der effiziente Mensch: Zur Dynamik von Raum und Zeit in mediatisierten Arbeitswelten.* transcript.

Roth-Ebner, C. (2016). Spatial phenomena of mediatised work. In J. Flecker (Ed.), *Space, place and global digital work* (pp. 227–245). Palgrave Macmillan.

Rothe, K., & Schade, A.-K. (2009). Transnational, national, lokal. Proteströume im Internet. In I. Köster, & K. Schubert (Eds.), *Medien in Raum und Zeit: Maßverhältnisse des Medialen* (pp. 193–221). transcript.

Schittich, C. (Ed.). (2012). *In detail: Work environments: Spatial concepts, Usage strategies, communications.* Institut für internationale Architektur-Dokumentation.

Schivelbusch, W. (1977). *Geschichte der Eisenbahnreise: Zur Industrialisierung von Raum und Zeit im 19. Jahrhundert.* Carl Hanser.

Schmiede, R. (2006). Knowledge, work and subject in informational capitalism. In J. Berleur, M. I. Nurminen, & J. Impagliazzo (Eds.), *Social informatics: An information society for all? In remembrance of Rob Kling: Proceedings of the Seventh International Conference on Human Choice and Computers (HCC7), IFIP TC 9, Maribor, Slovenia, September 21–23, 2006* (pp. 333–354). Springer Science and Business Media.

Schmiede, R., & Will-Zocholl, M. (2011). Engineers' work on the move: Challenges in automotive engineering in a globalized world. *Engineering Studies, 3,* 101–121.

Schörpf, P., Flecker, J., Schönauer, A., & Eichmann, H. (2017). Triangular love–hate: Management and control in creative crowdworking. *New Technology, Work and Employment, 32,* 43–58.

Sostero, M., Milasi, S., Hurley, J., Fernández-Macías, E, & Bisello, M. (2020). *Teleworkability and the COVID-19 crisis: A new digital divide?* (JRC working paper series on labour, education and technology 2020/05). European Commission.

Thakur Varma, S., & Devi Mishra, K. (2020). Media blogs in the prosumer culture: A study of social media narratives in Indian political communication. *International Journal of Advanced Science and Technology, 29*(9), 5920–5931.

Van Marrewijk, A. H., & Yanow, D. (Eds.). (2010). *Organizational spaces: Rematerializing the workaday world.* Edward Elgar.

Von Streit, A. (2011). *Entgrenzter Alltag – Arbeiten ohne Grenzen?: Das Internet und die raum-zeitlichen Organisationsstrategien von Wissensarbeitern.* transcript.

Warf, B., & Arias, S. (2009). Introduction: The reinsertion of space in the humanities and social sciences. In B. Warf & S. Arias (Eds.), *The spatial turn: Interdisciplinary perspectives* (pp. 1–10). Routledge.

Webster, J., & Randle, K. (2016). Positioning virtual workers within space, time, and social dynamics. In J. Webster & K. Randle (Eds.), *Virtual workers and the global labour market* (pp. 3–34). Palgrave Macmillan.

Will-Zocholl, M. (2016). New topologies of work: Informatisation, virtualisation, and globalisation in automotive engineering. In J. Flecker (Ed.), *Space, place and global digital work* (pp. 31–51). Palgrave Macmillan.

Will-Zocholl, M. (2021). Information space(s). In R. Appel-Meulenbroek & V. Danivska (Eds.), *Workplace theories: A handbook of theories on designing alignment between people and the office environment* (pp. 82–93). Routledge.

Will-Zocholl, M., Flecker, J., & Schörpf, P. (2019). Zur realen Virtualität von Arbeit. Raumbezüge in digitalisierter Wissensarbeit. *AIS-Studien, 12*(1), 36–54.

Open Access This chapter is licensed under the terms of the Creative Commons Attribution 4.0 International License (http://creativecommons.org/licenses/by/4.0/), which permits use, sharing, adaptation, distribution and reproduction in any medium or format, as long as you give appropriate credit to the original author(s) and the source, provide a link to the Creative Commons license and indicate if changes were made.

The images or other third party material in this chapter are included in the chapter's Creative Commons license, unless indicated otherwise in a credit line to the material. If material is not included in the chapter's Creative Commons license and your intended use is not permitted by statutory regulation or exceeds the permitted use, you will need to obtain permission directly from the copyright holder.

Part I

Geographies of Digital Work

2

The Geography of the Digital Freelance Economy in Russia and Beyond

Andrey Shevchuk, Denis Strebkov, and Alexey Tyulyupo

With the emergence of information and communication technologies (ICTs), work has been increasingly digitalised and delocalised. Ever more people use digital tools to create value from the use and manipulation of digital data. New ways of working and organising increasingly rely on the growing opportunities for effective coordination of spatially dispersed economic actors. Multiple overlapping terms, such as telecommuting, telework, remote work and virtual work, have been used to highlight the idea that work can be done away from traditional locations and delivered electronically via ICTs (Bailey & Kurland, 2002; Messenger & Gschwind, 2016; Nicklin et al., 2016). Recently, researchers from

---

The reported study was funded by the Russian Foundation for Basic Research (RFBR), project number 20-011-00587.

A. Shevchuk (✉) · D. Strebkov · A. Tyulyupo
Higher School of Economics (HSE University), Moscow, Russia
e-mail: shevchuk@hse.ru

various fields have been paying increasing attention to the digital freelance economy and online labour markets that operate across spatial and national borders (Agrawal et al., 2015; Aguinis & Lawal, 2013; Hong & Pavlou, 2013; Horton, 2010; Huws, 2017; Kässi & Lehdonvirta, 2018). Digital labour platforms (freelance online marketplaces) provide sophisticated infrastructure for distant interactions between millions of independent contractors (freelancers) and their clients (individuals, small firms and large corporations) from all over the world.[1] This new model is also referred to as crowd work, because required skills are outsourced through an open call to a geographically dispersed crowd (Berg et al., 2018). The online work ranges from simple micro-tasks (such as data entry or text transcribing) to high-skilled occupations (such as website building, software development, graphic design and consulting).

In the digital age, labour can move and migrate over long distances without the worker's body. These patterns of "virtual migration" (Aneesh, 2006) create a new spatial division of labour and complex economic geographies. The digital freelance economy is based on a new model of outsourcing and offshoring, where one-person micro providers serve clients around the world in transactions conducted via online platforms (Kuek et al., 2015; Lehdonvirta et al., 2019). In contrast to traditional outsourcing and offshoring of digital labour, as exemplified by overseas programming shops and call-centres, the digital freelance economy avails itself of the radical disruption of standard employment relationships and the proliferation of the so-called *gig economy*, comprising contract on-demand work mediated by digital platforms (Codagnone et al., 2018; Kalleberg & Dunn, 2016). Recently, the gig economy has been gaining much attention in public and academic debates. More empirical research is needed to reveal the models, structures and outcomes of the gig economy. The geography of the digital freelance economy is one important issue.

The extant literature on the digital freelance economy and online labour markets deals with geography in several ways. Researchers seek to conceptualise the digital freelance economy as a global phenomenon, reveal the spatial division of labour and workflows, and understand what it all means for workers in different parts of the world. In other words, two basic questions are typically asked. What is the geography of the digital freelance economy? And does place matter?

The data suggest that the digital freelance economy has been growing rapidly and has a global reach (Kässi & Lehdonvirta, 2018; Kuek et al., 2015). It is argued that online labour markets may level the playing field, removing spatial barriers for workers from depressed regions and less developed countries, who may rely on *virtual migration* in order to gain access to better paid jobs (Friedman, 2007; Malone et al., 2011). However, as online platforms provide companies with a potentially limitless pool of workers from all over the world competing with each other, fears arise about the overall race to the bottom (Graham & Anwar, 2019). The growing body of empirical studies indicates a number of restraints for allegedly meritocratic online labour markets, where work is remunerated regardless of a worker's location. Powerful factors such as time zones, language and culture make it challenging for freelancers and clients to work together across spatial and national borders (Gefen & Carmel, 2008; Hong & Pavlou, 2017; Horton et al., 2017; Lehdonvirta et al., 2019).

However, current research on the geography of the digital freelance economy contains some important gaps. Three interrelated issues should be acknowledged that may mislead or oversimplify our understanding of how place matters in the digital freelance economy. First, researchers focus almost exclusively on English-language platforms (Kässi & Lehdonvirta, 2018). However, Chinese platforms may compete with their Western counterparts as far as the number of users is concerned (Carmel et al., 2012; Kuek et al., 2015; To & Lai, 2015). Russian-language platforms also attract millions of users (Shevchuk & Strebkov, 2015), and freelance platforms in other languages such as Spanish (Galperin & Greppi, 2019) or Arabic (Kuek et al., 2015, p. 17) exist. By every measurement, the share of freelancers and businesses that work with each other beyond English-language platforms is not negligible. Second, the digital freelance economy is typically approached with the North–South distinction, where freelancers from less-developed parts of the world work for clients from the USA and Western Europe. This ignores other centres of economic development such as China and Russia, also showing significant demand for online labour, which becomes invisible when exploring exclusively English-language platforms (see the contribution by Jian Lin in this volume). The implied role of these countries in the digital freelance economy as simply suppliers of labour to the Global North needs reassessment. Third, both neoliberal and critical scholars tend to share the unidimensional vision of the "global gig economy" and the "planetary labour market" (Graham & Anwar, 2019), oversimplifying the complex geography of digital labour. In parallel with the global freelance economy, distinct regional and transnational online labour markets have emerged, which are shaped by common language, history, culture and other factors (see the contribution by Anna Ozimek regarding the digital games industry in this volume). We conclude that by focusing exclusively on the English-language freelance platforms, extant literature overlooks important developments in other parts of the world and obscures the real geography of the digital freelance economy as an emerging phenomenon.

In this chapter, to partially fill these gaps we make a case for the digital freelance economy in Russia and beyond. We examine how the Russian language and specific socio-economic factors facilitate a distinct online labour market with millions of participants, which include not only citizens of the Russian Federation, but also people from countries that were previously part of the former Soviet Union, as well as from any other countries where Russian-speaking people currently live (Shevchuk & Strebkov, 2015). We use the data from a leading Russian-language freelance platform for creative and knowledge work to reveal the complex geography of the digital freelance economy in Russia, and some important trends over an almost fifteen-year period. Following previous research on the online labour markets, we show how geographical location matters in the allegedly "flat" digitally-interconnected world.

1 The Geography of Online Labour in the Globalising World

The digital freelance economy, where electronically connected freelancers (e-lancers) work remotely on temporary projects, was first envisioned by Malone and Laubacher (1998), and then facilitated by dedicated websites (*online labour platforms or freelance online marketplaces*) around the turn of the millennium. On these websites, freelancers create professional profiles and clients post projects or contests.[2] Online labour platforms seek to provide comprehensive technical and institutional support for communication and transactions between distant parties, including sophisticated search engines, collaboration tools, certification of skills, reputation systems (ratings and reviews), safe pay (escrow) options, dispute assistance and arbitration, and so forth. Platforms earn revenue in various ways including membership fees, ad valorem charges on contract payments, and charges for additional services.

Online labour markets represent a distinct segment of the wider gig economy involving digitally-mediated on-demand labour (Codagnone et al., 2018; Kalleberg & Dunn, 2016). In contrast to local gig work (such as ride-hailing, delivery and handyman services) that implies the physical presence of a worker and a customer, online labour markets deal with remote work that can be delivered electronically. An important distinction within online labour platforms is between *microwork* or *piecework* platforms for low-skilled repetitive tasks such as data entry, classifying images, and text transcribing (e.g., Amazon Mechanical Turk) (Berg et al., 2018), and freelance platforms such as Upwork and Freelancer, comprising creative and knowledge work by software developers, graphic designers, writers, and consultants (Hong & Pavlou, 2013; Horton et al., 2017). Whereas local gig work apps typically announce a list of cities in which they operate, online labour platforms can be easily accessed remotely from anywhere in the world. For example, Uber as a platform offering locally bound services, reportedly covers more than 700 cities in sixty-three countries, whereas Freelancer.com as a platform for remote work, has users from 247 countries.

Digitalisation and globalisation are often presented as processes which inevitably signal the "death of distance" (Cairncross, 2001) and the emergence of the "flat world" (Friedman, 2007), making spatial location increasingly irrelevant for economic activity. To all appearances, an online labour market is very close to the idealised "flat world", where not only countries and firms, but also individuals can compete and collaborate worldwide, acting as one-person micro providers. The entry barriers to this kind of labour market are very low, consisting of a reliable Internet connection, reasonable command of English as the global lingua franca, and any skills that are tradable online. Digital labour platforms connect workers to global reservoirs of jobs (projects), overcoming distances and constraints of local demand through *virtual migration*. Workers from depressed regions and less developed countries get access to better-paid jobs without physical mobility (Horton, 2010; Malone et al., 2011). Through digital labour platforms, offshoring becomes available not only to large corporations, but also to small firms and individuals (Kuek et al., 2015).

Several studies shed light on where workers and clients on the leading global platforms are situated around the world (Agrawal et al., 2015; Gefen & Carmel, 2008; Graham et al., 2017; Horton et al., 2017; Kuek et al., 2015). Although using different measurement techniques and data from different platforms, all these studies deliver similar patterns. Overall, clients are primarily concentrated in the advanced industrial economies, while the providers are dispersed around the world in both rich and poor countries. The United States is the largest player in the global online labour market in terms of demand, and one of the largest (depending on the platform) in terms of supply. For instance, researchers from Oxford Internet Institute introduced the "online labour index" (OLI) aimed at tracking the utilisation of online labour across countries and occupations based on the data about the number of projects (tasks) posted on the major five English-language online platforms (Kässi & Lehdonvirta, 2018). About half of all projects come from US clients. Other prominent countries on the demand side include the United Kingdom, Australia, Canada and India. India, the only developing country in this list, has a large IT sector that may generate domestic demand for online workers. Leading countries show a rather similar skills demand with roughly one third of the jobs posted in software development and technology, followed by creative and multimedia work, followed by writing and translation. According to the OLI worker supplement, the largest suppliers of online labour are India (24%), Bangladesh (16%) and the United States (12%). The other countries in the top fifteen include Pakistan, Philippines, United Kingdom, Ukraine, Canada, Romania, Egypt, Germany, Russia, Kenya, Nigeria and Italy (Lehdonvirta, 2017). Freelancers from different countries bring different skills to the global market. For instance, India, Pakistan, Russia and Ukraine focus mainly on software development and technology.

According to the economists' view, due to increased "tradability" of services (Blinder, 2006) and "global labour arbitrage" (Roach, 2004) aimed at getting labour services at the lowest price, jobs should inevitably migrate to low-cost nations. However, empirical evidence from online labour markets suggests that domestic providers continue to get some preference. Although freelancers from less developed countries can offer lower prices, clients often choose domestic contractors (Gefen & Carmel, 2008). The only marked exceptions are clients from the USA who give relatively less preference to domestic providers. Several studies demonstrated that workers from less developed countries have less chances of winning a contract, when controlled for the contract price (Agrawal et al., 2013; Galperin & Greppi, 2019), and earn less money for the same job, although there is some wage convergence (Beerepoot & Lambregts, 2015). Clients from English-speaking countries tend to prefer freelancers from these countries over those for whom English is a foreign language, making the case for "nearshoring" where linguistic and cultural proximity can ease offshoring (Gefen & Carmel, 2008). Clients also might prefer to deal with people of the same ethnicity, as demonstrated by the observation that ethnic Indians are tilted to contract workers from India (Ghani et al., 2014). These barriers to outsiders' entrance into an online labour market is coined as the "liability of foreignness" (Lehdonvirta et al., 2019).

Researches offer several explanations, arguing that language, time zones, cultural and institutional differences make it challenging for clients and freelancers to work together around the world (Gefen & Carmel, 2008; Hong & Pavlou, 2017; Horton et al., 2017; Lehdonvirta et al., 2019). Clients might experience inconveniences and coordination problems when working with freelancers from different time zones. While contracting with foreign providers, clients are more likely to encounter cultural miscommunications and misunderstandings. The language barrier disadvantages workers from non-English-speaking countries who may experience difficulties communicating with the majority of clients. The limited amount of verifiable information about platform workers may foster statistical "geographical discrimination"

(Galperin & Greppi, 2019) based on geographic stereotyping. Clients may view the country as a marker of the worker's reliability and skills, therefore, workers from developing countries have more difficulties when it comes to gaining first contracts, resulting in significantly higher dropout chances during the first month on the platform and consistently lower earnings (Agrawal et al., 2013; Beerepoot & Lambregts, 2015). However, online reputation as exemplified by ratings and reviews may somewhat mitigate negative effects for foreign workers (Kanat et al., 2018; Lehdonvirta et al., 2019).

While creating jobs in economically disadvantaged areas, concern has been rising about the precariousness of online platform work. The fact that platforms avoid national labour legislation and prefer to treat their workers as independent entrepreneurs rather than employees warrants the speculation, whether this new form of employment is a genuine innovation or whether the platforms just thrive on "regulatory arbitrage" (Codagnone et al., 2018). Furthermore, oversupply of labour encourages price competition, presenting a serious problem even for workers in poorer countries, while the lack of physical proximity, common culture and social ties prevents any attempts by workers to stand up for their rights, rendering labour into a state of commodity to be easily bought and sold (Graham & Anwar, 2019).

2   History and Context of the Russian Online Labour Market

For most of the twentieth century in the Soviet Union, any type of independent contracting, self-employment, and entrepreneurship was completely illegal. All people were supposed to work for state-owned enterprises, which were allocated across the vast territory according to central planning (Markevich & Mikhailova, 2013). The Soviet Union covered an area of approximately one-sixth of the earth's land surface, which is more than twice as large as China, and nearly three times as big as the United States or Australia. Today, Russia is still the largest country in the world, taking up 11.5% of the world's landmass (however, the majority of this vast territory is virtually uninhabited).

The collapse of the Soviet Union in 1991 led to the emergence of fifteen independent states with many millions of people along with a common historical past and a common language divided by new political borders. Although dramatic political, economic and social disintegration has occurred since then, the Russian language still plays an important role in the post-Soviet space. Not only do many ethnic Russians live beyond Russia, but also many people in the former Soviet republics speak Russian as a first language or learned Russian at school (Cheskin & Kachuyevski, 2019; Mustajoki et al., 2019). Russian is the second official language in Belarus, Kyrgyzstan and Kazakhstan. Moreover, several waves dispatched Russian-speaking immigrants to far-flung countries during the Soviet and post-Soviet periods. Russian is Europe's largest native language and the world's seventh largest language by number of speakers. Overall, approximately 260,000,000 people in the world speak Russian, and out of these, about 150,000,000 are native speakers. More than 90,000,000 speakers of Russian live outside Russia in former Soviet republics. A significant proportion of speakers of Russian live in the USA, Canada, Australia and New Zealand (4,000,000), Western Europe (7,000,000), Eastern Europe and the Balkans (13,000,000), Asia (1,300,000), and other countries (Aref'ev, 2014). This fact has important consequences for the development of Runet, a segment of the Internet that uses the Russian language. Recently, the total Russian-speaking Internet audience reached 110,000,000 and is ranked ninth in the world for number of Internet users, surpassing German speakers (97,000,000) (Internet World Stats, 2019).

Contemporary post-Soviet Russia could not rely on strong and long-lasting traditions of independent work, self-employment rates are still very low, and the general entrepreneurial spirit is fairly weak (Chepurenko, 2015). Moreover, self-employment in Russia is seen mainly in traditional sectors, primitive technologies and manual labour. However, in the past two decades, freelance work through online platforms emerged as a new phenomenon that gradually became a distinctive feature of the Russian labour market. Although some attempts to establish an online infrastructure for freelance work had been piloted earlier, the first successful Russian-language platform Free-lance.ru, was founded in 2005 (in 2013 it was rebranded as FL.ru). For many years, FL.ru has been the leading freelance platform in the post-Soviet space and one of the largest in Europe and also in the world. Recently, it has been experiencing fierce competition from other Russian-language platforms and has lost its dominant position. However, with over 1,600,000 registered users it still stands among the main Russian-language freelance platforms. Overall, five leading Russian-based platforms have more than 1,000,000 users each, accounting for about 8,000,000 users in total (however, not all of them are active).

3 Methodological Approach and Data

Digitalisation not only transforms labour markets but also provides researchers with a new kind of data. Websites record a vast amount of information about their users, commonly referred to as "big data" or "digital traces" (Horton & Tambe, 2015; Lazer & Radford, 2017; Salganik, 2018). Although not originally created for research purposes, these data provide a unique opportunity for exploring work and employment in the digital age. Although far from the ideal of representative survey research, using digital traces data from online labour platforms became standard in the research of interactions between workers and clients, as well as for assessing the spatial distribution and the dynamics of digital labour. However, obtaining such *big data* directly from freelance platforms is problematic, as companies are often unwilling to share them with the researchers (Horton & Tambe, 2015). Alternatively, data can be gathered directly from the webpages using dedicated software. The extant literature on online labour markets relies equally on both methods: proprietary company datasets (Galperin & Greppi, 2019; Graham et al., 2017; Hong & Pavlou, 2017) as well as web-scraped data (Kässi & Lehdonvirta, 2018; Lehdonvirta et al., 2019).

In this chapter, we use the data from the Russian-language platform FL.ru for several reasons. FL.ru is one of the first large freelance platforms in the region, where we can observe users' activity over many years starting as early as 14 May 2005. Using these data, one can trace the historical evolution of online platform work in Russia for almost fifteen years. Although a single platform cannot be representative of the whole Russian-language online labour market in terms of the exact number of users, it can shed light on the geography of the digital freelance economy in Russia in terms of spatial distributions and their dynamics.

The data were obtained between 26 October 2019 to 31 October 2019, by scraping publicly available personal profiles of the clients and workers at FL.ru. The data encompasses most users who signed up between 14 May 2005 and 31 December 2018. This list, however, is not comprehensive because, on the one hand, some users deleted their personal accounts themselves, and, on the other hand, some users were blocked by the platform for violating the user agreement. Moreover, accounts of freelancers who did not fill out the portfolio section of their profiles and did not appear on the site for more than six months become invisible to the public and unavailable for research. However, the accounts of clients do not disappear for these reasons. Thus, our database comprises profiles of all the clients registered on FL.ru over the entire period, and profiles of freelancers that demonstrated at least minor activity on the platform during this time. We assume that this limitation of our data makes it difficult to accurately estimate the total number of users registered on the platform, but does not seriously affect the spatial distribution of freelancers and clients in question. Overall, our analytic sample includes 1,280,814 users, including 403,425 freelancers (31.5%) and 877,389 clients (68.5%).

The dataset includes information about user type (freelancer or client), registration and last visit dates, self-reported gender, date of birth, country and city of residence, professional specialisation and some other personal characteristics reflecting their activity on the site. Unfortunately, the key parameter for the current research—the location of residence—was reported by only 40% of users (66% of workers and 26% of clients). This is a significant, though typical limitation for research based on digital traces. The information about a user's city of residence was used to infer the part of the world, time zone, federal districts and regions of Russia. To assess the dynamics of indicators, we assume that the user was present on the site in a given year if he registered on the site in this or some earlier year, and the date of his last visit to the site fell within this or a later year.

Unfortunately, the information about the quantity and characteristics of all the projects executed on the platform is hidden and not available for research purposes. However, we can estimate workflows indirectly by investigating reviews which clients submit after the project has been completed. The limitation of such an approach is that according to the platform rules it is not compulsory to leave a review. That is why not every transaction is accompanied by a review. However, presumably, this fact does not seriously affect the spatial distribution of reviewers. We gathered all client reviews received by freelancers between 2005 and 2018. There were a total of 559,766 such reviews left on the platform, and in 71% of them (396,559), we were able to trace the location of both the reviewer and reviewee from their profiles on FL.ru. The vast majority of reviews (88.4%) were from Russian clients, 5.9% of reviews were written by clients from Ukraine, 1.7% from Belarus, 1.6% from other former Soviet republics, 2.4% from other countries.

To analyse the data, we performed statistical calculations using frequencies, cross-tabulation and correlation tables. All analyses were conducted using IBM SPSS software version 21.0.

4 The Geography of Supply and Demand

First, we present cumulative data about all users (both freelancers and clients) of the leading Russian-language freelance platform FL.ru who had registered on this website during the whole period of observation from 2005 to 2018. This approach allows us to estimate the overall geographical reach of the Russian-language online labour market. The data reveal a vast geographical coverage with users spanning 180 countries, although only thirty-six countries had more than a hundred users, and twenty-eight countries had only one user. Besides Russia, the FL.ru users live in all fourteen former Soviet Union republics, most of them in Ukraine, Belarus and Kazakhstan. Freelancers and clients reside in more than 3800 cities and towns,[3] 1665 of which are in Russia, 954 are in former Soviet republics and 1200 are in other countries around the world. The list of Russian cities by the number of FL.ru users is topped by Moscow, followed by other cities with a million-plus population, that are important national and regional centres of economic development such as St Petersburg, Yekaterinburg, Novosibirsk and Krasnodar. The cities with the largest number of users from the countries that used to be part of the former Soviet Union are Kyiv, Minsk, Kharkiv, Odesa, Dnepropetrovsk and Almaty. Among the countries outside the post-Soviet space, the prominent user locations are Prague, New York, London, Berlin, Tel Aviv, Warsaw and Barcelona. The general overview highlights that the Russian-language online labour market is truly transnational, connecting freelancers and clients from thousands of locations in the vast majority of countries across all inhabited continents. In terms of the geographical coverage, the leading Russians-language freelance platform is comparable with its Western counterparts.

4.1 Freelancers

In the next three sections we explore the current geographical distribution of freelancers and clients. The data is limited to 166,885 freelancers and 174,753 clients who visited FL.ru in 2018, of whom only 101,598 freelancers and 54,916 clients indicated their place of residence (country and city). Overall, in 2018 freelancers resided in 118 countries. The majority of freelancers were located in Russia (77.2%) and more than one fifth (21.1%) in the former Soviet Union republics, including Ukraine (12.4%), Belarus (4.0%), Kazakhstan (1.8%) and the other eleven post-Soviet countries (2.9%). As these numbers are affected by the population of the nations, weighting them helps to reveal the incidence of working on the leading Russian-language online platform. There were 10.3 online freelancers/10,000 of the labour force in Russia; 8.0 in Belarus, 7.0 in Ukraine and 2.0 in Kazakhstan.[4] These figures demonstrate that in fact, freelancers from Belarus are slightly more oriented to the Russian-language market compared with Ukrainian freelancers who also have several national platforms (Aleksynska et al., 2018). The countries outside the post-Soviet space accounted for the remaining 1.7% of labour supply on the platform. More than one hundred freelancers were from Poland, Germany and the United States; between fifty and one hundred users were from Thailand, Italy, the Czech Republic, Spain, Israel, Bulgaria and China.

As most of the freelancers reside in Russia, it is important to explore their spatial distribution within the country. In 2018, freelancers registered at FL.ru lived in all eighty-five Russian regions (the constituent entities officially referred to as the subjects of the Russian Federation) and represent all eight federal districts (the groupings of the federal subjects). More than half of the freelancers (55%) lived in the European part of Russia in the Central and North-West federal districts. The Southern and North-Caucasian districts cover 11% of Russian freelancers, 22% of them live in the Urals and Volga districts, and 12% in Siberia and the Far East. The largest populations of freelancers in Russia are in Moscow and the adjacent Moscow Region (31%), in St Petersburg and the adjacent Leningrad Region (13%), in Krasnodar Territory, Sverdlovsk Region, Novosibirsk Region, and Rostov Region (3–4% each).

In 2018, FL.ru freelancers resided in 2168 distinct locations, with about half of them (1093) situated in Russia. The largest cities with over 1000 online freelancers were Moscow, St Petersburg, Novosibirsk, Yekaterinburg, Krasnodar, Rostov-on-Don, Nizhny Novgorod, Kazan, Samara, Chelyabinsk, Voronezh and Ufa. Figure 1 suggests the positive relationship between the whole population of each city (natural logarithm) and the share of freelancers per 1000 of its citizens. Overall, the larger the city, the higher the percentage of its citizens who engage in online labour. This trend may be due to better Internet access, higher quality of skills as well as to the "creative city" phenomenon that encourages innovative models of work and digital lifestyles (for the description of a different situation in Japan see Keita Matsushita's contribution in this volume).

About a quarter of all cities and towns (585) where the freelancers lived in 2018 were located in the other post-Soviet countries, including Ukraine (308), Belarus (97), and Kazakhstan (61). Overall, fifty-nine cities on the territory of the former Soviet Union were prominent centres of freelance activity with more than 300 online freelancers living in each. Most of these cities were located in Russia (45) and Ukraine (8) (Kyiv, Kharkiv, Odesa, Dnepropetrovsk, Donetsk, Zaporizhzhia, Mykolaiv, Lviv). Other prominent cities from the post-Soviet

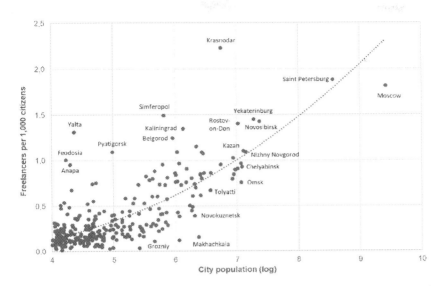

Fig. 1 The density of freelancers in Russian cities depending on their whole population in 2018

space with a relatively large number of Russian-speaking freelancers were Minsk, Gomel (Belarus), Almaty (Kazakhstan), Yerevan (Armenia), Chisinau (Moldova) and Tashkent (Uzbekistan).

There were not many Russian-speaking freelancers living outside post-Soviet countries. However, overall, freelancers covered 490 cities. In particular, freelancers from FL.ru represented forty-five cities in the USA (New York, Los Angeles, Boston, Chicago, San Francisco, Seattle, etc.), forty-six cities in Germany (Berlin, Munich, Stuttgart, Hanover, Frankfurt-on-Maine and others), and twenty-six cities in Poland (Warsaw, Wroclaw, Krakow, Poznan, etc.). Cities from other countries with the largest number of freelancers were Prague, London, Ko Samui, Sofia, Tel Aviv, Barcelona, Varna, Milan, Bangkok and Istanbul.

4.2 Clients

The clients active on FL.ru in 2018 resided in 121 countries. The demand on the platform was much more concentrated than the supply, as the vast majority of the clients resided in Russia (87.9%). Demand in terms of money was even more concentrated, with 91.5% of the total transaction value paid by clients from Russia.[5] A small percentages of clients resided in Ukraine (5.4%), Belarus (2.1%) and Kazakhstan (1.4%), and only 1.0% of clients lived in the other former Soviet Union republics. The remaining 2.2% of clients were located in other countries, the most prominent of which were Germany, the United States, Israel, the Czech Republic, Great Britain, Thailand and Spain. Overall, demand-side data suggest that the Russian-language online labour market serves mainly businesses based in the Russian Federation, with only a small number of clients from other countries. In this regard, freelancers from other countries could be treated as virtual migrants, contributing their skills to the Russian economy. The major consumer of digital labour was Moscow (42% of all clients), followed by St Petersburg (13%), Kyiv, Minsk, Yekaterinburg, and Novosibirsk (2% each).

4.3 Demand–Supply Ratio

Using data on the active FL.ru users, we calculated individual coefficients of demand–supply ratio for thirty countries sufficiently represented in the dataset (with more than fifty freelancers and clients in total in 2018) (see Fig. 2). The overall coefficient indicated that there were thirty-seven clients/one hundred workers on the whole platform during that period (1.0 to 2.7).[6] Further, the FL.ru data reveal that the demand for Russian language freelancers was much higher in developed countries such as Israel, USA, UK, Germany, Canada, Australia and the Czech Republic (from sixty-three to ninety-six clients/one hundred workers). Evidently, immigrants from Russia, starting businesses abroad, prefer to hire Russian-language workers. On the other hand, most post-Soviet countries seem to be the suppliers of digital labour. For instance, countries such as Armenia, Uzbekistan, Tajikistan, Moldova, Kyrgyzstan and

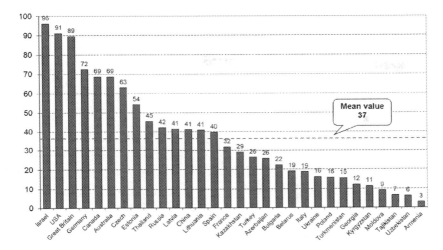

Fig. 2 Number of clients per 100 freelancers in different countries in 2018

Georgia had less than tweve clients/one hundred workers, Ukraine had sixteen, and Belarus nineteen. Compared to these two groups of countries, Russia was in an intermediate position with forty-two clients/one hundred workers.

5 Main Trends in an Emerging Market

In the following sections, we analyse the main trends in the Russian-language online labour market, including geographical clustering of economic activity, spatial division of online labour and decentralisation.

5.1 Geographical Clustering

Although online labour platforms have been designed to facilitate distant transactions, previous research provides strong evidence that spatial and cultural proximity affects the choice of a contractor (Gefen & Carmel, 2008; Ghani et al., 2014; Hong & Pavlou, 2017; Horton et al., 2017; Lehdonvirta et al., 2019). Moreover, clients tend to prefer domestic freelancers even in situations when all potential candidates are native-speakers and share a similar culture (Galperin & Greppi, 2019).

In this section we are going to see how spatial proximity affects market transactions. For this purpose, we use the data on the geographical distribution of clients and freelancers in reviews left by clients at the end of completed projects. The data reveal that 38.4% of all contracts fulfilled at FL.ru connected workers and clients who were actually residing in different countries, although on the leading global platforms such as Upwork, this figure can be as high as 90%. In turn, the share of contracts between freelancers and clients from different locations (cities) was about 87.3%. This is a significant indicator of the distant and transregional nature of the market. However, the share of non-proximate freelance contracting may be overstated as clients and workers from the same location may be more inclined to connect directly, avoiding platforms as mediators.

Figure 3 strongly suggests that clients tend to prefer contractors from the same country or their geographical region. For instance, 65.4% of all Russian client reviews were left to freelancers from Russia, while 57.1%

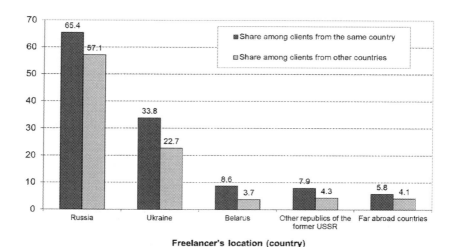

Fig. 3 Share of reviews left for freelancers by clients from different countries from 2005 to 2018 (percentages)

of all foreign client reviews were left to freelancers from Russia. This pattern emerges even more clearly in the case of former Soviet republics such as Ukraine, Belarus and others. For example, 33.8% of reviews by Ukrainian clients did not cross national borders, while only 22.7% of reviews by clients from other countries went to Ukrainian freelancers. This reflects an interesting fact, namely that clients from Ukraine and Belarus use the Russian-based platform to find freelancers from their own countries.

A similar pattern also appears in the analysis of Russian territories, as clients tend to prefer contracting with freelancers from the same region or federal district (see Fig. 4). Clients from Moscow, on average, work more often with freelancers from Moscow, clients from St Petersburg—with freelancers from St Petersburg, and so forth.

Although the data from FL.ru proves the transnational and transregional span of the Russian-language online labour market, it also reveals geographical clustering of economic activity. In line with previous research, we found some tendencies towards geographically proximate transactions. Clients tend to contract with freelancers from the same

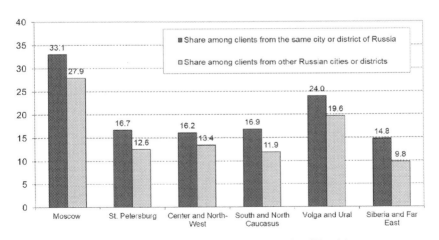

Fig. 4 Share of reviews left for freelancers by clients from main Russian cities and different federal districts from 2005 to 2018 (percentages)

country and region. It is noteworthy that about two thirds of all transactions on the Russian-language online labour market occur within Russia, including about one third that is concentrated in Moscow.

5.2 Spatial Division of Online Labour

This section explores how skills are distributed across the Russian-language online labour market to reveal the occupational patterns of virtual migration. Table 1 sheds light on the geographical distribution of freelancers by different occupations. Freelancers from Russia are better presented in business services (consulting, advertising and marketing, management, teaching), photo, audio, video and engineering services (82–85% vs. 77.1% among all workers). Ukrainian freelancers specialise more in IT services, as well as copywriting and editing (14–16% vs. 12.3%). Translators are over-represented in countries outside the post-Soviet space, since foreign residence might correspond to a better command of the language and serve as a marker for potential clients.

Table 1 Geographical distribution of Russian-language freelancers by different occupations from 2005 to 2018 (percentages)

Occupation	Freelancer's location			
	Russia	Ukraine	Other former USSR countries	Non post-Soviet countries
Websites, computer programming	71.6	**16.1**	10.8	1.5
Graphic design, creative arts	77.2	11.6	9.3	1.8
Engineering and manufacturing	**85.2**	8.1	6.1	0.5
Photography, audio, video	**82.3**	9.1	7.2	1.3
Copywriting and editing	76.5	**13.8**	8.1	1.6
Translating	76.8	7.8	8.7	**6.7**
Business services	**85.0**	7.7	5.8	1.6
Total	77.1	12.3	9.0	1.6

The data from client reviews to freelancers help to better understand the actual spatial patterns of various skills' utilisation, revealing the share of domestic and international transactions. In this case, we are not just looking at the geographical distribution of workers in different occupations, but also take into account the matchings between freelancers and clients from different countries for each specialisation. We are going to explore this matching in the case of Russia (see Table 2).

Russian clients tend to award contracts, more often, to domestic rather than foreign providers in the fields of engineering or manufacturing (70.2%) and business services (such as legal, advertising, consulting, etc.) (75.2 vs. 65.4% among all cases). By contrast, IT services (38.0%) and translating (38.1%) are more often imported by Russian clients from other countries (in comparison with 34.6% among all cases). It is interesting that for translating jobs, Russian clients turn to people who live outside Russia and the post-Soviet countries, much more often than for other skills (7.9 vs. 4.8%).[7] As for the export of skills from Russia, clients from other countries contract Russian freelancers more often when they

Table 2 Connections of clients with freelancers from Russia and other countries by different occupations from 2005 to 2018 (percentages)

Occupation	Clients from Russia — Freelancers from Russia	Clients from Russia — Freelancers from other countries	Clients from other countries — Freelancers from Russia	Clients from other countries — Freelancers from other countries
Websites, computer programming	62.0	**38.0**	55.8	**44.2**
Graphic design, creative arts	65.7	34.3	59.5	40.5
Engineering and manufacturing	**70.2**	29.8	51.8	**48.2**
Photography, audio, video	64.9	35.1	61.4	38.6
Copywriting and editing	66.4	33.6	58.5	41.5
Translating	61.9	**38.1**	60.1	39.9
Business services	**75.2**	24.8	**66.8**	33.2
Total	65.4	34.6	58.6	41.4

need business services such as marketing, management, consulting, and so forth. On the other hand, freelancers from Russia are less in demand when foreign clients require the services of engineering and manufacturing along with IT skills such as websites, computer programming and so forth.

Overall, the data reveal the spatial division of online labour that may be affected by many factors, including educational systems, size of the domestic markets, compensation gaps and general transferability of skills. The results may suggest that some skills (such as engineering and various business services) are less transferable across borders due to differences in the national technical standards and business regulations.

5.3 Decentralisation

In this section we use the overall data related to users registered on FL.ru from 2005 to 2018 to shed light on the main tendencies within the Russian-language online labour market (see Figs. 5 and 6). Various

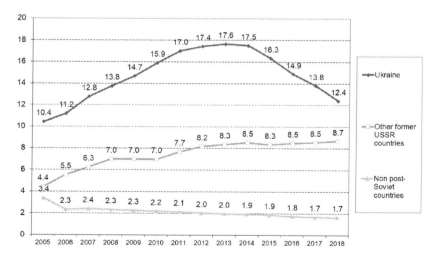

Fig. 5 The share of freelancers from different countries on FL.ru from 2005 to 2018 (percentages)

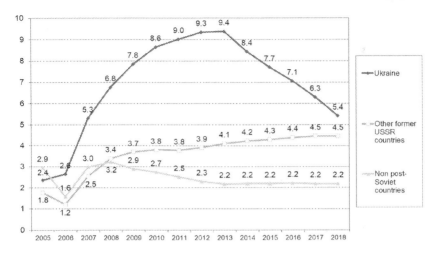

Fig. 6 The share of clients from different countries on FL.ru in 2005 to 2018 (percentages)

indicators over the entire period suggest the trend toward spatial decentralisation.

For many years, the shares of workers and clients from outside Russia have been increasing. Ukraine was the major driver of this development until 2014 when a severe political conflict between Russia and Ukraine erupted. Enormous controversy between both countries triggered a withdrawal of Ukrainian users from the Russian-based platform and prevented new registrations. The share of Ukrainian freelancers gradually increased from 10.4% in 2006 to 17.6% in 2013, and then returned almost to its original level (12.4% in 2018). A similar pattern was observed in the case of clients. In the early years (from 2005 to 2009), the share of Ukrainian clients at FL.ru grew actively and reached its maximum in 2013. After that, this indicator began to decline rapidly and by 2018 it had returned to the level of 2007 (5.4%). The share of users from other post-Soviet countries rose constantly over the entire period (among freelancers from 4.4% in 2005 to 8.7% in 2018, and among clients from 1.8 to 4.5%). However, the share of users from non post-Soviet countries has been dwindling somewhat gradually.

Overall, from 2005 to 2018, the share of freelancers at FL.ru from outside Russia increased from 18.2 to 22.8%, with a maximum of 27.9% in 2013/2014. The share of clients from outside Russia increased during the same time period, from 7.1 to 12.1%, with a maximum of 15.7% in 2013. We conclude that the consistent trend to international decentralisation of the Russian-language online labour market, driven by post-Soviet countries, was seriously affected by the political conflict between Russia and Ukraine from 2014 onwards.

Decentralisation of the online labour market, both for freelancers and clients, is even more evident within Russia (see Figs. 7 and 8). Over the fourteen years studied, the share of freelancers from Moscow had dropped by half, from 58 to 29%, the share of St Petersburg freelancers did not change greatly (15% in 2005 and 13% in 2018), while the share of freelancers from the all other Russian regions more than doubled, from 27 to 59%. Among clients, the share of workers from Moscow decreased from 78 to 48%. The share of St Petersburg clients remained at roughly the same level (12% in 2005 and 14% in 2018), while the share of clients from all other regions nearly quadrupled, from 10 to 38%. Thus,

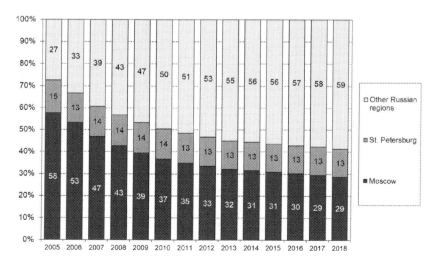

Fig. 7 The share of freelancers from Russian regions on FL.ru from 2005 to 2018 (percentages)

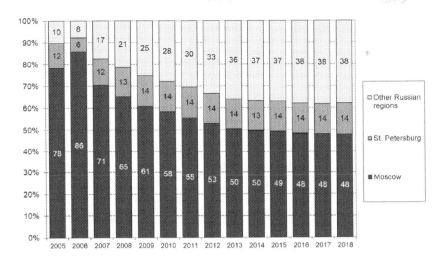

Fig. 8 The share of clients from Russian regions on FL.ru from 2005 to 2018 (percentages)

Moscow's share of the online labour market has decreased dramatically, both in terms of supply and demand. During 2005 to 2018, the share of freelancers from large cities with over 1,000,000 people (excluding Moscow and St. Petersburg) increased from 10 to 21%; the share of cities with populations between 500,000 and 1,000,000 increased from 8 to 14%. Freelancers and clients from smaller cities were drawn into the online labour market (cities under 250,000 saw a threefold increase, and for cities between 250,000 and 500,000 citizens there was a twofold increase). This development was most intense in the first years of the platform's operation and has been slowing down ever since, and the trend was the same for freelancers as well as for clients. We conclude that there is a strong trend toward the decentralisation of the online labour market within Russia. Moscow is gradually losing its prominence as the main location of clients and especially freelancers.

6   Conclusion

Online labour markets serve as a suitable case for researching how processes of digitalisation and globalisation create new and complex economic geographies by fundamentally altering the way people work and interact (Agrawal et al., 2015; Graham & Anwar, 2019; Kässi & Lehdonvirta, 2018; Kuek et al., 2015). A growing body of literature puts the "flat world" hypothesis (e.g., Friedman, 2007) under scrutiny and provides evidence of how location still matters in the digital freelance economy (Galperin & Greppi, 2019; Gefen & Carmel, 2008; Graham et al., 2017; Hong & Pavlou, 2017; Horton et al., 2017; Lehdonvirta et al., 2019). Making the case for the Russian-language online labour market, this study contributes to the emerging scholarship on the geography of digital labour in several ways.

First, we showed how common language, culture, history and other socio-economic factors facilitate a distinct online labour market that spans vast territories and political borders. Some dozens of online labour platforms that operate in the Russian language already have several millions of registered users. Most of them live in Russia and other countries that used to be part of the former Soviet Union. However, our data from just one leading Russian-language freelance platform, FL.ru, revealed the coverage of 180 countries. Overall, we demonstrated that presenting Russia as a mere supplier of digital labour to the Global North is misleading. We argue that the real geography of the digital freelance economy includes not only an emerging planetary labour market, but also an array of smaller online markets that operate across spatial borders in languages other than English (Galperin & Greppi, 2019; Kuek et al., 2015; Shevchuk & Strebkov, 2015; To & Lai, 2015). Future research should pay more attention not only to these non-English language markets in different parts of the world but also to the complex ways they intertwine and interact. Freelancers and clients may use many platforms simultaneously and switch over from one online market to another.

Second, we provided new empirical evidence on some important issues discussed in the extant literature on the geography of the digital freelance economy (Galperin & Greppi, 2019; Gefen & Carmel, 2008; Graham & Anwar, 2019; Graham et al., 2017; Hong & Pavlou, 2017; Horton et al.,

2017; Lehdonvirta et al., 2019). Our results support some regularities and patterns known from the previous studies of English-language platforms. For instance, demand for digital labour is far more concentrated than supply, revealing the few dominant centres of economic activity and vast areas of virtual migration. In our study, the vast majority of the clients lived in Russia (and particularly in Moscow) with freelancers scattered mainly across post-Soviet space and beyond, around the world. The study also suggests that clients in online labour markets tend to prefer contractors from the same country or geographical region, however, these preferences differ for various occupations illuminating the spatial division of online labour. We propose that this occupational dimension deserves more attention in future studies.

Third, unique data comprising a period from 2005 to 2018 helped to reveal the consistent trend towards spatial decentralisation in the Russian-language online labour market that manifests itself both internationally and within the territory of the Russian Federation. This means that more and more freelancers and clients from countries other than Russia and cities other than Moscow are participating in the Russian-language online labour market. We explain this by spatial diffusion of the online platform work as an innovative phenomenon from an economically more developed centre to less developed territories. We also showed how political factors such as the conflict between Ukraine and Russia can affect established trends. We encourage using long-term data to trace the changing geography of online labour.

Fourth, we explored not only the international dimension of the online labour market, but also the regional dimension within the territory of the Russian Federation, including the level of cities. We demonstrated that Russian regions are involved in the digital freelance economy to varying degrees. This may reflect strong inequalities in the regional economic development, including local labour market conditions, educational institutions and access to the high-speed Internet. We also found that the share of freelancers increases with the city population size, suggesting that online platform work is still a big-city phenomenon, although the share of freelancers from smaller cities in the online labour market is growing steadily (see the contribution by Jian Lin for different outcomes in China). Overall, researching the digital freelance economy at the regional and city levels allows for a more nuanced picture that reflects the uneven spatial development of different territories and could yield interesting results.

Notes

1. In this chapter, we use the terms *digital freelance economy* and *online labour market* to describe correspondingly the new economic model and the new type of labour market, and distinguish them from *digital platforms* or *online marketplaces*—dedicated websites (such as Upwork or Freelancer) that serve as mediators in online labour markets and provide basic infrastructure for the digital freelance economy. However, in the economic literature *online labour markets* are often conflated with websites (Hong & Pavlou, 2013; Horton, 2010).
2. On these online marketplaces workers typically appear as autonomous service providers. That is why in the identification of the opposite contracting party the term *employee* is usually avoided in favour of *client*, *buyer* or *requester*.
3. We found an interesting fact that neatly reflects the costs of self-reporting data: thirty-three users reported that they live in Baylam—the capital of Arulko, the fictional country from the computer game *Jagged Alliance 2*: https://en.wikipedia.org/wiki/Jagged_Alliance_2. Accessed 21 February 2021.
4. We used the International Labour Office data on total country labour force in 2018: https://ilostat.ilo.org/topics/population-and-labour-force. Accessed 21 February 2021.
5. This statistic is based on 12,460 projects that started in 2018 where a client left a review and indicated the amount of remuneration.
6. Our estimate of demand–supply ratio on the platform is limited by the lack of a complete set of all freelancers in 2018 and by a disproportionately large number of clients not recording their place of residence. To allow the comparison, we applied the adjustment coefficient based on the proportion between freelancers and clients signing up within two months preceding data collection, as FL.ru sitemap lists all users who signed up in the last six months. While due to computational confoundedness the coefficient might be biased in estimating the exact ratio of clients to freelancers, it is nevertheless valid for a between-countries comparison.

7. Complete results for individual countries are not presented in Table 2, but are available upon request.

References

Agrawal, A. K., Lacetera, N., & Lyons, E. (2013). *Does information help or hinder job applicants from less developed countries in online markets?* (NBER Working Paper No. 18720). National Bureau of Economic Research.

Agrawal, A., Horton, J., Lacetera, N., & Lyons, E. (2015). Digitization and the contract labor market: A research agenda. In A. Goldfarb, S. M. Greenstein, & C. E. Tucker (Eds.), *Economic analysis of the digital economy* (pp. 219–256). UCP.

Aguinis, H., & Lawal, S. O. (2013). eLancing: A review and research agenda for bridging the science–practice gap. *Human Resource Management Review, 23,* 6–17. https://doi.org/10.1016/j.hrmr.2012.06.003

Aleksynska, M., Bastrakova, A., & Kharchenko, N. (2018). *Work on digital labour platforms in Ukraine: Issues and policy perspectives.* International Labour Office.

Aneesh, A. (2006). *Virtual migration: The programming of globalization.* Duke University.

Aref'ev, A. L. (2014). The Russian language in the world: Past, present, and future. *Herald of the Russian Academy of Sciences, 84,* 357–364. https://doi.org/10.1134/S1019331614050050

Bailey, D. E., & Kurland, N. B. (2002). A review of telework research: Findings, new directions, and lessons for the study of modern work. *Journal of Organizational Behavior, 23,* 383–400. https://doi.org/10.1002/job.144

Beerepoot, N., & Lambregts, B. (2015). Competition in online job marketplaces: Towards a global labour market for outsourcing services? *Global Networks, 15,* 236–255. https://doi.org/10.1111/glob.12051

Berg, J., Furrer, M., Harmon, E., Rani, U., & Silberman, S. S. (2018). *Digital labour platforms and the future of work: Towards decent work in the online world* (Resource document). International Labour Office. https://www.ilo.org/global/publications/books/WCMS_645337/lang--en/index.htm. Accessed 21 February 2021.

Blinder, A. S. (2006). Offshoring: The next industrial revolution? *Foreign Affairs, 85*, 113–128.

Cairncross, F. (2001). *The death of distance: How the communications revolution is changing our lives*. HBSP.

Carmel, E., Hou, C. Q., & Olsen, T. (2012). The human cloud in China: An early inquiry and analysis. In *Proceedings of the Annual Workshop of the AIS Special Interest Group for ICT in Global Development, USA, 5*. https://aisel.aisnet.org/globdev2012/7/.

Chepurenko, A. (2015). Entrepreneurial activity under 'transition.' In R. Blackburn, U. Hytti, & F. Welter (Eds.), *Context, process and gender in entrepreneurship: Frontiers in European entrepreneurship research* (pp. 6–22). Edward Elgar.

Cheskin, A., & Kachuyevski, A. (2019). The Russian-Speaking populations in the post-Soviet space: Language, politics and identity. *Europe-Asia Studies, 71*, 1–23. https://doi.org/10.1080/09668136.2018.1529467

Codagnone, C., Karatzogianni, A., & Matthews, J. (2018). *Platform economics: Rhetoric and reality in the "sharing economy"*. Emerald.

Friedman, T. L. (2007). *The world is flat 3.0: A brief history of the twenty-first century*. Picador.

Galperin, H., & Greppi, C. (2019). Geographic discrimination in the gig economy. In M. Graham (Ed.), *Digital economies at global margins* (pp. 295–318). MIT.

Gefen, D., & Carmel, E. (2008). Is the world really flat? A look at offshoring at an online programming marketplace. *MIS Quarterly, 32*, 367–384.

Ghani, E., Kerr, W. R., & Stanton, C. (2014). Diasporas and outsourcing: Evidence from oDesk and India. *Management Science, 60*, 1677–1697. https://doi.org/10.1287/mnsc.2013.1832

Graham, M., & Anwar, M. A. (2019). The global gig economy: Towards a planetary labour market? *First Monday, 24*(4). https://doi.org/10.5210/fm.v24i4.9913.

Graham, M., Hjorth, I., & Lehdonvirta, V. (2017). Digital labour and development: Impacts of global digital labour platforms and the gig economy on worker livelihoods. *Transfer: European Review of Labour and Research, 23*, 135–162. https://doi.org/10.1177/1024258916687250.

Hong, Y., & Pavlou, P. A. (2013). *Online labor markets: An informal freelancer economy* (IBIT report). Institute for Business and Information Technology.

Hong, Y., & Pavlou, P. A. (2017). On buyer selection of service providers in online outsourcing platforms for IT services. *Information Systems Research, 28*, 547–562. https://doi.org/10.1287/isre.2017.0709

Horton, J. J. (2010). Online labor markets. In A. Saberi (Ed.), *Internet and network economics* (pp. 515–522). Springer.

Horton, J. J., & Tambe, P. (2015). Labor economists get their microscope: Big data and labor market analysis. *Big Data, 3*(3), 130–137. https://doi.org/10.1089/big.2015.0017

Horton, J., Kerr, W. R., & Stanton, C. (2017). *Digital labor markets and global talent flows* (NBER Working Paper No. 23398). Link to resource document. National Bureau of Economic Research. http://www.nber.org/papers/w23398. Accessed 21 February 2021.

Huws, U. (2017). Where did online platforms come from? The virtualization of work organization and the new policy challenges it raises. In P. Meil & V. Kirov (Eds.), *Policy implications of virtual work* (pp. 29–48). Springer.

Internet World Stats. (2019). *Top Ten internet languages in the world*. Miniwatts Marketing Group. https://www.internetworldstats.com/stats7.htm. Accessed 21 February 2021.

Kalleberg, A. L., & Dunn, M. (2016). Good jobs, bad jobs in the gig economy. *Perspectives on Work, 20*(1), 10–13, 74.

Kanat, I., Hong, Y., & Raghu, T. S. (2018). Surviving in global online labor markets for IT services: A geo-economic analysis. *Information Systems Research, 29*, 893–909. https://doi.org/10.1287/isre.2017.0751

Kässi, O., & Lehdonvirta, V. (2018). Online labour index: Measuring the online gig economy for policy and research. *Technological Forecasting and Social Change, 137*(12), 241–248. https://doi.org/10.1016/j.techfore.2018.07.056

Kuek, S. C., Paradi-Guilford, C., Fayomi, T., Imaizumi, C., Ipeirotis, P., Pina, P., et al. (2015). *The global opportunity in online outsourcing* (Resource document). The World Bank. http://pubdocs.worldbank.org/pubdocs/publicdoc/2015/6/212201433273511482/Global-OO-Study.pdf. Accessed 21 February 2021.

Lazer, D., & Radford, J. (2017). Data ex machina: Introduction to big data. *Annual Review of Sociology, 43*(1), 19–39. https://doi.org/10.1146/annurev-soc-060116-053457

Lehdonvirta, V. (2017). *Where are online workers located? The international division of digital gig work*. Oxford Internet Institute. https://ilabour.oii.ox.ac.uk/where-are-online-workers-located-the-international-division-of-digital-gig-work/. Accessed 21 February 2021.

Lehdonvirta, V., Kässi, O., Hjorth, I., Barnard, H., & Graham, M. (2019). The global platform economy: A new offshoring institution enabling emerging-economy microproviders. *Journal of Management, 45*, 567–599. https://doi.org/10.1177/0149206318786781

Malone, T. W., & Laubacher, R. J. (1998). The dawn of the e-lance economy. *Harvard Business Review, 76*(5), 144–152, 189.

Malone, T. W., Laubacher, R. J., & Johns, T. (2011). The big idea: The age of hyperspecialization. *Harvard Business Review, 89*(4), 56–65.

Markevich, A., & Mikhailova, T. N. (2013). Economic geography of Russia. In M. Alexeev & S. Weber (Eds.), *The Oxford handbook of the Russian economy* (pp. 617–642). Oxford University Press.

Messenger, J. C., & Gschwind, L. (2016). Three generations of telework: New ICTs and the (r)evolution from home office to virtual office. *New Technology, Work and Employment, 31*, 195–208. https://doi.org/10.1111/ntwe.12073

Mustajoki, A., Protassova, E., & Yelenevskaya, M. (2019). *The soft power of the Russian language: Pluricentricity, politics and policies*. Routledge.

Nicklin, J. M., Cerasoli, C. P., & Dydyn, K. L. (2016). Telecommuting: What? Why? When? and How? In J. Lee (Ed.), *The impact of ICT on work* (pp. 41–70). Springer.

Roach, S. (2004). *How global labour arbitrage will shape the world economy* (Resource document). Hussonet. http://ecocritique.free.fr/roachglo.pdf. Accessed 21 Feb 2021.

Salganik, M. J. (2018). *Bit by bit: Social research in the digital age*. Princeton University Press.

Shevchuk, A., & Strebkov, D. (2015). The rise of freelance contracting on the Russian-language internet. *Small Enterprise Research, 22*, 146–158. https://doi.org/10.1080/13215906.2015.1052341

To, W.-M., & Lai, L. S. L. (2015). Crowdsourcing in China: Opportunities and concerns. *IT Professional, 17*(3), 53–59.

3

Supporting the Global Digital Games Industry: Outsourcing Games Production in Poland and Estonia

Anna Ozimek

In recent years there has been growing interest in investigating the digital games culture and production in various sociocultural and socio-economic contexts (e.g., Huntemann and Aslinger, 2013). This body of research provides important insights into understanding the extent and complexity of digital games production networks and the variety of game-making practices. These studies investigated the gendered labour in hardware production (Huntemann, 2013), working conditions of community managers in Ireland (Kerr & Kelleher, 2015) and informal game-making practices in Australia (Keogh, 2021). Furthermore, studies about varieties of game-making experiences problematise questions about who is working on digital games, where and how (e.g., Keogh, 2021). As a result, efforts to expand scholarly understanding of games production

---

A. Ozimek (✉)
Department of Theatre, Film, Television and Interactive Media, University of York, York, UK
e-mail: anna.ozimek@york.ac.uk

© The Author(s), under exclusive license to Springer Nature Switzerland AG 2021
M. Will-Zocholl and C. Roth-Ebner (eds.), *Topologies of Digital Work*, Dynamics of Virtual Work,
https://doi.org/10.1007/978-3-030-80327-8_3

and workforce are uncovering increasingly complex, tangled relationships among the global game market, international production networks, regional support measures, local policies and a highly mobile, creative workforce. Therefore, like other examples of digital labour, work in digital games is characterised "by both 'placelessness' *and* [emphasis in the original] stickiness, by both dispersion *and* [emphasis in the original] spatial concentration" (Flecker, 2016, p. 2).

This chapter contributes to this growing body of research on digital games production by exploring outsourcing work in Poland and Estonia. Outsourcing is defined as "a business activity (involving the production of either goods or services) which is purchased by an organisation from an external supplier rather than being carried out internally" (Huws et al., 2004, p. 4). In other words, outsourcing is synonymous with subcontracting work. Since the late 1980s, outsourcing has become the fastest-growing management practice supported by the extensive development of the Information and Communication Technologies (ICT) infrastructure and the Internet (Davis-Blake & Broschak, 2009). The prevalence of outsourcing and its impact on employment relations have been extensively discussed in studies about software development (e.g., Flecker, 2009). Outsourcing is also not a novelty in games development where the rising cost and complexity involved in games production leads to increasing reliance on subcontracted labour (Thomsen, 2018). In fact, some national and regional industries historically developed from providing subcontracted work in their region to international clients (Chung, 2016). Despite the growing importance of outsourcing for the digital games industry (Nichols, 2014, p. 82) it remains "a less visible facet of the globalization" (Dyer-Witheford & de Peuter, 2009, p. 50). The reasoning behind outsourcing parts of production in cultural industries comes from complex decisions regarding finding locations with access to a capable workforce, relatively lower labour costs, availability of flexible employment arrangements, lack of strong unionisation tendencies or a favourable climate for foreign investments, national regulations and policies (Huws et al., 2004, p. 19). Consequently, subcontracting of work in the games industry raises questions about the dynamics of the industry development, complex networks of companies supporting global games production and about the workers' position within these relations.

Drawing on semi-structured interviews with people engaged in games production, and analysis of secondary sources (e.g., industry reports), this contribution presents a variety of approaches to and practices of outsourcing in the context of Eastern European countries. The findings in this contribution are based on data from two research projects concerning the development of games industries in Poland and Estonia. After the collapse of the Soviet Union, the Eastern bloc countries underwent rapid political, economic and social changes. The bloc's transformation at the beginning of the 1990s contributed to significant changes in labour markets, a shift of economic development to the service sector, increased interest in attracting foreign investments to the countries and the local governments' interest in the digital economy sector (e.g., Hardy, 2009). In addition, ICT-related outsourcing services provided by Eastern European countries grew in importance and developed a significant IT-support services base. Huws et al., (2004, p. 2) argued that this increase in outsourcing was motivated by a geographical and historical proximity to Western European countries. In this contribution, I will specifically investigate game work in subcontracted arrangements because, inevitably, the restructuring of companies and value chains contributes to the fragmentation of employment and composition of labour (Flecker, 2009).

The chapter has two aims: First, it provides an empirical contribution to studies about national and regional digital games production and specifically games production in the Central and Eastern Europe (CEE) region. Previous studies about the CEE region encompass historical investigations of informal digital games distribution networks and game cultures (Švelch, 2018) and discussions about the CEE region in comparative studies about different national digital games industries, including the Czech Republic and Iran (Šisler et al., 2017) and Germany, Sweden and Poland (Teipen, 2008). This chapter expands these studies by investigating subcontracted work in the CEE region. Second, this chapter focuses on work arrangements, which are often excluded from national statistics and reports about the workforce in the games industry (e.g., Bobrowski et al., 2017). While workers engaged in subcontracted work provide vital services to the industry, they are often not defined as a "core" or "creative" workforce. However, their work and the extent of fragmented and decentralised production networks indicate that both identifying game workers and precisely defining extensive games production networks are becoming increasingly more difficult.

The chapter is structured as follows. The next section describes studies regarding the spatialisation of games production. The third section outlines the study's research design. The findings and discussion section is divided into two parts: The first part provides contextual background about the organisation and composition of games industries in Poland and Estonia. The second part describes three different examples of outsourcing practices. In the conclusion section, I will demonstrate that the popularity of outsourcing work in the CEE countries is associated with the histories of the national games industries, and—after the collapse of the Soviet Union—access to a capable workforce, cheaper labour and countries with an increased interest in attracting foreign investments and supporting entrepreneurial endeavours. Furthermore, I argue that the digital games workforce and the experiences of its members are locally embedded; influenced by the available infrastructure, resources and regulations; and positioned to compete with other actors within the global games market.

1 Spatial Relations of Digital Games Production

The digital games industry is often emblematic of contemporary transnational informational capitalism (Bulut, 2015; Dyer-Witheford & de Peuter, 2009; Kerr, 2017). The industry evolved from companies engaged in the development of military research, ICT infrastructure and toy industries at the beginning of the 1970s (Kerr, 2017, p. 61). By quickly adapting to new technologies, developing new business models and mobilising global networks of creative labour, the global digital games industry's revenue in 2019 grew to an estimated 120,100,000,000 USD (Takahashi, 2020).

Media and cultural industries have always been connected through complex production networks and have operated across local, regional and global boundaries (Christopherson, 2006). Asymmetrical power relations in media industries have been addressed by scholars interested in the political economy of communication, such as Mosco (1996). Drawing on the work of Henri Lefebrve (1974/1991), Mosco discussed the concept of "spatialisation" to indicate the importance of investigating meaning of place, space and power in media industries studies and he addressed spatialisation as "the process of overcoming the constraints of space and time in social life" (Mosco, 1996, p. 157). Through this concept, political economists demonstrate how the capitalist mode of production uses the power of transportation and communication to transform spatial relations among various institutions, companies, commodities and people (Mosco, 1996). Kerr (2014, p. 28) argued that the concept of spatialisation offers a useful theoretical framework to analyse the internationalisation of media industries, including games industries. Kerr (2014, p. 28) also demonstrated that while Mosco's (1996) approach to spatialisation attends mostly to actions of corporations and states, Lefebrve's idea of spatialisation focuses not only on structures and actions of given institutions but also on various aspects of power in relation to the meaning of space. Lefebrve (1974/1991) engages with other elements of the social production of space, such as spatial practice (space perceived), representation of space (discourse *on* space) and spaces of representation (discourse *of* space). Through this understanding, space is both produced and productive, and it evolved historically rather than being created separately from a society (see the contribution by Christian Oggolder in this volume). This perspective provides a useful starting point in thinking about the sociohistorical development of spaces in digital games production beyond assigning them to only national or regional boundaries. As Mosco (1996, p. 179) argued, "the choice of the term spatialisation is precisely intended to underscore the process of constant spatial change, which geography has documented over the range of configurations of absolute, space, time–space, cost-space, social space and cultural space". Thinking about spatialisation of digital games production allows for the discussion of the extent and variety of production networks spanning national, regional and international boundaries and changes in power relations.

Early studies about games production networks (e.g., Johns, 2006) demonstrated that software and hardware production in the industry are highly regionalised. From the beginning of the 1980s, the digital games industries were dominated by companies from North America and Japan (Kerr, 2017). However, since 2010, Chinese and South Korean companies have grown in importance (Kerr, 2017). Since the digital games industry development began, many of these companies have come from the ICT sector (e.g., Apple, Google) or entertainment sector (e.g., Sony, Vivendi, Time Warner). In addition, digital games markets include a variety of segments ranging from PC and console gaming to mobile and online games. Software production can be divided further into companies specialising in publishing, development, middleware development and related activities (e.g., service-support companies). Game development can be carried out by in-house development studios owned by publishers (i.e., first-party studio), by second-party development studios working on the basis of external contracts for publishers or by third-party developers (independent game developers) who develop their own games and self-publish them or try to gain contracts with external publishers (see Kerr, 2006). With the development of ICT infrastructures, the Internet, online distribution, new business models in digital games and access to development tools, new models of games development have been established from informal forms of game development (Keogh, 2021) to geographically dispersed networks of subcontracted work (e.g., Chung, 2016). These practices and networks span different geographical locations, while the political, economic and social histories of a given region play a role in the formation of national games industries.

Digital games industries are developing in relation to their historical embeddedness and local infrastructure because "the spatial distribution of the games industry is complex and linked in part to the history of the games industry but more significantly to the regional structure of software production networks interacting with local and regional financial, cultural, and labour markets" (Kerr, 2014, pp. 28–29). Studies on national games production demonstrated that the pre-existing infrastructure, connection to other cultural industries and recognition of cultural legitimacy of digital games are important in understanding the historical trajectories and development of games industries. Izushi and Aoyama (2006) discussed how the well-established manga and animation industry in Japan supported the development of the Japanese digital games industry. Chung (2016) described how the online games industry has been developed in Southeast Asia through reliance on outsourcing and contracting work within the region. Kerr and Cawley (2012) explained why Ireland became an important place for providing middleware and community services for the global digital games industry while having a weak base for its own intellectual property (IP) games development. Furthermore, scholars argue that the involvement of national and intranational institutions in providing support measures for the industry contributes to defining their economic potential and cultural legitimacy (e.g., Sotamaa et al., 2019). This diversity of production networks raises questions about the labour behind digital games production, that is, labour based in different geographical locations, labour in different organisational structures and labour performed in a variety of occupational tasks.

2 Research Methods and Methodology

This chapter draws on data from two projects on the development of the digital game industries in Poland (from 2014 to 2018) and Estonia (from 2019 to 2020). The presented findings are based on an investigation of the relationship between the development of local games production and the global power dynamics influencing the games production space documented between 2014 and 2020.

The chapter primarily focuses on data from semi-structured interviews ($n = 67$) with game workers and other interviewees associated with a given national games industry (e.g., educators, community organisers or local industry representatives). The interview data are supported by the analysis of secondary sources (e.g., industry reports, policy documents and archival game magazine documents) to contextualise interviewees' perspectives. The interview schedule was prepared based on a review of previous studies about games production and an analysis of secondary sources. Overall, I conducted forty-four interviews in Poland and twenty-three in Estonia; interviewees were identified based on purposive snowballing sampling. My approaches to collecting and conducting interviews were informed by recognising the fragmented nature of the industries in Poland and Estonia, wherein the majority of workers in the games industries escape strict categorisations of occupational and professional backgrounds. In the presented research projects, I have acknowledged that my interviewees had a wide variety of industry-related work experience in independent game development, Triple-A[1] productions, game testing, software engineering and game designing.

Interviews were conducted in person or with the use of the software application Skype. The interviews had an average length of between forty-five and ninety minutes. Interviews were conducted either in Polish or English, depending on the respective interviewee's background.[2] I transcribed all interviews and have provided translations of the interviews conducted in Polish. I decided to anonymise the interviewees' quotes to protect them and possible third parties. In rare circumstances where parties could not be anonymised, for example, where an interviewee represented an institution or community, interviewees gave permission to include information that rendered them identifiable. I analysed all collected data through thematic analysis using the Nvivo Pro 11 qualitative analysis software.

3 Digital Game Industries in Poland and Estonia: Findings and Discussion

My intention in this chapter is neither to compare the two countries nor to claim that the situation experienced by game workers in Poland and Estonia is unique. On the contrary, the structure of the global digital games market and its competitiveness require game workers to engage in subcontracted work around the world (e.g., Chung, 2016; Keogh, 2021). Instead, the focus of this chapter is on the sociohistorical development of service providers in the CEE region and the variety of work organisations related to outsourcing in the digital games industry. Obvious differences between Poland and Estonia cannot be underestimated, including national histories, national and religious identities, and the size of the local games industries. Poland is a country of approximately 38,000,000 inhabitants based in an ethnically homogenous state. Estonia, on the other hand, has slightly more than 1,300,000 inhabitants in a multinational state with significant participation from the Russian-speaking community.

Despite these differences, Poland and Estonia share some similarities. They are both historically defined as a part of the Eastern bloc: Poland as a satellite country under the USSR's influence, and Estonia as one of the Soviet republics. Poland and Estonia share some similar histories and experiences that have had an impact on the development of the technology and games industries in the region. Both countries experienced challenges in accessing technology due to the embargo imposed by the Coordinating Committee for Multilateral Export Controls (CoCom). The imposed embargo prevented the Eastern bloc from obtaining technological equipment and exchanging engineering knowledge. After the collapse of the Soviet Union, both countries underwent significant social, economic and political changes. Due to the transition towards a capitalist market economy, rapid social, economic and political reforms occurred, resulting in, inter alia, the introduction of flexible work arrangements, dismantled welfare provisions and increased interest in attracting foreign investments to the region (see also Hardy, 2009). Achieving an understanding of the concept of spatialisation in the context of games production in Eastern Europe is to position games production within the broader socio-economic and historical changes that are taking place in Poland and Estonia. Consequently, the production of space in the CEE context involves the ongoing construction of economic, ideological and everyday social relations, which have an impact on understanding work in digital games production.

The foundations of the Polish digital games industry were established during the era of the Polish People's Republic (from 1947 to 1989). The downturn in Poland's communist economy resulted in the local games culture developing through grey technology markets, which acquired and distributed foreign software and hardware in Poland through informal channels (Kosman, 2015). The heritage of informal distribution and games production became an important part of the Polish industry's cultural identity, as major Polish digital games developers and publishers, such as CD Projekt and Techland, started their operations through the distribution or localisation of foreign software on the Polish market. In 1990, Polish game production began experiencing challenges related to the country's transition to a capitalist economy: increased interest in attracting foreign investors to Poland, struggles against persistent software piracy and the increased competitiveness of the global digital game market (see Kosman, 2015). Despite its turbulent past, the Polish digital games industry has become a poster child for success in the CEE region. According to industry reports, the contemporary Polish games industry consists of approximately 400 companies (Bobrowski et al., 2017) that are consolidated mostly in major urban locations such as Warsaw (Mazovian region) or Krakow (Malopolska) (Bobrowski et al., 2017).

The majority of production in Poland, as in many other countries, consists of small- and medium-sized developers that self-fund and self-publish their productions (Bobrowski et al., 2017). However, Poland is also home to well-known Triple-A developers and publishers (e.g., CD Projekt, Techland) and service-support companies specialising in game testing, localisation and porting (e.g., QLOC, Lionbridge). The workforce engaged in digital games production in Poland includes various actors with different experiences and specialisations, such as creative directors in Triple-A companies, 3D graphic design freelancers and digital game testers based in service-support companies. Game workers based in Poland experience similar challenges as discussed in studies on game workers in other countries; their work is often precarious, project-based and marked by prolonged periods of overtime (see Ozimek, 2018). The exact number of game workers working in Poland is unknown, as estimations vary, given the reports' methodological approaches and used terminology.

Estonia is often associated with the idea of a "digital" society due to the country's extensive investments in e-government infrastructure. The Estonian government's interest in digital technologies might be associated with the country's difficult past of being one of the Soviet republics and experiencing significant economic limitations. Therefore, as stated by some interviewees, the country openly embraced investments in the broadly defined ICT sector due to the lack of other economic development alternatives. The country made efforts to attract foreign investments and support local entrepreneurs by facilitating the opening of companies, introducing a transparent tax system and simplifying communication with authorities (Kaminska-Korolczuk & Kijewska, 2017, p. 141). However, some interviewees argued that while the embracing of a digital economy in Estonia is visible from the outside, digital games production is not part of this narrative. Interviewees engaged in local games production admitted that the developing industry lacked appropriate support measures, opportunities for career progression and recognition from the government.

Little information is available regarding the history of the Estonian game culture and industry. The earliest records discussed the game *SkyRoads* from 1993, developed by Bluemoon game studio, as the first internationally successful Estonian production. In early 2000, the majority of digital games companies based in Estonia offered services such as development of art assets for international clients (e.g., Ringtail Studios). According to interviewees, the development and expansion of companies related to games production in the country started much later, in the mid-2000s, with the emergence of major games studios that specialised in mobile games (e.g., Creative Mobile) and entrepreneurial initiatives dedicated to supporting small game developers (e.g., GameFounders accelerator). According to a database of companies curated by the International Game Developers Association Estonia (IGDA),[3] the Estonian games industry includes eighty companies as of 2020. Further analysis of the listed companies indicates that only thirty-three of the included entities are directly engaged in digital games development, while the other companies include service providers (thirty-six), online casinos (four), community organisations (three) or unidentified companies (seven). Unsurprisingly, most digital games companies and related companies are based in Estonia's capital city, Tallinn.

According to the interviewees, the structure of the Estonian digital games-related companies is highly fragmented, and the leading positions are filled by developers who specialise in mobile games production.

According to the report about creative industries prepared by the Estonian government, games industry data are included in a broader subcategory of creative industries defined as "entertainment software" (Estonian Institute of Economic Research, 2018, pp. 15–16). It has been estimated, according to data from 2015, that there are 989 workers employed in the entertainment software sector in Estonia. However, according to the report, the majority of workers from this sector are employed in the online gambling industry rather than in digital games production (Estonian Institute of Economic Research, 2018, pp. 15–16). The inclusion of the online gambling industry inflates the numbers of companies and workers employed in the entertainment sector, and detailed data on workers in the digital games industry are not presented. Interviewees demonstrated that PC and console digital games production are mostly carried out by small development teams or individual creators who supplement their income through work as contractors for other entertainment and non-entertainment software productions.

4 Subcontracting Work in the Digital Games Industry

In contrast to the outsourcing of hardware production, the outsourcing patterns of software production are less rigidly defined (Kerr, 2006, p. 78). Eastern Europe is often mentioned as a desired destination for outsourcing parts of games production; however, the different forms of the subcontracted work experience in the region are comparatively less explored (Nichols, 2014, p. 151). Investigation of subcontracting arrangements in the digital games industry draws attention to the multiplicity of spatialities at work: from companies offsetting the risk of cultural production, to destinations with lower labour costs, to locating productions in places of social and cultural proximity (e.g., shared language). Therefore, while the use of ICT and Internet infrastructure allows games companies to subcontract parts of production to different countries and regions, cultural production is spatially distributed based on sociohistorical, economic and cultural factors (Kerr, 2014, p. 30).

To investigate the process of spatialisation of games software production in Eastern Europe is to acknowledge the economic and sociohistorical trajectories of the development of these games industries. It is not only to acknowledge the development of amateur game developers' communities, but also the political and economic position of Eastern European countries (i.e., Poland and Estonia) and the dynamics of the interaction between national, regional and international actors and institutions. Consequently, this contribution turns to the process of spatialisation to acknowledge the variety of actors and influences that contribute to shaping the organisation of subcontracted work in Poland and Estonia.

Outsourcing of digital software production to Eastern Europe is not a novelty. On the contrary, in the late 1980s and the beginning of the 1990s, companies based in Poland and Estonia often provided support for the development of digital games in other countries, mostly North America and Western Europe. The digital games industries in Poland and Estonia have been established under the influence of differences in political, economic and technological development, with digital games companies based in the USA, Japan and Western Europe establishing their leading positions in the market as developers and publishers, while game development in Eastern Europe remained mostly a small-scale and hobbyist activity (Kluska & Rozwadowski, 2011). While digital games development was not economically viable for early games enthusiasts in Poland and Estonia, establishing support-services companies in these countries was deemed to be more profitable, often offering foreign clients access to cheaper labour and early international investments in Eastern European markets (Kosman, 2015).

The closest approximation to professional digital games production in the Polish People's Republic came in the form of development studios established for porting and developing digital games from the US market. The only game studio established in 1983 that reflected the standards of game studios in the United States was created by Lucjan Wencel, a Polish immigrant from California (Kluska, 2019). The company mainly prepared conversions of American games (for the US market) on a variety of hardware platforms, such as the game Computer Quarterback (1980) from Apple II to Commodore 64 and Atari (Kluska,

2019). However, the company closed its doors in 1993 as the currency exchange rate between the US dollar and Polish zloty at the beginning of the 1990s made digital game production in Poland less cost-efficient for foreign investors (Kluska, 2019). After 1989, many Polish companies that specialised in games development specifically invested their resources in digital games distribution, localisation and support services (Kosman, 2015).

A similar motivation to subcontract work to the CEE has been seen in Estonia (see Stone et al., 2006). While Estonian service-support companies were established later than in Poland, the core of the industry's development is based on providing opportunities for subcontracting work. One of the oldest professional studios in Estonia, Ringtail Studios (1999), specialises in providing art assets for Triple-A games. However, due to the country's geographical proximity and historical relations, Estonian companies cooperate closely with service-support companies from Russia, for example, through opening new studios in countries outside its Eastern border. Both examples demonstrate the construction of Poland and Estonia as places for subcontracted work based on political, economic and technological power asymmetries in the development of game production between "Eastern" and "Western" countries.[4]

In the following sections, I will explore the different subcategories of subcontracted work in the digital games industries in Poland and Estonia. The aim of this chapter is not to compare subcontracted work organisations in both countries but to demonstrate the variety of practices observable in defining outsourcing relations. I will discuss the following three examples:

- the outsourcing of digital games testing work to Poland;
- the subcontracting of freelance artists from Eastern Europe by companies based in Estonia; and
- the subcontracted work performed by small development teams in Estonia.

4.1 Digital Game Testers

Service-support companies often specialise in providing multiple services to external clients, such as testing, porting and localisation solutions. In Poland, these entities are established by regional companies (e.g., QLOC) or by companies representing an office of international corporations (usually North American) specialising in supporting digital media industries (e.g., Lionbridge). Such companies' scope of operation is largely unknown as they are often omitted in official reports about national digital games industries (e.g., Bobrowski et al., 2017). The establishment of service-support companies in Poland continues the expansion of foreign investment in the ICT sector and service economy of Central and Eastern Europe that was observed at the beginning of the 2000s.

Companies operating in Poland provide services to international clients from various parts of the world, including Western Europe, North America and East Asia. The presence in Poland of international corporations specialising in support services for various media productions reflects corporate expansion to new territories in search of cheaper labour, a workforce with particular skills (both testing and language abilities) and, potentially, favourable foreign investment policies. In addition to the economic and political rationales, the expansion to Poland is dictated by the desire for new markets and audiences. Poland-based service-support companies offer testing and localisation support and consequently draw from a local pool of workers with specific skills (e.g., in the use of Eastern European languages).

The increased use of ICT networks, continuing expansion of international operations and increased complexity of digital games production resulted in companies' outsourcing parts of their production to third-party companies, significantly changing game workers' status in the industry (Flecker, 2009). The service providers (or outsourcing companies) offer their clients access to a skilled workforce with cheaper labour defined not only by local workers' lower wages but also by very flexible employment arrangements. This view was universally shared by the study's interviewees who had worked in such companies. The service-support companies were able not only to freely adjust the number of workers in projects but also to release their clients from responsibility for the workers and their working conditions.

The interviewees with outsourcing work experience toiled mostly in the digital games testing sector known as quality assurance (QA), which entails testing the functionality and playability of digital games and reporting any observed problems to external clients (see Ozimek, 2018). Because of QA's association with standardised tasks and the non-core elements of development, game developers often outsource most or all testing activities to third-party companies, which are obligated not only to deliver the task on time to the clients but also to preserve the confidentiality of ongoing external projects. Therefore, testers often experience high levels of work surveillance to prevent data breaches.

The barriers to finding jobs in service-support companies, specifically testing jobs, are relatively low in comparison to those associated with finding direct employment in game development studios. Prospective employees are required to be fluent in English and perceptive in finding errors in software. Some interviewees considered finding employment in a service-support company to be the first step in breaking into the highly competitive digital games industry, but the interviewees indicated that work in service-support companies was neither financially rewarding nor stable. Testers were paid by the hour and generally hired through flexible contracts that did not grant them the protections offered by Polish labour law. Consequently, the risk associated with the company's operation is transferred to the contracted employees.

The organisation of service-support companies demonstrates the interplay of sociohistorical, economic and cultural factors that affect how the social production of space in Poland's games industry is organised. The example of Poland is not unique as similar patterns of outsourcing game development are seen in other countries (e.g., Chung, 2016). From the perspective of international publishers and developers, the spatial relocation of digital work is motivated by perceived benefits related to wages, employment conditions (e.g., types of available contracts) and the desire to expand to new markets and audiences (e.g., different language abilities). This spatial relocation further fragments not only the labour process but also employment organisations, contributing to the precarity of digital game testers. While digital games production is inevitably mobile, it has a clear logic and direction that relies on the local embeddedness of digital games work for reasons of cost, flexibility and desired sociocultural attributes.

4.2 Remotely Working Artists

Although Estonia hosts no game development studios specialising in Triple-A production, companies based in the country nevertheless support internationally recognised digital games productions. Companies such as Ringtail Studios and Fox3D Entertainment, both based in the capital city of Tallinn, provide support to a variety of well-known companies, including Activision or Avalanche Studios. The engagement with Triple-A international games production is visible mostly in the outsourcing sector specialising in "art" support, including 3D modelling, 3D environments, motion capture and cinematics. However, some service providers operate without physical office space, instead relying on an extensive ICT infrastructure to find, maintain and cooperate with networks of freelancers in other countries. During an interview with the public relations (PR) manager of a local service provider, he described the structure of the company.

> Our business model is now becoming the leading model for many companies in the world. It's not to have a centralised office but to work with everybody remotely ... We started working with Triple-A titles so, by now, we have over 100 different designers. All of them are located in this part of Europe. In Estonia, we have only our business development. There are maybe four to five people [in the Estonian office]. (Vladimir, PR manager)

Apart from its headquarters in Tallinn, Estonia, the service provider also has studios in Russia and Lithuania. However, the company's main business model involves contracting a variety of freelancers who work remotely on assigned tasks. In this sense, the company acts as an intermediary between international clients and specialised artists. This setup further complicates employment relationships in which an intermediary company is positioned between subcontractors and the client. Vladimir, the PR manager, also discussed the company's preference for hiring artists from Eastern Europe: "The majority of our artists come from Russia, Ukraine and Lithuania. I would say that these are the three main ones [countries]." Furthermore, the company representatives noted that they often rely on informal recommendations when expanding their access to the region's skilled workforce. This example demonstrates that spatialisation in the region's digital games production is distributed in relation to historical, economic and cultural factors.

The preference for hiring artists from other Eastern European countries is based on the same principles that motivate major service companies to hire testers in Poland: the company benefits from cheaper labour and access to a skilled workforce. As one contractor argued on the Fox3D company's Glassdoor (2020) review page, "Sometimes [there is a] very heavy workload without an adequate compensation. Here is no super high budgets and payment [but better than Russian average salary]."[5] The organisational model of the discussed companies suggests that increasing virtualisation provides an opportunity to establish freelancer networks that support companies from diverse locations. Furthermore, the recruitment of freelancers from, for example, Russia demonstrates the possibility of reducing labour costs thanks to the different salaries offered in the two countries. The companies also benefit from regulations and initiatives introduced by the Estonian government, such as support for entrepreneurial endeavours. However, as in the case of digital game testers, this situation exacerbates the financial insecurity and employment instability of the freelance artists hired through such companies.

This example also demonstrates that regional and international service-support companies expand their reach by hiring a workforce from other Eastern European countries. The decision to hire from other Eastern European countries is also dictated by the historical connections of the countries in the region, as exemplified by the observed significant participation of Russian and Russian-Estonian communities in games production and related services. These sociocultural and economic relations influence the spatialisation of game production in Estonia and neighbouring countries. Consequently, they demonstrate not only a flow of capital and investment from Western countries to Estonia, but also a dynamic entanglement among international, national and regional production networks, including further Eastern European production networks. This example demonstrates that the trend of outsourcing parts of digital game production is motivated not only by an economic rationale but also by sociohistorical and cultural proximities.

4.3 Hybrid Companies: Subcontractors Who Just Want to Make Games

Along with companies dedicated mostly to providing services to local and international publishers and developers, smaller game developers and individual creators commonly offer outsourcing services and digital games development. The work-for-hire practices of smaller development studios are not limited to Poland and Estonia; in fact, it is a common type of digital games work in various regions.

A reliance on subcontracted work was visible in the Estonian digital games industry. The interviewees argued that the majority of game developers based in Estonia are mostly aspiring developers who are engaged in developing their first projects. The interviewees who defined themselves as independent game developers often experienced extremely precarious working conditions, and they admitted to having difficulty in achieving financial sustainability and to engaging in extensive subcontracting work to maintain their livelihood and fund further game projects. The skills offered by smaller and solo developers ranged from software programming and graphic design to others broadly connected to digital media products. The following is a typical description of such companies in Estonia. "We are specialised in brand management, visual identity and social media management. We help you in growing your business. This is our mission. Also, we make indie videogames" (Dev9K, 2020).

Alice Arno, a project manager for IGDA Estonia who observed the development of the local community argued that the majority of digital games companies in Estonia are hybrids that pursue diverse activities in a desperate bid to stay financially secure.

> In Estonia, not all of them [digital games companies] are directly in game development. Some of them are what I would call hybrid companies.

> They're basically, let's say, working for a few years on making their own games, and then they can do some sort of service, like outsourcing. (Alice, project manager)

Like every creative production, digital games development is a high-risk undertaking that may not yield the expected profit. Furthermore, as the interviewees argued, digital games production is not afforded the same level of cultural legitimacy as other cultural industries in Estonia. Game developers based in Estonia rarely enjoy sufficient support from publishers and investors for their productions. According to interviewees and external sources (Tartu City Government, 2019), investment in Estonian games production is still considered too risky for external investors. Like other small games developers around the world, Estonian developers bear the risk associated with digital games production. Mosco acknowledges the dynamic between major international publishers and independent companies: "Although the number of 'independent' production companies grow[s], these absorb high product risks and labour costs for the giants, which maintain their control over the critical areas of finance and distribution" (Mosco, 1996, p. 109). The interviewees who worked for hybrid companies admitted that they rarely made any profit from their games. Consequently, reliance on additional contracted work was one of the easier ways by which local games production could be established.

> Freelancing keeps on paying for the game development and for the living. ... At the moment, I would say, even though it takes more time than freelancing, it's still the side activity because it's not producing enough money to be the main activity [games production]. (Edward, independent game developer)

Most interviewees specialising in game development were also actively engaged in subcontracted work for various local and international clients. They also argued that working for international clients while living in Estonia was beneficial from a financial perspective due to the relatively low cost of living and good quality of life in Estonia coupled with higher salaries from countries with higher labour costs.

The interviewees' views on the role of outsourcing in the Estonian digital games industry were related to its sociohistorical development. The Estonian industry remains young and fragmented and is primarily characterised by small teams or solo developers and informal forms of game production. Therefore, the limited access in Estonia to infrastructure and the exchange of knowledge for games development (e.g., a number of experienced workers, variety of established companies) makes the country a challenging place for most local game-makers. Because digital games are produced for a global market, Estonian game-makers face a variety of obstacles related to differences in available resources from the access to professional networks (such as attending conferences, mentoring support), the language barriers (English as a universal language in the industry) to access to support measures. While outsourcing was not considered as prestigious as work on one's own intellectual property (IP) projects, it was approached as a means of sustaining the interviewees' livelihood. Subcontracted work was seen as a necessity and as a potential source of the stability that could not be found by investing only in digital games development.

5 Conclusion

This chapter demonstrates the complexity of production networks in the games industry, which spans regional, national and international boundaries. The examples show how the multilayered spatialities of game outsourcing in Poland and Estonia are distributed along historical, economic, social and cultural lines. While this contribution takes the national boundaries of digital games industries as a starting point, it highlights the importance of acknowledging diverse international flows (e.g., services, workers and practices, e.g., policies) in discussing work in digital games (see Kerr, 2014, 2017), from international and regional companies that are establishing service-support businesses in Poland to Estonian companies that are hiring remote workers from other Eastern European countries.

I argue that the spatial relocation of organisations, game production and workers does not make the meanings of place and space obsolete.

Undoubtedly, ICT and Internet infrastructures have facilitated and accelerated the use of subcontracted work in the digital games industry (see Flecker, 2016). These technologies do not make digital game production placeless but rather emphasise that its spatial organisation has become more multilayered and entangled in networks of international, regional and national actors (Flecker & Schönauer, 2016). This contribution touches only partially on the concept of spatialisation in demonstrating that these digital games spaces did not emerge spontaneously with the increased use of ICT and the Internet but rather grew from a continuation of the spatial relocation of work along sociohistorical, economic and cultural lines.

Outsourcing parts of digital game production to Eastern European countries is not a novelty; Polish and Estonian companies have supported the development of digital game software since the late 1980s (Kluska, 2019). However, differences in the political and economic development between Western and Eastern countries have contributed to significant asymmetries in power relations and the availability of resources, infrastructure and knowledge about game software development in different spaces and places.

International companies' decisions to outsource digital game production to Poland and Estonia are motivated by the search for cheaper labour, preferable regulations, flexible employment relations and low levels of unionisation as well as the expansion of their cultural products' reach to new markets and audiences (see Huws et al., 2004). Each of the three examples of outsourcing demonstrates how the specific positionality of subcontracted work results from economic, regulatory, social and cultural processes that lead to a particular social construction of the spaces of digital game production.

The spatial localisation of game software production networks results in fragmented employment and unstable working conditions. While the interviewees differed in their approach to outsourcing from precarity, as discussed by game testers, to subcontracted work as their main source of income in hybrid companies in Estonia, they were all experiencing precarity that is associated with work in a flexible service economy. The social and cultural connotations of subcontracted work in the industry also influenced the interviewees' approaches to this work, which was not considered a creative part of the games industry. The division between different tasks, occupational positions and their spatiality also reflects the power dynamics between places that are considered creative in terms of establishing and working on videogames and places that are considered a support base for wider digital games industries.

Acknowledgements This project was funded by the Estonian Research Council grant (European Regional Development Fund and the programme Mobilitas Pluss (MOBJD380)).

Notes

1. Triple-A refers to digital games development which specialises in the production of big budget games.
2. Interviews with interviewees from Estonia were conducted in English.
3. Data from the IGDA database was revised following the information from reports and interviews with game workers based in Estonia.
4. I use the terms "Western" and "Eastern" (countries) to designate dialectically constituted spaces shaped by historical discourses, social imaginaries and material inequalities.
5. Direct quote from the review web page.

References

Bobrowski, M., Rodzińska-Szary, P., Krampus-Sepielak, A., Śliwiński, M., Rudnicki, S. (2017). Kondycja Polskiej Branży Gier. Raport 2017. Resource document. *Krakowski Park Technologiczny*. https://www.cdprojekt.com/pl/wp-content/uploads-pl/2016/03/kondycja-polskiej-branzy-gier17.pdf. Accessed 21 February 2021.

Bulut, E. (2015). Glamor above, precarity below: Immaterial labour in the video game industry. *Critical Studies in Media Communication, 32*, 193–207. https://doi.org/10.1080/15295036.2015.1047880

Christopherson, S. (2006). Behind the scenes: How transnational firms are constructing a new international division of labor in media work. *Geoforum, 37*, 739–751. https://doi.org/10.1016/j.geoforum.2006.01.003

Chung, P. (2016). Revisiting creative industry models for game industry development in Southeast Asia. In A. Fung (Ed.), *Global game industries and cultural policy* (pp. 125–151). Palgrave Macmillan.

Davis-Blake, A., & Broschak, P. (2009). Outsourcing and the changing nature of work. *Annual Review of Sociology, 35*, 321–340. https://doi.org/10.1146/annurev.soc.34.040507.134641

Dev9k (2020). Main page. http://www.dev9k.com. Accessed 15 October 2020.

Dyer-Witheford, N., & de Peuter, G. (2009). *Games of empire: Global capitalism and video games.* UMP.

Estonian Institute of Economic Research (2018). 12 Meelelahutustarkvara. https://www.kul.ee/sites/kulminn/files/12._meelelahutustarkvara.pdf. Accessed 21 February 2021.

Flecker, J. (2009). Outsourcing, spatial relocation and the fragmentation of employment. *Competition & Change, 13*, 251–266. https://doi.org/10.1179/102452909X451369

Flecker, J. (2016). Introduction. In J. Flecker (Ed.), *Space, place and global digital work* (pp. 1–8). Palgrave Macmillan.

Flecker, J., & Schönauer, A. (2016). The production of 'placelessness': Digital service work in global value chain. In J. Flecker (Ed.), *Space, place and global digital work* (pp. 11–30). Palgrave Macmillan.

Glassdoor (2020). Fox3D entertainment [Reviews]. https://www.glassdoor.com/Reviews/Fox3D-Entertainment-Reviews-E1144625.htm. Accessed 21 February 2021.

Hardy, J. (2009). *Poland's new capitalism.* Pluto.

Huntemann, N. B. (2013). Women in video games: The case of hardware production and promotion. In N. B. Huntemann & B. Aslinger (Eds.), *Gaming globally: Production, play and place* (pp. 41–58). Palgrave Macmillan.

Huntemann, N. B., & Aslinger, B. (Eds.). (2013). *Gaming globally: Production, play, and place.* Palgrave Macmillan.

Huws, U., Dahlmann, S., & Flecker, J. (2004). *Outsourcing of ICT and related services in the EU: A status report (report for the European foundation for the improvement of living and working conditions).* Office for Official Publications of the European Communities.

Izushi, H., & Aoyama, Y. (2006). Industry evolution and cross-sectoral skill transfers: A comparative analysis of the video game in Japan, the United

States, and the United Kingdom. *Environment and Planning A, 38,* 1843–1861. https://doi.org/10.1068/a37205

Johns, J. (2006). Video game production networks: Value capture, power relations and embeddedness. *Journal of Economic Geography, 6,* 151–180. https://doi.org/10.1093/jeg/lbi001

Kamińska-Korolczuk, K., & Kijewska, B. (2017). The history of the internet in Estonia and Poland. In G. Goggin & M. McLelland (Eds.), *The Routledge companion to global internet histories* (pp. 135–150). Routledge.

Keogh, B. (2021). The cultural field of video game production in Australia. *Games and Culture, 16,* 116–135. https://doi.org/10.1177/1555412019873746

Kerr, A. (2006). *The business and culture of digital games: Gamework and gameplay.* Sage.

Kerr, A. (2014). Placing International Media Production. *Media Industries, 1*(1), 27–32. https://doi.org/10.3998/mij.15031809.0001.106

Kerr, A. (2017). *Global games: Production, circulation and policy in the networked era.* Routledge.

Kerr, A., & Cawley, A. (2012). The spatialisation of the digital games industry: Lessons from Ireland. *International Journal of Cultural Policy, 18,* 398–418. https://doi.org/10.1080/10286632.2011.598515

Kerr, A., & Kelleher, J. D. (2015). The recruitment of passion and community in the service of capital: Community managers in the digital games industry. *Critical Studies in Media Communication, 32,* 177–192. https://doi.org/10.1080/15295036.2015.1045005

Kluska, B. (2019, November 23). Karen, logical design works i dzial oprogramowania eksportowego. *Pixelpost.* http://pixelpost.pl/karen-logical-desing-works-i-dzial-oprogramowania-eksportowego/. Accessed 21 Februar 2021.

Kluska, B., & Rozwadowski, M. (2011). *Bajty polskie.* Samizdat Orka.

Kosman, M. (2015). *Nie tylko wiedźmin: Historia polskich gier komputerowych.* Open Beta.

Lefebrve, H. (1974). *La production de l'espace.* Anthropos. English edition: Lefebrve, H. (1991). *The production of space* (trans: Nicholson-Smith, D.). Blackwell.

Mosco, V. (1996). *The political economy of communication.* Sage.

Nichols, R. (2014). *The video game business.* Palgrave Macmillan.

Ozimek, A. M. (2018). *Videogame work in Poland investigating creative labour in a post-socialist culture industry* [Doctoral dissertation]. University of Leeds.

Šisler, V., Švelch, J., & Šlerka, J. (2017). Video games and the asymmetry of global cultural flows: The game industry and game culture in Iran and the Czech Republic. *International Journal of Communication, 11*, 3857–3879.

Sotamaa, O., Jorgensen, K., & Sandqvist, U. (2019). Public game funding in the Nordic region. *International Journal of Cultural Policy, 26*, 1–16. https://doi.org/10.1080/10286632.2019.1656203

Stone, T., Belgrave, J., & Kovacevic, S. (2006). *The games industry in Eastern Europe*. Department of Trade and Industry.

Švelch, J. (2018). *Gaming the iron curtain: How teenagers and amateurs in communist Czechoslovakia claimed the medium of computer games*. MIT.

Takahashi, D. (2020, January 2). SuperData: Games hit $120.1 billion in 2019, with Fortnite topping $1.8 billion. *VentureBeat*. https://venturebeat.com/2020/01/02/superdata-games-hit-120-1-billion-in-2019-with-fortnite-topping-1-8-billion/. Accessed 21 February 2021.

Tartu City Government. (2019). Engaging with industry and public authorities: Part 4—Estonia—Tartu. Resource document. *BGZ Berlin International Cooperation Agency GmbH*. http://baltic-games.eu/files/bgi_goa2-2_output_4_es-ta.pdf. Accessed 21 February 2021.

Teipen, C. (2008). Work and employment in creative industries: The video game industry in Germany, Sweden and Poland. *Economic and Industrial Democracy, 29*, 309–335. https://doi.org/10.1177/0143831X08092459

Thomsen, M. (2018, February 6). The universe has been outsourced: The unseen labor behind the video game industry's biggest titles. *The Outline*. https://theoutline.com/post/3087/outsourcing-blockbuster-video-games-made-in-china-horizon-zero-dawn?zi=blsj76ob&zd=2. Accessed 21 February 2021.

4

Automating Labour and the Spatial Politics of Data Centre Technologies

Brett Neilson and Ned Rossiter

Without data centres, automation stops. Data centres are communication infrastructures that store, process and transmit digitally encoded data. They offer cloud-based services to clients that include the automation of organisational routines such as workflow processes and systems management. Promoted as optimising efficiencies, data centres automate task-oriented work while also impacting on labour practices in ways that calibrate work to computational activity. One of the key functions of data centres over the coming decades will consist in supporting automated economies with the integration of artificial intelligence, machine learning and robotics into processes of capital valorisation and accumulation. Stemming from a project entitled "Data Farms: Circuits, Labour, Territory" (http://datafarms.org) that investigates the expansion of the

---

B. Neilson · N. Rossiter (✉)
Institute for Culture and Society, Western Sydney University, Sydney, NSW, Australia
e-mail: n.rossiter@westernsydney.edu.au

data centre industry in Asia, this chapter engages the spatial politics of data infrastructures in the age of automation. We focus on data centres in Singapore, which is renowned as a growth hub for data storage and processing installations. Because data centres are themselves automated environments and provide infrastructure that enables automation in workplaces located in diverse and often physically distant sites, they offer a strategic object for research on the uneven and varied implications of automation for labour.

In this chapter, we tackle the nexus of automation and labour by investigating Singapore's data centre industry across diverse milieus. These include the historical legacy of colonialism in Southeast Asia, the continuities between data extraction enabled by data centres and other extractive practices, the capacity for automated technologies to acquire sovereign-like powers, the aesthetic dimensions of data's relations to natural and artificial environments, and the significance of automation for state transformation. Our wide-ranging approach reflects the variety of ways in which data centres recast automation's consequences for labour. Although the issue of whether automation displaces jobs or moves them across sectors is part of our analysis, we do not seek to resolve this age-old question that generates both fantasies and fears about the eradication of work by machines. Rather, we approach the human–machine nexus from diverse angles to suggest that the bond of automation and labour has broader relevance for changing relations between space, economy and politics. In this regard, we understand data centres not merely as technical infrastructures but also as political institutions, which shift power relations across wide spatial vistas and contribute to changing patterns of geopolitics and governance across diverse geographical scales.

Data centres lend an infrastructural dimension to labour politics. The material qualities of data centres—which include hardware and software capabilities along with the architectural form of the buildings, environmental impact of operations and geographical settings—become evident when political strategy and organising approach these digital infrastructures as relevant to understanding labour's situation in changing economic circumstances. Our analysis expands the debate on automation and labour to encompass issues of media, extraction, standards, geopolitics, territory and infrastructure. We ask how the division of labour across the spectrum of data servicing industries generates spatial formations that standard accounts of political economy in the tech industry struggle to explain. Focusing on Singapore's data centres and their positioning within wider vistas of capitalist activity and institutional transformation gives a geopolitical anchor to our investigation of how labour transitions to a society of automation.

How can we understand the variation of labour within the footprints generated by data centres when automation threatens to displace the human from the machinery of capital? Answering this question in the context of data centres in Singapore means positioning these installations in relation to other forms of digital infrastructure as well as considering their interaction with forms of political power vested in the state. Our approach combines an empirical concern for the technical operations of data centres with an investigation of the material effects of these operations at sites where labour forces interact with client machines that connect remotely to data centres by means of network topologies that take infrastructural form in cabling technologies and data transfer protocols. We question zero sum narratives of automation and job loss in an analytical frame at once attentive to local conditions and the wider spatial and temporal transformations of digital capitalism.

The history of communications media and transport technologies shows how space and time are endowed with tendencies and propensities specific to the material properties of these systems (Innis, 1951). Similarly, infrastructural facilities such as data centres generate spatialities and temporalities coincident with the operational logic of machines. Such a feature runs against the grain of conventional understandings in international relations and area studies of space as the object of an inter-state contest between civilisational cultures. Temporal features such as low-latency, speed, switching and computational decision-making are likewise antithetical to modern tropes of time as linear, progressive and evolutionary. Machine time and infrastructural space have implications for the performance and experience of work in ways that inform our analysis of labour regimes in contemporary capitalism.

Automated technologies operating from data centres reconfigure key industries, including transport and logistics, manufacturing, education and training, health and medical services, finance and banking. However, because the data economy extends beyond industry as narrowly conceived, we also consider the labour of data production as it applies to the use of social media and other digital services. These services, which expand labour socially beyond the confines of industry, generate large datasets by drawing upon forms of social cooperation often pursued for pleasure or convenience. Indeed, data harvested in this way can provide a basis for training automated technologies. They thus supply a resource for firms that seek to profit by developing and renting out artificial intelligence capacities. We draw attention to the material infrastructures that enable such data extraction (Couldry & Mejias, 2019; Mezzadra & Neilson, 2017).

Our inquiry is geopolitical in its focus on Singapore, an important data centre hub where both Chinese and US tech companies are active. Aside from the question of how Singapore's data centres establish territorial reach that crosses and reconfigures the Southeast Asian region, the competition between Chinese and US tech firms is evident in this context. The ownership and control of standards is an aspect of this competition. We argue that the tussle to institute and spread standards for data transfer and artificial intelligence registers a mode of power that shifts relations between businesses and states. Accordingly, we position Singapore as a laboratory for geopolitical entities intent on expanding their power and influence across regional and global scales.

1   New Dreams—Old Nightmares

Since its separation from Malaysia in 1965, Singapore's economic prosperity has been built on subjecting state capitalism to market competition and attracting foreign investment, initially in the manufacturing and petroleum industries and then in more capital intensive sectors such as technology. Starting in the mid-2000s, the government has supported the island's emergence as a data centre hub by offering foreign tech companies attractive tax rates, flexible labour arrangements, ready electricity and water supplies and lucrative research and development opportunities. Singapore now hosts around seventy state-of-the-art data centres, attracting approximately 50 per cent of the market share in Southeast Asia (BroadGroup, 2016) and positioning it to benefit from artificial intelligence and machine-learning technologies.

Data centres in Singapore establish infrastructural connections with territorial reach that extends across and reconfigures the Southeast Asian region. To enter one of these installations is to encounter a sterile and securitised environment. Flashing lights and humming fans register the presence of workforces that occupy the client end of network architectures that connect data centres to the outside world. Server load indexes distant labour. Whenever a firm locates servers in a data centre or hires services from a cloud provider, its workforce begins to interact with machines whose location may be unknown to them. This creates infrastructural relations and business possibilities between otherwise disconnected labour forces. For instance, a securely employed office worker in Malaysia and a precarious data entry worker in Indonesia may interact with servers in the same Singapore installation, or even use services delivered by the same physical machine. Because data centres obscure connections between parties that sit on the client end of server/client architectures, relations of this kind among labour forces are not evident to those without inside knowledge about the network topologies and client list of data centres. The world of business enters into a kind of transactional promiscuity not foreseen in strategic planning documents. Such operational obscurity enables data centre companies to recommend business relations of potential interest to their clients, opening additional revenue streams for data facilities and further consolidating their capacity to make worlds.

The example of workers in Indonesia and Malaysia interacting with servers in the same Singapore facility gives an idea of how data centres create connections across the global division of labour, crossing differences of space, gender, race, citizenship, occupation and employment status and social identity. To understand more fully the extent and implications of these connections, we must register how interaction with servers in data centres supports the development of machine learning and other artificial intelligence technologies. Data extracted from the activities of workers and users of digital services such as social media platforms provide the raw material from which tech companies build automated services. This situation means that the jobs of workers who interact with servers in data centres are increasingly at risk of elimination through automation. The keystrokes and other inputs provided by these workers provide data that can potentially train artificial intelligence to perform the same tasks. The current wave of fear surrounding the automation of labour extends not only to manufacturing jobs that new-generation robots might perform. Although such displacement is a growing concern in Southeast Asia (Chang & Hunyh, 2016), the jobs of service, mental or immaterial labourers who interact with digital technologies are also at stake.

New dreams of artificial intelligence inspire old nightmares of labour loss. In recent years, a raft of news reports and policy documents have delivered fearful prognoses of job displacement due to automation (see e.g., Frey & Osborne, 2013; Méda, 2016; Regalado, 2012). A prominent claim in these reports and documents is that these jobs will not shift to the science and technology sectors that drive technological change, as supposedly has been the case in previous waves of automation. In other words, the structural ascent of workers into high-level tertiary industries and economies has hit a peak over the last thirty years and is now facing gradual termination. A contrasting response from feminism and science and technology studies envisions the reabsorption of work by other means, insisting that futures are always social rather than driven by markets and technologies (see e.g., Wajcman, 2017). Another prevalent argument stems from versions of accelerationism that imagine an elimination of work and a repurposing of modes of production to invent post-capitalist futures (Srnicek & Williams, 2016).

Overall, the debate is stuck between arguments about job loss that repeat positions on mechanisation and labour derived from early political economy and claims for the powers of automation based on technical knowledge of code, algorithms, neural networks and other relevant programming techniques. We seek to move beyond this impasse by placing the question of automation and labour in the context of the data storage and processing facilities that allow artificial intelligence and machine learning to proceed. Our argument has affinities with that of Benanav (2019, p. 121), who contends that automation technologies may lead to an under-demand for labour but that the primary reason for this waning of labour demand is "the absence of a corresponding pace of job creation in the wider economy". In highlighting the dependency relation between labour, automation technologies and data regimes specific to the operational logic of data centres, we seek to examine how this situation shifts unevenly across spatial variegations in the global economy that are increasingly shaped by routines and topologies of digital networking.

2   Racking and Stacking

Automation has a long history. From the jacquard loom to the centrifugal governor, the Taylorist production line to just-in-time logistical systems, automation has tied industrial modernity to the experience and conditions of labour. Automation has functioned as a connecting device across racial and gendered divisions of labour. To what extent do the relations between automation and labour shift with technologies of artificial intelligence and machine learning? A familiar claim is that earlier techniques of automation used data to perform linear and repetitive tasks whereas contemporary artificial intelligence allows pattern recognition and learning that can mimic human behaviour and thus replace or augment mental labour tasks (Miller, 2018). Beatrice Fazi (2018) argues that artificial intelligence is alien to human thought and thus the relation between automation and labour is not one of simulation. Whatever the limits of machine learning and artificial intelligence, their political and economic significance cannot be underestimated, particularly when services based on them increasingly inform the business models of tech firms spearheading research and development in this field. Ideology and cultural values influence technology design, and therefore hold a shaping force on the experiences and position of people who interact with automated technologies. Business models, in other words, are not merely fanciful discourses, vision statements and marketing campaigns divorced from the social world in which they circulate.

The extraction and aggregation of data is a precondition for contemporary artificial intelligence and machine learning. Systems complexity can only evolve from the volume and quality of data available for these techniques to crunch. Such an operational requirement situates the data centre as the optimal storage facility and repository for artificial intelligence and machine learning. There is also a political economy at work here. The commercial ownership of data centres frequently does not coincide with the ownership of data trafficking through such installations. Data centres store, process and transmit data whose provenance potentially stretches across many quite different firms and clients. These installations can occupy a meta-operational role by drawing on and accessing a substantial corpus of data for artificial intelligence and machine learning purposes, developing commercial applications on this basis. Storage, transmission and processing, in other words, are just one dimension of the business model of data centres, which are poised to expand services and capacity in the realm of computational cognition.

Advances in machine learning algorithms are central to optimising data centre operations. Some of these applications address problems of energy efficiency and long-term environmental prediction or the optimisation of computational processing power through the development of neural networks and cloud delivery services. However, the automation of labour in data centres is also on the frontier of developments in machine learning. Take the example of data centre jobs at Google, just to name one prominent operator in the Singapore environment. While data centre jobs at Google have expanded tenfold over the past decade, employment rates are now on the decline. The human is now effectively interchangeable with the machine: "The ability to pull together disparate bits of information", as one Google executive explains. As this executive goes on to say: "The cut-and-dry division of labour, where some people did racking and stacking, some provisioned servers and installed operating systems, some oversaw network connections and others did service maintenance in production, has been replaced by automation" (Sverdlik, 2017, n.p.).

As far as data centre management goes, functions usually divide between infrastructure and business management. The former has itself become a profuse field of automation with the introduction of "data centre infrastructure management" (DCIM) software in a range of corporate packages with names like Sunbird, Nlyte and Tuangru. These packages bridge information across organisational domains, including data centre operations, facilities and information technology to configure workflows, power use and the like. We can think of them as kind of a meta-automation that works across different datasets and infrastructural elements to make routine automation possible. DCIM packages also enable remote operation of data centres, meaning that management can push staff on the ground to a minimum—a minimum that nonetheless is usually gendered male.

The high degree of automation in data centres does not correspond to the making of a business environment where availability of personnel presents no challenge. A French national working for a major tech firm in Singapore told us: "The more you go to the north of Asia, the more arms and legs there are running the things". He referred to Malaysian government efforts to attract data centres with real estate costs, electricity tariffs and water availability. While finding personnel to perform routine tasks in data centres poses no problem, the availability of skilled individuals to intervene at the level of infrastructure management presents difficulties. Cultural variations are relevant, for instance, in running data centres in Thailand, the Philippines or Japan. According to our informant, if companies are building "solutions" to address the local market, they need to hire local players. If they are trying to go beyond the local market, they need technical and management personnel to align with the culture of the client, meaning that more cosmopolitan and outward-looking attitudes become a component of employability. As a consequence, in-house expertise is distributed according to the cultural variation of markets and client needs. Automation does not simply subtract labour from capital, in other words, but rather multiplies the geocultural settings that supply data capitalism with knowledge that services machine operations. This multiplication and supply involves people as much as machines, and political terrains of population and culture as much as digitally networked topologies of communication.

Whatever the significance of automation for labour within data centres, it is at the client end of the architectures that extend from these installations that the nexus of labour and automation is most intense. We have already discussed how users and workers who interact with client machines that connect to data centres furnish data that can train algorithms to perform their jobs, or at least tasks that are part of their jobs. In the case of data centres in Singapore, this possibility extends across wide regional vistas due to the extensive network capabilities of these installations. To understand how server–client architectures extend the net of automation beyond the data centre, we must account for the way in which these architectures interact with technologies of virtualisation within the data centre.

In the contemporary data centre, east–west traffic (between servers in the same facility) exceeds north–south traffic (between servers and clients beyond the data centre). Different topologies with names like Clos, fat-tree, Dcell, BCube, c-Through, Helois, PortLand and Hedera physically connect servers to each other within data centres (Liu et al., 2013, pp. 7–23). Each of these configurations has its own purpose and implies trade-offs between network qualities such as speed, redundancy, accessibility, power use and scalability. Consisting of wires, servers and switches, these physical networks can also be hybrid or, through use of optical as opposed to electronic switches, reconfigure during runtime. On top of these variously designed hardware networks, DCIM software controls the virtualisation process, assigning load to different physical machines and moving virtual machines across them in variable patterns to optimise operations. One reason why this east–west traffic is so important is because it underlies peering relations that allow firms to realise comparative advantages by creating connections with the servers of other firms in the same installation. Peering arrangements enable the elimination of intermediaries and the reduction of transit times for data packets that would otherwise run through external networks such as the Internet. They also allow rapid sharing and agglomeration of data that can train machine learning and other artificial intelligence algorithms. Without understanding the network topologies and virtualisation processes operative within data centres, it is difficult to track or intervene in the application of automated technologies along the server–client axis where labour becomes vulnerable.

Like other technologies of logistical coordination and automation, these developments seek to reduce the turnover time of capital. Such efforts are pronounced in high-frequency trading, a financial sector renowned for its requirements of low-latency computing. New routines of remote sensing and edge computing feed the fantasy that the data centre might begin to stand free of the human labour forces that operate at its client end. That millisecond differences are at stake makes it seem as if all this proceeds inevitably and beyond the reach (or at least the speed) of human cognition. As Harney and Moten (2013, p. 87) write: "Logistics wants to dispense with the subject altogether". Ultimately, however, a server cannot eliminate its clients. This is true even if a front-end machine usually needs to consult several other servers in the same data centre before it can send an aggregated response back to a client. To recognise the server's need for clients is not to perpetuate the perversion of the master–slave dialectic or to suggest that clients come first, as twentieth-century corporations once claimed of their customers. Rather, it is to register capital's increased dependence on so-called externalities. In the data economy, capital extracts value from fronts of social cooperation that it does not necessarily control or coordinate in the manner that it once did in the industrial factory.

If, from the viewpoint of media theory, automation presents the growing ubiquity of autonomous systems, from the perspective of capital it creates a scenario of increased reliance on its outsides. Data are the index of this reliance. While the data centre load may register distant labour and thus the continued presence of living knowledge, intelligence and subjectivity, the data generated by this labour, paid or unpaid, present capital with new frontiers of accumulation. In this sense, we cannot immediately equate the extraction of value that fuels data economies with the extraction of surplus value that characterises so-called free wage labour. Recalling Rosa Luxemburg's (1913/2003) argument that accumulation requires a society that consists of more than capitalists and workers, we can register how data provide capital with an outside to prospect and draw upon. To understand data as such an outside is to recognise that they arise from forms of human cooperation and social activity that capital does not necessarily organise, even if they are subject to a kind of projective logic by which capital constructs them as susceptible to appropriation. If, for Luxemburg, writing in the early twentieth century, the outside of capital consisted of different territories that could be colonised and integrated into the capitalist world system, the fronts presented by data today are more profuse and topologically variegated. The data centre is the infrastructural facility that sucks in and agglomerates these diverse bodies of data, subjecting them to forms of analysis and extraction that can themselves be automated and serve the ends of further automation at the client interface. The location of data production sites with respect to standard topographies of national political space and international territorial borders remains relevant for legislation and policy. However, such arrangements are increasingly inflected and challenged by topologies of digital connection that support processes of extraction, valorisation and accumulation that national governments struggle to control.

3 Installing Data

How then are we to understand the relations between labour, capital and data? In an article entitled *Data: The Currency of Tomorrow*, Jayson Goh, the former Executive Director of the Infocomms and Media Division of Singapore's Economic Development Board, writes: "Data is a raw resource, just like labour and capital, but one that needs to be farmed, milled and modelled into an effectively usable form" (Goh, 2013, p. 8). The metaphor of data as a raw resource is dominant in industry and government attempts to make sense of data's relation to labour and capital. Present whenever there is talk of data mining, the implication of the metaphor of raw data is that data are there for the taking, like resources in the ground. Even in the case of resource mining, however, capital and labour are necessary to make the extractive process productive. Tsing (2005) gives the example of the sorting, grading and transportation that are necessary to make a coal supply chain function, beyond the extraction of raw material from the earth. The same applies to data, where the extracted material is not natural resources but patterns of social cooperation. Data, in this sense, are always "cooked" (Gitelman, 2013), regardless of whether they are produced by human input, as in the case of social media, or by social practices and activities detected through remote sensing or other Internet of Things technologies. As Goh

(2013) recognises, such data must be "farmed, milled and modelled" into a usable or, perhaps better, a fungible form. This work of aggregation, processing and analysis occurs in data centres, where the smoothing out or cleaning of data makes them machine readable and thus ready to train algorithms to perform automated tasks.

However securitised the data centre may be, and whatever the protocols of commercial secrecy that apply to its operations and clientele, such farming, milling and modelling does not take place in a vacuum. Just as automation requires machines to interact with their environments or external conditions of operation, rather than performing a series of mandated tasks in serial patterns, the data centre is an installation that situates itself in diverse material contexts. If environments of automation consist increasingly of data themselves, drawn in from various kinds of sensing technologies, the environments of data centres remain physical as well as computational. These environments are multiple and include the urban milieus to which data centres maintain weak social ties. They also include national environments that partially set regulatory frames for data centre operations and infrastructural environments provided by electrical grids, cable networks and the like. Routines of supply and maintenance furnish hardware environments, while software environments encompass different aspects of code and algorithms. Finally, natural environments supply the energy and water resources for which data centres have a seemingly insatiable thirst.

The load of data centres on natural environments is an important area of social and ecological concern. Research connects data centres to the energy infrastructures on which they depend and, in turn, to the intensification of global warming (see, e.g., Carruth, 2014; Hogan, 2015; Starosielski, 2014). Aware of its environmental footprint, the data centre industry responds by setting its own green standards and handing out awards on their basis. Whatever the impact of data centres on natural environments, and undoubtedly it is significant, the need of these facilities for power and water draws arguments about them back to the fundamentals of agrarian political economy: The dispossession of land, water, forests and other common property is part of the conditions of their existence. However, a mere quantification of the power and water data centres use cannot account for the multiple environments in which these installations exist. These environments, importantly, are not merely technical and ecological but also social and cultural. They encompass the urban milieu in which data centres are set, the shifting social relations that result from the communicative and locational media they support, and, more widely, the aesthetic environments that their operations culturally inflect and which, in turn, react back upon public consciousness of these infrastructures. An example of such an aesthetic environment is the spectacle generated by Karl Lagerfeld's transformation of the Grand Palais catwalk into a makeshift data centre for the launch of Chanel's 2017 *prêt-à-porter* line at Paris Fashion Week (Stinson, 2016).

Not by accident do we refer to data centres as installations. The aesthetic medium of the installation, which is blatant in the Lagerfeld example or in artworks and films that take data centres as a theme, is also evident in the infrastructure and design of data centres themselves. The title of Cisco IT architect Douglas Alger's book *The Art of the Data Center* (2012) registers how the aestheticisation of the data centre is not merely an act carried out by external agents such as artists or fashion designers but integral to the technological environment of data centre design itself. Another example of this aestheticisation comes in the work of cable technicians responsible for wiring together servers. For all of the standardisation of communication protocols, there is remarkable variation in the aesthetics of cable and wiring configurations twisting across the ports of server racks. Many data centres present uniform cabinets of servers in stark contrast to the chaotic tangle of cables that snake across the hot and cold aisles of patch panels that bring servers into communicable relation. Other installations display a splendour that resembles a cadaver splayed out for the acquisition of scientific skills. Revered as art among technicians, cabling establishes the distributed topology of routers and switches in data centres. What qualifies as art for technicians passes as porn for other kinds of spectators. A prominent aggregator site where these punters share their art features the byline: "A place for sharing links to good-looking cabling (primarily data centres) that could be considered art (or porn)" (Cable Porn; the art of tidy data centres, 2018).

The aesthetics of cable configurations index the spatial distinction of data centre installations on global scales. As one Singapore-based company specialised in data centre infrastructure and management solutions touts on their site: "Standard rack configurations won't work well in every data centre. Space constraints, cable routing, power configurations and cooling environments vary" (DC Gears, 2018, n.p.). Not only, then, do external conditions influence the orchestration of cable configurations. These installations also support a range of data centre functions. Whether configured for faster backup and retrieval speeds, scalability for storage, flexibility, security or management considerations, data centre cabling provides an optic of data typologies not easily gleaned from conventional ethnographies of infrastructure.

Regardless of the network topology chosen for a data centre, the large number of switches and servers in these installations means that faults and failures are a regular feature of their operations. Routing mechanisms must make use of redundancies offered by hardware. Not by accident is one of the main industry bodies in the data centre industry known as the Uptime Institute. As Mosco (2014, p. 9) writes: "cloud companies promise and their customers expect, that data centres will operate with no down time". Many data centres run diesel power generators, which are kept turning over so that they can kick in in the event of an external power failure. Typologies of fault tolerance move us into different classifications of data centre failure: failure type, failure region, failure neighbourhood, failure mode and failure time (Liu et al., 2013, pp. 51–53). Failure in the form of "crashes and viruses, bloatware, malware and vaporware", as media theorist Cramer (2005, p. 9) notes, comprises the "irrationality of rational systems".

An aesthetic allure crosses the spectrum of failure. Contingency, like failure, is multihued. A particular state may be, during the course of economic history, notable as an infrastructural centre or growth area for one technological form or another. This does not mean *ipso facto* that these technological forms harmonise with others in ways that avoid failures of interoperability. Nor does it mean that a dominant technological form generates social harmony within or beyond the state. Singapore's data centres position the island-state as an infrastructural hub. Managers seek to assure system stability and longevity with an eye to not just internal machine operations but also to burgeoning competition in the market throughout the Asian region. More particularly, the materiality of data centres as an infrastructural form is spatially extensive and prone to vagaries of failure that do not always conform to those listed in manuals. As we argue in the next section, the effort to introduce standards is a bulwark against failures, and not accidentally has the production of standards for artificial intelligence become a sharp area of geopolitical competition that shapes the contemporary world across its spatial and economic dimensions.

4 The Automated State

We earlier suggested that Singapore provides a strategic site to observe the growing competition between China and the US to set artificial intelligence standards because firms from both these states are active in the island's data centre industry. Singapore, for its part, has sought to play a role as an intermediary to Chinese business since the Deng Xiaoping era of opening. More recently, Singapore has opened its doors to Chinese data centre operators such as Aliyun (Alibaba Cloud), Tencent and China Mobile. The Chinese search engine provider Baidu runs an artificial intelligence research centre in the island's Fusionopolis technology park (Apostolou, 2012). In turn, Singapore has invested in data centres in China via the government-linked corporation Singapore Technology Telemedia, which has a stake in twenty-six mainland data centres (Choudhury, 2017). Singapore's sovereign wealth fund Temasek Holdings is an investor in Chinese artificial intelligence startups such as Sensetime, which specialises in surveillance, and Rokid, a robotics firm with voice technology capabilities. While it is true that Chinese firms also set up data centres in neighbouring countries like Malaysia and Thailand, Singapore remains their main launch pad for expansion in Southeast Asia and provides a context where they mingle and compete with US operators such as Google, Amazon and Microsoft. This means Singapore's future as a data centre hub rests largely in the race between China and the US to establish standards for artificial intelligence.

Although China's data protectionist policies have generally been interpreted in relation to the Great Fire Wall and issues of freedom and democracy, they also mean that the country has amassed a great deal of data on which to build artificial intelligence. As opposed to nations who opened their doors to US tech giants and have thus had data generated by users in their territories drained out and used to generate services that might potentially be sold back to them, China has extracted its own data and set its own digital industry standards. While this poses business advantages, it also presents challenges when it comes to international expansion, especially as most standards have been set in the US. Perhaps this is why China has prepared a New Generation Artificial Intelligence Development Plan (State Council of China, 2017) and a follow-up White Paper on Artificial Intelligence Standards (Standards Administration of China, 2018) to lay out a strategy for shaping artificial intelligence governance and policy at the international level (Ding et al., 2018). Huawei senior director Wael Diab has become chairperson of the subcommittee of the International Standards Organisation and the International Electrotechnical Commission working on artificial intelligence standards. Not accidentally did this body, formed in 2017, hold its first meeting in Beijing.

While the outcomes of China's effort to shape artificial intelligence standards are unknown, they are important not only for commercial but also geopolitical reasons. China seeks a "right to speak" at the international table of technology development and is also keen to ensure the roll out of automated governance technologies, such as its social credit system, without a huge social backlash, as occurred with India's introduction of its Aadhaar social identity number. China's claims for assuring the safety and social acceptance of artificial intelligence are serious, even if its international expansion in the field is likely to proceed in the absence of the civil society voices that shape the debate in Europe and North America. Playing a key role in standardisation promises to increase the value derived from automated technologies due to data pooling and interoperability. China's intervention also seeks to improve the competitiveness of its firms by working essential patents into protocols and thus obliging other firms to pay royalties when building equipment. With its long-standing practice of piracy and violation of intellectual property rights, China suffered humiliation from signing up to the World Trade Organisation's Agreement on Trade-Related Aspects of Intellectual Property Rights in 2001. Never admitted as a board member of the US dominated Internet Corporation for Assigned Names and Numbers (ICANN), the Chinese government maintained its own regulatory processes and engaged ICANN through the organisation's Governmental Advisory Committee. China also played an obstructionist role in the United Nation's World Summit on the Information Society multistakeholder Internet governance meetings held in the early 2000s. Now China intends to exact recompense by building its own artificial intelligence capabilities. Such a project, particularly when it takes the form of standard setting, promises to change the global business environment, giving Chinese technology firms greater leverage to enter new markets, particularly but not only in the developing world.

As the unravelling of neoliberalism brings more countries to favour the models of state capitalism developed in China and Singapore, the relations between states and tech companies are likely to shift. Such changes are particularly relevant in contexts where automation technologies threaten job loss. Call centre jobs in the Philippines, for instance, are currently under threat from the Google automated voice response system Duplex (Gonzales, 2018), which would doubtless be served from its data centre in Singapore. However, the Duplex roll out is delayed due to ethical questions of machines imitating humans (Lomas, 2018), and Chinese firms such as the aforementioned Rokid, financed by Singapore's sovereign wealth fund, are not far behind in developing their own voice recognition chip (Jao, 2018). Chinese influence on technical and ethical standards could open new channels of investment and automation in the Philippine call centre market. Tracing these possible changes is a task for future research. For now, a focus on the territorial and operative dimensions of data centres promises to give a more nuanced picture than either the vision of Morozov (2018), for whom states retain the capacity to rein in tech companies, or Bratton (2015), whose totalising vision of information infrastructures posits a global nomos that eclipses state power. States do not go away, but neither are they singular entities. Morozov (2018) remains wedded to an order of international states, while Bratton's (2015) preference is for a politics of things in which humans drift into aesthetic reverie.

If automation creates autonomous systems, we need to ask how such autonomy measures up in the political sphere. In political theory, autonomy registers either as an attribute of sovereignty or as a characteristic of independent political organisation that exists beyond the state. Tech companies market automated services not only to commercial entities but also to political bodies such as states and municipalities. The discourse of the smart city is the most obvious symptom of such efforts, raising the question of how economic returns and political powers of surveillance, control and decision flow to corporations and algorithms rather than to formally constituted political bodies and the citizens, or denizens, that compose them. We think the nexus of automation and sovereignty is more complex than smart city debates allow.

To claim that states retain the ability to control autonomous systems is to underestimate the extent to which automation contributes to governance. The demise of censuses and other state-run statistical surveys in the face of the vast amounts of data held by social media and other tech companies is a register of this. Similar observations apply to other areas of government, including healthcare, taxation, welfare and policing. Today, even military applications run from the securitised environment of commercial data centres. Yet to pretend that infrastructures of automation float free from established political institutions—states, parties, bureaucracies and the like—is to enter a fantasy world where clear cut-divisions between politics and commerce structure the articulation of power. We can certainly recognise data centres as autonomous infrastructures that operate in parallel, rivalry and partnership with states. This vision can take multiple shapes, from Robert MacBride's (1967) call in The *Automated State* for a national computing centre (in the United States) that would remain independent from any one of the government's arms to Keller Easterling's (2014) more recent and transnationalised mapping of emergent infrastructural powers in *Extrastatecraft*. But everywhere states are hitting back against the autonomy of data, whether it be through routine protocols of surveillance, firewalls, national nets, policy visions that make "smartness" a principle of nationalism or legislation that mandates so-called data sovereignty.

Data sovereignty measures, in particular, are a front of state paranoia in the face of the proliferation of data. As Chander and Lê (2015, p. 680) explain, there are many ways in which states seek to encumber the transfer of data across national borders. These methods include:

rules preventing information from being sent outside the country, rules requiring prior consent of the data subject before information is transmitted across national borders, rules requiring copies of information to be stored domestically, and even a tax on the export of data.

Selby (2017, p. 213) argues that laws requiring data to be stored within a particular jurisdiction "are being supported by some countries not only as a means to reduce their comparative disadvantage in internet data hosting, but also to reduce their comparative disadvantage in internet signals intelligence". Whether they understand motives as economic or political, attempts to understand data sovereignty tend to assume a baseline model of the state more or less Weberian in provenance: a territorial entity that holds the legitimate monopoly of violence over a given community. We tend to think, by contrast, that data sovereignty laws represent an effort by states to assert themselves as such an entity within a global political situation that has drastically changed. The sovereignty of media arises at precisely the point the state presumes itself to wield authority within data environments already surrendered to the automation of decision.

Debates about the governmentalisation of the state have questioned its unity. At the same time, critiques of the state's exceptional powers haunt traditional visions of sovereignty. In the world of Marxist theory, it seems no longer possible for the state to act, to control, or mediate the aggregate operations of capital let alone vouchsafe the social reproduction of labour. We are neither enthusiastic for arguments about the withering away of the state nor for reactive positions that proclaim it has never changed. We also recognise, as Gupta (2012, p. 52) puts it, that arguments about the state must always ask the question "which state?" Nonetheless, we must measure the transformations of state power against the operative powers manifest in data centres. To contend that state legislation will bring these powers to heel is to make an assumption about where the seats of power lie these days. The situation, we think, is more open. The decision of a country like Singapore to welcome data centres to its shores by no means registers a dynamic of power where legislation and policy trump infrastructure every time.

5 Conclusion

If data centres crystallise political powers, they are likely to become a crucial point of investigation and intervention for movements that seek to change the world. Although debate has evolved in relation to the nexus of automation and labour, a widening ambit of political and economic analysis is necessary to pose accurate questions about the impact of automation on workforces. This chapter shows that such analysis is not possible in the absence of considerations of media, extraction, standards, geopolitics, territory and infrastructure that expand the ambit of political economy and science and technology studies. If our focus on the data centre industry in Singapore has drawn attention to developments in Southeast Asia, this interest has also been strategic insofar as it raises the issue of how data centres reconfigure world regions and highlights geopolitical struggles. The growing prospect of technological "decoupling" between China and the US is certainly relevant here, although its dynamics have played out somewhat more visibly in relation to 5G networking systems. What remains the case is that if regions such as Europe hope to establish some autonomy in the data economy, allowing for an escape from a zero sum choice between adopting US or Chinese technologies, the development of data centres within regulatory environments attentive to the ownership and sharing of data that undergird machine learning and automation routines will be key. Our point is that such regulation will not necessarily be delivered by state powers that must already reckon with the political relevance of automated decision-making. The prospect to recalibrate technologies of automation in ways that do not serve capital accumulation rests on ongoing struggles and modes of organisation that script new horizons as externalities not yet trafficked through global infrastructures of control. This is the art of installation without the sovereign.

Acknowledgements The Authors acknowledge the financial support by the Australian Research Council (ARC DP160103307).

References

Alger, D. (2012). *The art of the data center: A look inside the world's most innovative and compelling computing environments.* Prentice Hall.

Apostolou, N. (2012, July 27). Baidu opens R&D lab in Singapore: Chinese answer to Google gets into speech recognition. *The Register.* https://www.theregister.com/2012/07/27/baidu_opens_first_lab/. Accessed 21 February 2021.

Benanav, A. (2019). Automation and the future of work—2. *New Left Review, 120,* 117–146.

Bratton, B. (2015). *The stack: On software and sovereignty.* MIT Press.

BroadGroup. (2016). *Data centre South East Asia.* BroadGroup.

Cable porn; the art of tidy data centres. (2018). *Reddit.* https://old.reddit.com/r/cableporn/. Accessed 21 February 2021.

Carruth, A. (2014). The digital cloud and the micropolitics of energy. *Public Culture, 26,* 339–364.

Chander, A., & Lê, U. P. (2015). Data nationalism. *Emory Law Journal, 64,* 677–739.

Chang, J.-H., & Hunyh, P. (2016). *ASEAN in transformation: The future of jobs at risk of automation* (Bureau for Employers' Activities, Working Paper No. 9). International Labour Organization.

Choudhury, A. R. (2017, August 22). STT data centre arm set up for next stage of global expansion. *Business Times.* https://www.businesstimes.com.sg/technology/stt-data-centre-arm-set-for-next-stage-of-global-expansion. Accessed 21 February 2021.

Couldry, N., & Mejias, U. A. (2019). *The costs of connection: How data is colonizing human life and appropriating it for capitalism.* Stanford University Press.

Cramer, F. (2005). *Words made flesh: Code, culture, imagination.* Piet Zwart Institute.

DC Gears (2018). Customizable racks. http://www.dcgears.com.sg/racks-enclosures/racks/customizable-racks. Accessed 21 February 2021.

Ding, J., Triolo, P., & Sacks, S. (2018). Chinese interests take a big seat at the AI governance table: Government and industry team to shape emerging AI standards-setting process. *New America.* https://www.newamerica.org/cybersecurity-initiative/digichina/blog/chinese-interests-take-big-seat-ai-governance-table/. Accessed 21 February 2021.

Easterling, K. (2014). *Extrastatecraft: The power of infrastructure space.* Verso.

Fazi, M. B. (2018). Can a machine think (anything new)? Automation beyond simulation. *AI & Society, 34*, 813–824.

Frey, C. B., & Osborne, M. A. (2013). The future of employment: How susceptible are jobs to computerisation? Resource document. *University of Oxford*. http://www.oxfordmartin.ox.ac.uk/downloads/academic/The_Future_of_Employment.pdf. Accessed 21 February 2021.

Gitelman, L. (Ed.). (2013). *"Raw data" is an oxymoron*. MIT Press.

Goh, J. (2013). Data: The currency of tomorrow. Resource document. *Singapore Economic Development Board*. https://www.edb.gov.sg/content/dam/.../Singapore-Business-News-May-2013.pdf. Accessed 24 October 2018.

Gonzales, G. (2018, July 6). The Google tech that may threaten call centre jobs. *Rappler*. https://www.rappler.com/technology/features/google-duplex-call-center-philippines-threat. Accessed 21 February 2021.

Gupta, A. (2012). *Red tape: Bureaucracy, structural violence and poverty in India*. Duke University Press.

Harney, S., & Moten, F. (2013). *The undercommons: Fugitive planning & black study*. Minor Compositions.

Hogan, M. (2015). Facebook data storage centers as the archive's underbelly. *Television & New Media, 16*, 3–18.

Innis, H. A. (1951). *The bias of communication*. University of Toronto Press.

Jao, N. (2018, June 5). Chinese AI startup Rokid will mass produce their own custom AI chip for voice recognition. *TechNode*. https://technode.com/2018/06/05/rokid/. Accessed 21 Feb 2021.

Liu, Y., Muppala, J. K., Veeraraghavan, M., Lin, D., & Hamdi, M. (2013). *Data centre networks: Topologies, architectures and fault-tolerance characteristics*. Springer.

Lomas, N. (2018, May 10). Duplex shows Google failing at ethical and creative AI design. *TechCrunch*. https://techcrunch.com/2018/05/10/duplex-shows-google-failing-at-ethical-and-creative-ai-design/. Accessed 21 February 2021.

Luxemburg, R. (1913). *Die Akkumulation des Kapitals*. Heptagon. English edition: Luxemburg, R. (2003). *The accumulation of capital* (trans: Schwarzschild, A., foreword: Kowalik, T.). Routledge.

MacBride, R. (1967). *The automated state: Computer systems as a new force in society*. Chilton.

Méda, D. (2016). *The future of work: The meaning and value of work in Europe* (ILO Research Paper No. 18). International Labour Organization.

Mezzadra, S., & Neilson, B. (2017). On the multiple frontiers of extraction: Excavating contemporary capitalism. *Cultural Studies, 31*, 185–204.

Miller, S. M. (2018). AI: Augmentation, more so than automation: A managerial perspective on how firms can effectively deploy human minds and intelligent machines in the workplace. *Asian Management Insights, 5*(1), 1–20.

Morozov, E. (2018, April 1). After the Facebook scandal it's time to base the digital economy on public v private ownership of data. *The Guardian*. https://www.theguardian.com/technology/2018/mar/31/big-data-lie-exposed-simply-blaming-facebook-wont-fix-reclaim-private-information. Accessed 21 February 2021.

Mosco, V. (2014). *To the cloud: Big data in a turbulent world*. Paradigm.

Regalado, A. (2012, July 11). When machines do your job. *MIT Technology Review*. https://www.technologyreview.com/s/428429/when-machines-do-your-job/. Accessed 21 February 2021.

Selby, J. (2017). Data localization laws: Trade barriers or legitimate responses to cybersecurity risks, or both? *International Journal of Law and Information Technology, 25*, 213–232.

Srnicek, N., & Williams, A. (2016). *Inventing the Future: Postcapitalism and a World without Work*. Verso.

Standards Administration of China (2018). White paper on artificial intelligence standardization. Resource document. http://www.sgic.gov.cn/upload/f1ca3511-05f2-43a0-8235-eeb0934db8c7/20180122/5371516606048992.pdf. Accessed 24 October 2018.

Starosielski, N. (2014). The materiality of media heat. *International Journal of Communication, 8*, 2504–2508.

State Council of China (2017). New generation of artificial intelligence development planning. http://www.gov.cn/zhengce/content/2017-07/20/content_5211996.htm. Accessed 24 October 2018.

Stinson, E. (2016, April 10). Chanel turned its fashion show runway into a data centre. *Wired*. https://www.wired.com/2016/10/chanel-turned-fashion-show-runway-data-center/#:~:text=Chanel%20Turned%20Its%20Fashion%20Show%20Runway%20Into%20a,colorful%20ethernet%20cords%20spewed%20from%20stacks%20of%20servers. Accessed 23 February 2021.

Sverdlik, Y. (2017, February 13). How to get a data centre job at Google. *Data Centre Knowledge*. https://www.datacenterknowledge.com/archives/2017/02/13/how-to-get-a-data-center-job-at-google. Accessed 23 February 2021.

Tsing, A. (2005). *Friction: An ethnography of global connection*. Princeton University Press.

Wajcman, J. (2017). Automation: Is it really different this time? *The British Journal of Sociology*, 68, 119–127.

Open Access This chapter is licensed under the terms of the Creative Commons Attribution 4.0 International License (http://creativecommons.org/licenses/by/4.0/), which permits use, sharing, adaptation, distribution and reproduction in any medium or format, as long as you give appropriate credit to the original author(s) and the source, provide a link to the Creative Commons license and indicate if changes were made.

The images or other third party material in this chapter are included in the chapter's Creative Commons license, unless indicated otherwise in a credit line to the material. If material is not included in the chapter's Creative Commons license and your intended use is not permitted by statutory regulation or exceeds the permitted use, you will need to obtain permission directly from the copyright holder.

Part II

Places of Work

5

Doing Homework Again: Places of Work from a Historical Perspective

Christian Oggolder

Digitalisation and the virtual space of the Internet have created a new arrangement of space. Business, politics, culture and communication are shifting from physical places to virtual spaces. Clearly defined boundaries of real and virtual spaces are vanishing, just like the defined boundary between urban centres and the periphery, between work and leisure, between public and private (Felstead et al., 2005). Accordingly, these changes can provoke concerns for many people (Flecker, 2016). However, the modern way of separating work and leisure, public and private—and consequently the respective spheres of men and women—is a construction based on societal, technological and economic changes.

Therefore, dealing with the current phenomena concerning the changes of work environments and of social life needs a historical

C. Oggolder (✉)
Institute for Comparative Media and Communication Studies (CMC), Austrian Academy of Sciences / University of Klagenfurt, Vienna, Austria
e-mail: christian.oggolder@aau.at

perspective. Komlosy (2018b) claims that "the debate about how people assess work requires historical context", thus "work must be seen in discursive, relational categories instead of one fixed one" (ibid., p. 175).

In this chapter, the current changes in workplaces and production environments are therefore discussed from a historical perspective. Understanding modernity (Giddens, 1990) as the pivotal point between the early modern and the late modern period (Nerone, 2015), work in a late modern digitalised environment is consequently contrasted with both modern and premodern forms of work and social life.

1 Meanings of Work

Studying the history of work means constantly being asked about the actual meaning of work. What does it mean when we speak of work during a certain period of time, and of course, within a certain region? However, the history of work is mostly based on a "eurocentric grand narrative" (Komlosy, 2018a, p. 10). Apart from global aspects of work (Hofmeester & van der Linden, 2018), only focusing on historical changes of the societal perception of work, there are nonetheless still a multitude of different views on what work actually is and how work has been perceived by people who have worked and those who have not.

Given that the European narrative always starts with the ancient Greeks, this also applies to attitudes towards work (Lis, 2009). Thus, Greek philosophers developed a social and value system that formed the basis for the negative connotation of physical labour and the social discreditation of domestic work (Komlosy, 2018a, p. 10). Nevertheless, starting in classical antiquity, a "broad consensus existed on the principle that every person had to make efforts regardless of his or her status, and that idleness was both ethically and socially unacceptable" (Lis & Soly, 2019, p. 143f.).

The ancient scepticism about work that produced an antagonism of work and freedom is similar to the Jewish-Christian tradition where work was perceived as both a curse and blessing, punishment and divine order at the same time. The arduousness of work has always been understood as a form of penance for human sinfulness, mostly in the sense of Genesis (3:17–19): "By the sweat of your brow you will eat your bread, until you return to the ground" (Kocka, 2005, p. 188). At the same time, in the tradition of the three monotheistic religions, this bane could also be turned into a blessing from God, which made love for work a commandment through the formula "ora et labora" (Komlosy, 2014, p. 27).

During the early modern period, when traditional handcraft and trade emerged more and more as the socio-economic basis for European urban societies, work gained central importance. Thus, especially qualified and socially and culturally standardised work was now increasingly linked to freedom and urban rights, diametrically different to how it was regarded in the ancient polis. Becoming formative for the emerging urban culture, at the same time urban culture had a positive effect on work by honouring it and using it as a source of legitimation for property, wealth and social advantages (Kocka, 2005, p. 188). In contrast to the wealth of the nobility that was grounded solely on one's birth, increasingly perceived as unfair by the bourgeoisie, work not only opened the opportunity for non-aristocrats to attain wealth, but also to achieve this rightfully. As a result, since then being poor has been perceived as personal failure, resulting from personal idleness and a lack of effort. Furthermore, work has been evaluated and categorised as productive and unproductive work (Laibman, 1999).

In addition to the philosophical explanation of the concept of work, a process of economisation also took place. Toil, pain and contempt vanished from this economic understanding of work. This was the working concept of the breakthrough capitalism, even before the beginning of industrialisation, which was not established in England until the late eighteenth century, followed even later by the European continent in the nineteenth century (Kocka, 2005, p. 189).

However, everyday life and the experiences of the working population did not correspond entirely to the glorification of work that determined the discourse of the intellectuals. Industrialisation changed a lot. It was then that the "work society" emerged that still shapes our reality today, although many believe that its existence is waning and its time is running out (Kocka, 2005, p. 194). Following Aurell (2009), it is quite evident that "every evolved society possesses an ideology of work, in the sense of a social doctrine deployed to serve special interests" (ibid., p. 71). Depending on the ruling societal conditions, the respective division of tasks "is the result of such ideology" (ibid., p. 71). The division of tasks, however, is in turn closely linked to the respective places of work.

2   Places of Work

This section focuses on three historically relevant places of work. Accordingly, these three categories—the house, the city and the network—can also be used to characterise the organisation of work typical for certain historical periods. Thus, during the early modern period the concept of the house was of importance in the realm of work and production. As a consequence of industrialisation, mass production and urbanisation the city became the dominating sphere of work during modernity. Finally, digitalisation and the rise of the network society (Castells, 2010) has reduced the need for spatial concentration. Both the house and the city have now become nodes within networks.

2.1   The House

During the early modern period "the house" was not only a prominent place for work, but rather it can also be described as an entire concept, "as a basic unit of society and economy, in which living and working were closely interconnected and inseparably combined" (Ehmer, 2019, p. 83). Revived from classical Greek philosophers, notably Xenophon and Aristotle, during Renaissance and Humanism, these ideas were disseminated throughout Europe via domestic conduct books and various kinds of advice literature (ibid., p. 83). Besides that, this is also an early and vivid example of interrelated effects of media change, especially the invention of the printing press, and social change. The spread of the revived classical literature was promoted by the contemporary new media and vice versa: Gutenberg's invention had found both practical use and acceptance.

The concept of the house was based on "household workshops" (Roper, 1991), where the place for work and the living place shared a common spatial unit. Each of these workshops was run by a master and his wife. The master coordinated the work of the apprentices, journeymen and servants who lived in the craft house and the products that they manufactured were sold either in markets or directly from the workshop (ibid., p. 29). However, it is crucial not to focus exclusively on economic aspects in the household-workshop ideal. Roper (1991) argues that "a sexual economy mirrored the productive economy" (ibid., p. 31). Being married was of utmost importance for the master, because his wife guaranteed his "achieved adult masculinity", thus she "proved his masterhood, while at the same time being responsible for the food, light, bedding, heat, water, and other domestic needs of the shop's small labour force" (ibid., p. 31).

Nevertheless, this "household-workshop" ideal has to be seen as what it is, an ideal. Mentioning "the army of day-labourers, permanent servants, itinerates, and improvident craftsfolk", Roper (1991) names those people, for whom the idyll of the house "had probably never meshed with the reality of their lives" (ibid., p. 31). Taking into account social aspects in terms of places of work, Ehmer (2019) claims that we can observe "an increasing combination of several workplaces by individual men and women of lower classes due to their need to earn their income from various sources during their daily, weekly, or seasonal work and during their life course" (ibid., p. 87).

2.2 The City

Similar to the ideal-typical concept of the house during the early modern period, the city is considered to be the ideal-typical concept of the workplace for the modern era, particularly with regard to the twentieth century (Lefebvre, 1996).

Cities have been places of centralisation throughout history, when cultural, political and economic centres emerged from cult centres. However, premodern cities, consisting only of a few thousand inhabitants, were largely separated from their surroundings by massive city walls, protected by gates and connected with neighbouring cities by only a few prominent streets (Oggolder, 2013, p. 67). Following Ehmer (2019), in the sixteenth century only "about 10 percent of the European population lived in cities with more than five thousand inhabitants", but regardless of the actual size of the city, "all towns and cities were centres of crafts and trades" (ibid., p. 74), which were predominantly organised by the concept of the house. On the other hand, the vast majority of the European population lived in rural areas and laboured in agriculture.

In addition to constant improvements to the street systems (Laitinen & Cohen, 2009) that facilitated a more efficient exchange of people, goods and information, the invention of the printing press marked a qualitative advance in terms of the mutual convergency of urban centres. Printing accelerated and expanded access to information, it "modified practices of devotion, of entertainment, of information, and of knowledge" (Chartier, 1989, p. 1). Hence, printing did not only change the media, but the perception of people's reality as well (Giesecke, 1992, p. 21). Accordingly, this also applies to a change in people's spatial perception. Neighbouring cities moved closer via stories and news, which were printed on leaflets in circulation, and gave people an impression of distant regions.

Philosophers of the Enlightenment and early economists stood for an emphatic appreciation of work as a source of property, wealth and civility or rather as the core of human existence and individual fulfilment. Moreover, prevailing capitalism and technological progress as well as the internal state reforms and the formation of territorial states further promoted this trend (Kocka, 2005, p. 188). In addition to restructuring work and creating industrial centres, propelled by the spreading idea of (urban) work as source of wealth, massive movements of people towards cities became a matter of fact. The result was an explosive population growth in cities and the creation of new cities. "Industry gradually made its way into the city in search of capital and capitalists, markets, and an abundant supply of low-cost labor" (Lefebvre, 1970/2003, p. 13). Since then, living conditions have been linked to the realities of the city (Löw, 2010, p. 605) and as a result of industrialisation, "which is a process of domination that absorbs the agricultural production", the city emerged as what Lefebvre (1970/2003, p. 2) called "urban society". Hart (2019) claims that "the drive to make money reorganized workplaces that stood at the heart of new working cultures" (ibid., p. 75). How this reorganisation of workplaces was perceived by those who were affected, "depended on their gender, class, and, increasingly, on their race" (ibid., p. 75).

Besides, printing not only changed the perception of space in terms of news from abroad. Since publishing means conveying something to the public, the invention of the printing press also played a fundamental role with regard to changes in the perception of the public and the public sphere. Colman and Ross (2010) argue "that the public has no ontological essence prior to mediated representation" (ibid., p. 29). Richard Sennett (1977) claims that "'public' thus came to mean a life passed outside the life of family and close friends" (ibid., p. 17). When different areas of life were recognised as publicly defined, others subsequently became exclusively private (Jarvis, 2011, p. 69). Regarding places of work, this development led to a spatial separation of the production of goods and the reproduction of labour power. In other words, the fabrication and the trade of goods were assigned to the public, while the reproduction of labour power was still associated with the house, which was now perceived as private. These fundamental changes in the realm of public and public space on the one hand and privacy and family on the other hand have been providing constant conditions for centuries. This normative framework has only been seriously questioned in recent years as a result of digitalisation.

Finally, the concept of the city during the industrial era is closely related to the concept of mass society, mass production for the consumption of the masses (Adorno & Horkheimer, 1944/1997, pp. 120–167). The workplace here no longer functions solely as the place where products are manufactured, as was the case in the early modern house. Instead, the urban workplace has become the place where human labour is offered under precisely defined temporal and spatial conditions. Ruggiero (2001) states that "the birth of the factory system required the abandonment of previous habits, and the adoption of a new discipline, one to which workers were entirely unaccustomed" (ibid., p. 53). Work no longer means exclusively manufacturing products that meet the basic needs of life. The effort of wageworkers from now on serves as a medium of exchange for both products to meet basic needs of life and, more importantly, products that are essential for being able to participate in the culture of mass society. Ruggiero (2001) emphasises that "the history of the city can be read as the history of social conflicts simultaneously pursuing emancipation through and from work" (ibid., p. 55).

2.3 The Network

Networks are receiving a lot of attention today, but they are not a fundamentally new phenomenon (Windeler & Wirth, 2018, p. 238). As trading and communication networks, for instance, the famous one maintained by the Fugger family (Keller, 2016), networks played an important role even in the premodern era. Nevertheless, it would be inappropriate to call early modern societies network societies.

According to Castells (2010), the concept and the rise of the network society are of course strongly related to the emergence of the Internet. However, we basically have to differentiate between the network and the Internet. Castells (2001) identifies the former as the "organizational form of the Information Age", the latter, however, serves as its "technological basis" (ibid., p. 1). As a consequence of the introduction of computer-based information and communication technologies, networks—being "primarily the preserve of private life" in contrast to "centralized hierarchies [which] were the fiefdoms of power and production"—have been able "to deploy their flexibility and adaptability, thus asserting their evolutionary nature" (ibid., p. 2).

According to the decline of cities' centrality as simple nodes within a network (Oggolder, 2013), the urban space as a clearly defined entity concurrently dissolves itself. Arguing from a global economic perspective, Sassen (2001) on the other hand states that "cities concentrate control over vast resources, while finance and specialized service industries have restructured the urban social and economic order" (ibid., p. 4). For that reason, she claims the emergence of a new type of city that she calls the "global city" (ibid., p. 4). This reasoning, however, neatly underlines the changing nature of cities, which have now been integrated as nodes in a global network.

Moreover, the expansion of urban areas and the increasing number of road networks between cities lead to the absorption of smaller centres, and the boundaries between urban and rural areas have been becoming increasingly blurred (Castells, 2001, p. 207). Aurigi (2005) states that the crisis of current cities "is not just a matter of size", but rather, "it is also because the city is not a 'whole' any more or perhaps, it is not like the majority of us expect a 'whole' to be" (ibid., p. 10).

Since mobility—both physical and electronic—has dramatically increased during the last few decades, "the need for spatial concentration" has accordingly decreased (Carmona et al., 2010, p. 32). The city as a perceived place for work no longer exists in its traditional form, which was constitutive for the era of modernity. Digitalisation and the virtual space of the Internet have created a new arrangement of space. The image of two—originally—independent and self-contained territories is about to blur. Clearly defined boundaries between real and virtual spaces are vanishing, just like the definite boundary between urban centres and periphery, between work and leisure, between public and private. Burd (2007) claims a "new definition of the city" and suggests in particular that the wireless world "mixes and melds the virtual and real, forces old media to merge and readjust" (ibid., p. 40). Veel (2006) states that "also on a non-metaphoric level, the web and the city seem to be two increasingly intermingled entities" (Veel, 2006, p. 229). Accordingly, Gordon and de Souza e Silva (2011) argue that mediated interaction between people "does not spell the end of good urban spaces; but it does spell a change" (Gordon and de Souza e Silva, 2011, p. 86).

However, working with the help of digital technologies is considered a prototype of translocal and mobile work that appears to be detached from any temporal and spatial reference (Roth-Ebner, 2016, p. 233; Will-Zocholl et al., 2019, p. 37). Neither factory and office nor the city are therefore required as places of work anymore. Moreover, beside this spatial dimension we are at the same time confronted with changes concerning the temporal organisation of work. Both spatial and temporal independence can lead to problems regarding "extended availability" (Nöhammer & Stichlberger, 2019, p. 1193) for employees (see the contribution by Calle Rosengren, Ann Bergman and Kristina Palm in this volume). Furthermore, given that workplaces have become ubiquitous, worktime has slipped—at least partly—from the employer's direct control. For that reason, digital technology can also be used to partially overcome management's loss of control by installing employee-monitoring tools (Peetz, 2019; West & Bowman, 2014).

Furthermore, work processes have been made more flexible in terms of space and time in order to make them more effective (Roth-Ebner, 2015, 2016, p. 233). To be able to work anytime and anywhere and thus achieve a maximum increase in performance, employment has been removed from the operational framework (Müller, 2018, p. 218). Therefore, doing homework not only means doing work at home, but also doing work both detached from spatial and temporal limits and, what is even more relevant, with a need for personal responsibility—above all as a self-employed person. Thus, as the downside of flexibility and potential freedom, we also have to deal with precarious employment.

Beyond that, research on work and workplaces, taking networks and digital technology into account, should not ignore all other relevant meta processes of today, globalisation in particular (Thomas, 2020). It is essential, in this context, to advance beyond the Eurocentric perspective and not to focus exclusively on the global north. Hence, not the entire world and its working people are *directly* affected by digitalisation and may work under the conditions of digital workplaces. Hundreds of thousands of employees have to deal with working conditions that are no different from those of the modern era of factories, or even worse, for instance, thinking of miners who mine minerals for digital products used by societies of the late modern era (Fuchs, 2014, p. 155). Working under these conditions therefore also means working in the age of the network (Lipnack & Stamps, 1994).

3 Conclusion

The aim of this chapter was to add a historical perspective to the discussion about the current changes related to places of work as a result of digitalisation. It was therefore essential to focus on both the perception of work and the spatial organisation of work over the course of time.

Today we live in a transitional phase in a variety of areas of life, and the way we perceive and organise work is no exception from this. As Harison (2019) argues, it is evident that having changed significantly after 1800, work and workplaces are now "contrasting with the 'old regime' that went before it and leaving patterns we live with today" (ibid., p. 51). Thus, even today the conception of work is still influenced by ancient religious traditions on the one hand and, at the same time, organisational frameworks still follow the necessities of industrialisation on the other hand (Gregg, 2018, p. 10). Accordingly, Kocka (2005, p. 187f.) argues that a general concept of work was developed in the eighteenth century, which was indeed interpreted slightly differently by different authors, but was on the whole defined by the following key features: Work had a purpose outside of itself, namely, the purpose of producing something, and to achieve something (ibid.). However, work was also always arduous and some kind of required effort and a minimum of persistence were necessary. On the whole, this is an acceptable minimal description of work in a comprehensive sense, which is still appropriate today. Play, leisure, doing nothing have usually been terms that are contradictory to work. However, thinking of new, digitally supported forms of learning and working, discussed under the term "gamification" (Dale, 2014) shines a new light on this traditional definition of work.

In addition, it "is a sociological truism that industrialisation also created two distinct spheres of social life—home and work—that had previously been undifferentiated and interwoven" (Felstead et al., 2005, p. 3). Hence, the concept of the early modern house was characterised by the integration of work and both the production of goods and the reproduction of labour into everyday life.

With the advent of factories in the wake of industrialisation, centralised manufacturing plants replaced these small-scale, early modern workshops. Cities emerged as centres of work and life; however, the two spheres were spatially separated. Driven by the digitalisation (of work) and other parallel meta processes such as globalisation, these spheres transformed into increasingly indistinct entities.

Thus, *doing homework again*, working not in factories and offices, but in the living room, ultimately means returning to premodern forms of work. Moreover, "working at home involves undertaking employment-related tasks within a residential dwelling or household premises" (Felstead et al., 2005, p. 6). Regardless of the loss of these two previously separate areas of home and work, there are nevertheless still places of work which are based on modernity. The same holds true for the division of work between men and women as well as the separation of the private and the public. Returning to the early modern craftsperson who did his or her job in the house, independently of time and on his or her own economic responsibility, the circle closes in a way.

References

Adorno, T. W., & Horkheimer, M. (1944/1997). *Dialektik der Aufklärung*. Institute of Social Research. English Edition: Adorno, T. W., & Horkheimer, M. (1997). *Dialectic of enlightenment* (Cumming, J., Trans.). Verso.

Aurell, J. (2009). Reading renaissance merchants' handbooks: Confronting professional ethics and social identity. In J. Ehmer & C. Lis (Eds.), *The idea of work in Europe from antiquity to modern times* (pp. 71–90). Ashgate.

Aurigi, A. (2005). *Making the digital city: The early shaping of urban internet space*. Ashgate.

Burd, G. (2007). Mobility in Mediapolis: Will cities be displaced, replaced, or disappear? In S. Kleinman (Ed.), *Displacing place: Mobile communication in the twenty-first century* (pp. 39–58). Peter Lang.

Carmona, M., Tiesdell, S., Heath, T., & Oc, T. (2010). *Public places urban spaces: The dimensions of urban design* (2nd ed.). Architectural Press.

Castells, M. (2001). *The internet galaxy: Reflections on the internet, business, and society*. Oxford University Press.

Castells, M. (2010). *The rise of the network society* (2nd ed.). Blackwell.

Chartier, R. (1989). General introduction: Print culture. In R. Chartier (Ed.), *The culture of print: Power and the uses of print in early modern Europe* (pp. 1–10). Princeton University Press.

Colman, S., & Ross, K. (2010). *The media and the public: "Them" and "us" in media discourse*. Blackwell.

Dale, S. (2014). Gamification: Making work fun, or making fun of work? *Business Information Review, 31*, 82–90.

Ehmer, J. (2019). Work and workplaces. In B. de Munck, & T. M. Safley (Eds.), *A cultural history of work: In the early modern age* (Vol. 3, pp. 67–88). Bloomsbury Academic.

Felstead, A., Jewson, N., & Walters, S. (2005). *Changing places of work*. Palgrave Macmillan.

Flecker, J. (Ed.). (2016). *Space, place and global digital work*. Palgrave Macmillan.

Fuchs, C. (2014). *Digital labour and Karl Marx*. Routledge.

Giddens, A. (1990). *The consequences of modernity*. Stanford University Press.

Giesecke, M. (1992). *Sinnenwandel, Sprachwandel, Kulturwandel: Studien zur Vorgeschichte der Informationsgesellschaft*. Suhrkamp.

Gordon, E., & de Souza e Silva, A. (2011). *Net locality: Why location matters in a networked world*. Wiley-Blackwell.

Gregg, M. (2018). *Counterproductive: Time management in the knowledge economy*. Duke University Press.

Harison, C. (2019). Work and workplaces. In V. E. Thompson (Ed.), *A cultural history of work: In the age of empire* (Vol. 5, pp. 51–65). Bloomsbury Academic.

Hart, E. (2019). Work and workplaces. In D. Simonton & A. Montenach (Eds.), *A cultural history of work: In the age of Enlightenment* (Vol. 4, pp. 61–75). Bloomsbury Academic.

Hofmeester, K., & van der Linden, M. (Eds.). (2018). *Handbook the global history of work*. De Gruyter.

Jarvis, J. (2011). *Public parts: How sharing in the digital age improves the way we work and live*. Simon & Schuster.

Keller, K. (2016). Die Fuggerzeitungen: Geschriebene Zeitungen und der Beginn der periodischen Presse. Von den frühen Drucken zur Ausdifferenzierung des Mediensystems (1500 bis 1918)In M. Karmasin & C. Oggolder (Eds.), *Österreichische Mediengeschichte* (Vol. 1, pp. 27–50). Springer VS.

Kocka, J. (2005). Mehr Last als Lust. Arbeit und Arbeitsgesellschaft in der europäischen Geschichte. *Jahrbuch für Wirtschaftsgeschichte: Economic History Yearbook, 46*(2), 185–206.

Komlosy, A. (2014). *Arbeit: Eine globalhistorische Perspektive. 13. bis 21. Jahrhundert* (2nd ed.). Promedia.

Komlosy, A. (2018a). *Work: The last 1,000 years*. Verso.

Komlosy, A. (2018b). Western Europe. In K. Hofmeester & M. van der Linden (Eds.), *Handbook global history of work* (pp. 157–178). De Gruyter.

Laibman, D. (1999). Productive and unproductive labor: A comment. *Review of Radical Political Economics, 31*(2), 61–73.

Laitinen, R., & Cohen, T. V. (Eds.). (2009). *Cultural history of early modern European streets*. Brill.
Lefebvre, H. (1970). *La révolution urbaine*. Gallimard. English edition: Lefebvre, H. (2003). *The urban revolution* (R. Bononno, Foreword: N. Smith, Trans). University of Minnesota Physicians.
Lefebvre, H. (1996). *Writings on cities*. Blackwell.
Lipnack, J., & Stamps, J. (1994). *The age of the network: Organizing principles for the 21st century*. Oliver Wight.
Lis, C. (2009). Perceptions of work in classical antiquity: A polyphonic heritage. In J. Ehmer & C. Lis (Eds.), *The idea of work in Europe from antiquity to modern times* (pp. 33–68). Ashgate.
Lis, C., & Soly, H. (2019). Work and society. In B. de Munck & T. M. Safley (Eds.), *A cultural history of work: In the early modern age* (Vol. 3, pp. 129–144). Bloomsbury Academic.
Löw, M. (2010). Stadt- und Raumsoziologie. In G. Kneer & M. Schroer (Eds.), *Handbuch spezielle Soziologien* (pp. 605–622). Springer VS.
Müller, K. F. (2018). „Ein schön schrecklicher Fortschritt": Die Mediatisierung des Häuslichen und die Entgrenzung von Berufsarbeit. *M&K, 66*, 217–233.
Nerone, J. (2015). *The media and public life: A history*. Polity.
Nöhammer, E., & Stichlberger, S. (2019). Digitalization, innovative work behavior and extended availability. *Journal of Business Economics, 89*, 1191–1214.
Oggolder, C. (2013). Losing centrality: Urban spaces and the network society. In S. Tosoni, M. Tarantino & C. Giaccardi (Eds.), *Media & the city: Urbanism, technology and communication* (geography, anthropology, recreation, pp. 66–76). Cambridge Scholars.
Peetz, D. (2019). Management, culture and control. In D. Peetz, *The realities and futures of work* (pp. 113–140). The Australian National University.
Roper, L. (1991). *The holy household: Women and morals in reformation Augsburg*. Oxford University Press.
Roth-Ebner, C. (2015). *Der effiziente Mensch: Zur Dynamik von Raum und Zeit in mediatisierten Arbeitswelten*. transcript.
Roth-Ebner, C. (2016). Spatial phenomena of mediatised work. In J. Flecker (Ed.), *Space, place and global digital work* (pp. 227–245). Palgrave Macmillan.
Ruggiero, V. (2001). *Movements in the city: Conflict in the European metropolis*. Routledge.
Sassen, S. (2001). *The global city: New York, London, Tokyo*. Princeton University Press.

Sennett, R. (1977). *The fall of public man.* Cambridge University Press.
Thomas, H. (2020). Governing global production networks in the new economy. In A. Wilkinson & M. Barry (Eds.), *The future of work and employment* (pp. 189–203). Edward Elgar.
Veel, K. (2006). CyberCitizen: Urban identity in net art. In C. Emden, C. Keen & D. R. Midgley (Eds.), *Imagining the city, Volume 1: The art of urban living* (Vol. 7, cultural history and literary imagination series, pp. 229–245). Peter Lang.
West, J. P., & Bowman, J. S. (2014). Electronic surveillance at work: An ethical analysis. *Administration & Society, 48,* 628–651.
Will-Zocholl, M., Flecker, J., & Schörpf, P. (2019). Zur realen Virtualität von Arbeit: Raumbezüge digitalisierter Wissensarbeit. *AIS-Studien, 12*(1), 36–54.
Windeler, A., & Wirth, C. (2018). Netzwerke und Arbeit. In F. Böhle, G. G. Voß & G. Wachtler (Eds.), *Handbuch Arbeitssoziologie: Band 2: Akteure und Institutionen* (2nd ed., pp. 237–275). Springer VS.

6

The Spatial Production of Wanghong: Political Economy, Labour Mobility and the "Unlikely" Creativity

Jian Lin

Yuan San, a local resident from Jiangxi Province, livestreamed on Douyin when he was sleeping in February 2020, when most Chinese were quarantined at home due to the pandemic. Surprisingly, this sleeping-show quickly went viral online and attracted around 20,000,000 views in two days and generated over 70,000 CNY (8800 EUR) income from the platform. "I livestreamed my sleep because I was so bored", Yuan San speaks of the reason for his livestreaming, "but I didn't realize so many people are even more bored than me" (Phoenix New Media, 2020). When the Chinese as well as the global economy were severely disrupted by the coronavirus outbreak in early 2020, social media entertainment (Cunningham & Craig, 2019), often termed as "wanghong" (网红, web red) industry in Chinese, might be one of the very few that still manages

J. Lin (✉)
Centre for Media and Journalism Studies, University of Groningen, Groningen, The Netherlands
e-mail: j.lin@rug.nl

© The Author(s), under exclusive license to Springer Nature Switzerland AG 2021
M. Will-Zocholl and C. Roth-Ebner (eds.), *Topologies of Digital Work*, Dynamics of Virtual Work,
https://doi.org/10.1007/978-3-030-80327-8_6

to thrive and grow. The emerging digital economy and technological innovation give rise to China's own influencer culture and economy. The highly networked digital platforms incubate a seemingly "placeness", "virtual" or "cloud" creative economy to incorporate numerous disparate individuals as well as their creativities to participate as both creators and audience in the online wanghong communities. According to media reports, the daily average online time per user of Chinese leading social media platforms such as Douyin, Kuaishou, Taobao Live, Douyu and Huya increased by 70 min in the first quarter of 2020 (Youwenyouda, 2020). In the same period, the total revenue of Douyu and Huya, the two major livestreaming platforms in China, has been reported to have increased by 50% (Duan & Jiayan, 2020; Xu, 2020). If the pandemic inhibits social mobility, the Chinese wanghong economy seems to benefit from such physical immobility: Both its production and consumption are not necessarily restrained by creators' and consumers' geolocation.

Apart from this participation of grassroots individuals, even legacy entertainment industries have shifted their attention to the wanghong economy. During the outbreak, Chinese television networks (e.g., Hunan TV) and online portals (e.g., Tencent Video, Youku and Iqiyi) have lined up to create "wanghong-style" reality shows by inviting celebrities to document their performance at home or in their private studios (Cai, 2020). *Eat Well*, for example, a show created by Youku, invites celebrities such as Zhao Benshan, Pan Changjiang, Lin Yongjian and Ma Weiwei to livestream their cooking and dining experiences with their family members at home. In these new reality shows, we can detect an increasingly fluid boundary between wanghong and celebrities, whose distinction becomes blurred by the application of social media affordances.

These cases demonstrate the power and potential of the wanghong economy in today's China. With limited competition from, and access to, a relatively immature legacy media industry, social media provided the means for new forms of cultural expression coupled with state-driven incentives for growing the domestic consumption market and various channels for monetisation and entrepreneurship on the side of individual creators. Behind this networked social media economy is the mobilisation of "grassroots" creators, their labour and cultures, privileged by affordable access to high-speed and mobile technology that has caused digital divides in other cultures. As the author argued elsewhere, this industry has enabled an "unlikely" social mobility from rural, working or migrant class to the creative class (Lin & de Kloet, 2019), which has transcended the "urban", "professionally-educated", "fashionable" imagery of creative labour.

This social mobility brought by the wanghong economy raises questions concerning the implications of the social media economy for Chinese society: How does this networked economy fit into and reflect the large structure of Chinese political economy of communication industries? Why and how are these individual creators motivated and incorporated into the wanghong economy? How do they experience everyday life and work within the wanghong industry? Given the diversity in demography and geolocations of wanghong creators as I will explicate in this chapter, how do the practices of wanghong production and business implicate and shape the various local spatial and social relationships?

To explore these questions, this chapter first introduces the political economy of the wanghong industry in contemporary China, based on an archival research of policy documents and industrial reports. Though still subject to the state's cultural censorship and regulation, the wanghong economy fits into the state's agenda of digital economy, employment promotion and the recent "poverty alleviation" agenda, by incorporating the grassroots, marginal population and creating opportunities for employment and national economic restructuring. Various local places are connected by embedded advertising and e-commerce affordances of wanghong platforms, and are transformed into mediaspaces (Couldry & McCarthy, 2004), where individual personalities and identities are constantly reproduced as cultural commodities for the production, consumption as well as exploitation of wanghong culture.

On top of this political-economic analysis, the following sections explore the social mobility this economy enables, the social backgrounds as well as the labour conditions of wanghong creators. The analysis is based on the author's ethnographic research in China from 2017 to 2019. During these fieldtrips, the author visited the headquarters of Chinese leading Internet companies including ByteDance, Tencent,

Alibaba and Kuaishou. Twenty-one semi-structured interviews were conducted with wanghong creators, MCN entrepreneurs and managers of platform companies. Most of these interviews were conducted in Chinese and later translated by the author. Other than these fieldwork data, this chapter also includes archival research of secondary media reports on the experiences of wanghong creators. As I will show in the following sections, this study first investigates two forms of social mobility facilitated by the wanghong industry: It incorporates both professional media and cultural professionals who used to work for legacy media organisations, and those who often come from a more grassroots background and adopt an amateurish style in their content production. Enabled by the well-established ICT infrastructure across China, the Chinese wanghong economy has managed to include a far more diverse creative workforce than is the case in the Western social media entertainment studied by Cunningham and Craig (2019); it produces a vibrant socio-economic network that expands from the urban centres to the rural, marginal places and populations. In terms of labour experience, however, the emerging financial and employment opportunities also come with various aspects of uncertainty and precarity, caused by the stringent Internet censorship and competitive market. Creativity, life and individuality are constantly mobilised and calculated according to the workings of the social media platform, leading to a continuous self-governance including both self-censorship and emotional management.

Finally, the chapter offers a qualitative content analysis of selected popular wanghong content to explore the aesthetics and culture that the wanghong economy produces. Directly driven by the vernacular, grassroots and banal everyday life, the wanghong economy has produced "unlikely aesthetics" widely circulated in the online space. These online creativities may often be deemed as "inadequate", "unfulfilling" and even "unacceptable" in the context of the Chinese legacy screen culture and the offline social locations, where the hierarchical, patriarchal and normative values often dominate. The various local places serve as versatile workplaces for wanghong production, while simultaneously they are transformed into "the space of flows" (Castells, 2011) in both online culture and the socio-economic relations engendered by the wanghong industry. Local places and their identities still matter, but in the mediated online space they only exist on a surface level that can add to the performative authenticity creators attempt to claim and monetise. For creators and their online communities, however, the entertaining, simple and relevant wanghong creativity promises an approachable alternative, in which the vernacular can not only watch but participate—an "authentic" alternative to both the established screen culture and the banality of offline everyday life that are supposedly more artificial and restrained.

1 The State, Platformisation and the Wanghong Industry

The Chinese state has been a crucial agent in the development and transformation of the Chinese economy and society in the past decades. As Yu Hong (2017a, pp. 10–13) illustrates, the Chinese government has pledged to place information and communication at the centre of the national economic restructuring plan developed in response to the post-2008 global economic crisis, using information and communication technology (ICT) as industries and infrastructure to transform traditional industrial sectors. In his annual speech at the Chinese national congress in 2015, Premier Li Keqiang announced China's "Internet +" agenda. This is a new national development strategy that aims at boosting and restructuring the national economy through the upgrading of digital infrastructure and technological innovation (The State Council, 2015b). The new policy agenda puts the Internet at the centre, aiming to integrate network connectivity and the "disruptive business and managerial model" (of decentralised, private, post-Fordist corporate management) with a wide range of traditional sectors, from manufacturing, agriculture, energy, finance and transportation to public services and education (Hong, 2017b; The State Council, 2015b). Moreover, the "Internet + " strategy pledges to propel a new digital economy that can foster and benefit small startups, entrepreneurship and innovation. As such, it dovetails with another policy agenda championed by the state government under the name "Boosting Mass Entrepreneurship and Innovation" (大众创业万众创

新, *dazhong chuangxin, wanzhong chuangye*; The State Council, 2015a). The latter policy seeks to mobilise the creativity and innovative power of grassroots individuals for national economic growth. "Internet + " complements the "Mass Entrepreneurship" strategy in the sense that the prosperous digital economy provides opportunities for grassroots individuals to find employment and become entrepreneurs.

Following this spirit of "Internet +" and "Mass Entrepreneurship", the central government further specifies its policy measures in the *Guidelines on Developing Digital Economies and Expanding Employment* issued in 2018 (The State Council, 2018). In this document, employment has been given primary focus in developing digital economies, which are expected to create new employment opportunities through the new digital industries such as e-commerce and platform economy. At the same time, the convergence of traditional industries with digital technologies and platform services are believed to provide new and "better" opportunities of employment and entrepreneurship to the workforce in seemingly "outdated" sectors such as agricultural and manufacturing industries.

In practice, the state agenda of "Internet +" and "Mass Entrepreneurship" has greatly contributed to the surging digital and platform economy (Nieborg & Poell, 2018; van Dijck et al., 2018). According to *The 44th China National Statistical Report on Internet Development* published by the China Internet Network Information Center (CNNIC, 2019, p. 75), the total economic output of the Chinese digital economy in 2018 rose to 31,300,000,000 CNY (3872,000,000,000 EUR), constituting 34.8% of Chinese GDP (Gross Domestic Product) and creating 191,000,000 job positions. Among these, various digital platforms and apps such as Taobao (e-commerce), WeChat (social media), Didi (transportation), Eleme (food delivery) and Kuaishou (short video and livestreaming) have created over 60,000,000 jobs (平台经济破解"成长烦恼", 2019). The retail sales through e-commerce platforms in the first half of 2019 reached 3,810,000,000,000 CNY (471,000,000,000 EUR), making up 20% of the total retail sales of consumer goods. Geographically, this thriving digital economy is not necessarily limited to the urban, previously developed regions. As disclosed by the *White Paper on Chinese Digital Economy and Employment 2019* published by the China Academy of Information and Communications Technology (CAICT, 2019), in 2018 there were over 9,800,000 e-commerce companies located in Chinese rural areas, creating 28,000,000 employment opportunities for local farmers (ibid., p. 37). The online retail sales of agricultural products increased by 33.8%, to 231,000,000,000 CNY (29,000,000,000 EUR) in 2018. Less developed provinces like Anhui and Guizhou and second- and third-tier cities such as Chengdu and Wuhan have been lining up to promulgate incentive policies to promote digital industries and digital convergence. Advocated by the Chinese authorities, the digital economies seem to break the existing regional and spatial barriers and contribute to a more balanced and diversified regional economic structure (CNNIC, 2019, p. 74).

Resembling their Western counterparts like Google, Apple, Facebook, Amazon and Microsoft, Chinese Internet giants such as Alibaba, Tencent, Bytedance and Baidu together with various platforms such as Taobao, Didi, WeChat and Toutiao have played a dominant role in the process of platformisation. Operating as business intermediaries (Nieborg & Poell, 2018), these platforms enable a massive incorporation of multiple stakeholders—to name but a few, advertisers, service or product providers, end-users and audience—and identify them as platform users in their online ecosystem, in which these platform companies hold the most dominant position. In the media and cultural sectors, according to the *White Paper* (CAICT, 2019, p. 34), this platformisation has contributed to 55.5% of overall economic growth in broadcast, television, film and recording industries. The convergence blurs the boundary between the traditional media forms and gives rise to an exponential growth of user-generated content production, forming the basis of the wanghong industry. Short video platforms such as Douyin (Chinese version of TikTok) and Kuaishou, for example, managed to have a user base of over 648,000,000 with an average usage rate at 78.2% (CAICT, 2019, p. 35). Both traditional media companies and grassroots individuals are facilitated to start and expand their content and business on these new media platforms. Considering that the state has controlled most of the traditional media sectors for decades, the rise of the digital media platforms, which are mostly private or shareholding platform companies, will definitely encroach on the larger cultural market and the dominant privilege of the state media.

Moreover, enabled by the data-driven digital technologies and built-in affordances of advertising and e-commerce, the influence of the wanghong economy reaches beyond the boundaries of the media and cultural industries. It first of all creates career and business opportunities for grassroots individuals to become online content producers—wanghong creators, which are not necessarily limited to those who are educated, located in urban areas, and are employed in legacy media and cultural sectors. By virtue of the integration of e-commerce and advertising affordances in video and livestreaming platforms, these diverse creators further bring financial and market opportunities to those working in the traditional sectors, such as farmers, craftsmen and consumer goods manufacturers. Chinese livestreaming platforms, for example, managed to attract over 500,000,000 users in 2019 and achieved total transactions through e-commerce of over 433,000,000,000 CNY (54,000,000,000 EUR) (Xiaoyan, 2020).

Together with platform companies, the above diverse actors form a platform-dominated network system—"the multisided markets" (McIntyre & Srinivasan, 2017; Nieborg & Poell, 2018), in which various places, localities, things and people are connected in a commercial and dynamic online ecology. Within this ecology, the wanghong economy seems to have the capacity to transform various local places into mediaspaces (Couldry & McCarthy, 2004), personalities and identities into cultural commodities, for the production, consumption as well as exploitation of wanghong culture. It fits, on the one hand, into the state's agenda of digital economy, employment promotion as well as the recent "poverty alleviation" agenda[1] by incorporating grassroots, marginal population and creating opportunities for employment and national economic restructuring. For example, livestreaming has been widely used by rural wanghong creators to sell products on Chinese e-commerce platforms such as Taobao and Pinduoduo. In April 2020, hundreds of Chinese local county majors even joined these livestreaming shows to help sell agricultural products, whose sales were heavily impacted by Covid-19 (Wang & Xiong, 2020). On the other hand, the network effects of the wanghong economy still follow the logic of platform capitalism, in the sense that the connectivity enabled by social media platforms always favours the interests of big Internet companies to collect and commodify as much data as possible, and "in their position as an intermediary, platforms gain not only access to more data but also control and governance" (Srnicek, 2016, p. 47).

Given that at the core of the wanghong industry is still the production of symbols, representations and even social relationships, the governance of the wanghong economy is further complicated by the Chinese regulatory framework of "cultural governance". The state not only wants to "profit" from information and culture, but also seeks to control and shape it. Demonstrated by many studies on Chinese media (Keane, 2013; Lin, 2019; Sun, 2010), Chinese authorities have been eager to promote its national imagery to wield Chinese "soft power"[2] on the global stage on the one hand, while they expect a conforming culture that ensures social stability and national unity on the other. These two threads of national discourse function as the fundamental baselines that all media platforms and creators must comply with in their everyday practice. For the wanghong economy, the establishing of the "Great Firewall" induces a geopolitical market segregation and restriction that not only shields the domestic Internet and platform companies from the global competition dominated by American imperialism (Jin, 2013) represented by its GAFAM (Google, Apple, Facebook, Amazon and Microsoft) platform ecosystem, but also curbs, if not excludes, active interaction between the Chinese wanghong culture and the global influencer community.

Against this background of the political economy of the Chinese wanghong industry, we still need to probe into the everyday experience of wanghong creators, especially with regard to their working and living conditions in the social media economy. If the network effects of the wanghong industry promise connectivity between different spaces and populations, what does this transforming spatial and social relationship mean for those diverse creator individuals? And how can we make sense of the vast popularity and connectivity brought by wanghong culture in the context of contemporary China? To explore these questions the following section will first analyse the social background of wanghong creators and the social and labour mobility engendered by the wanghong economy.

2   Becoming Wanghong

A middle-aged (in her 40 s) Chinese woman from a small city in Zhejiang Province resigned after working for sixteen years as a writer for a state-run magazine in late 2017 and started writing on the WeChat public account platform. Her channel now has over 60,000 subscribers and brings in 50,000 CNY (6300 EUR) advertising revenue per month (interview, April 2020). Not only is it profitable, the flexible work also allows her to stay at home and raise her two children. According to the statistics provided by an intermediary agency for Wanghong creators on WeChat, 80% of these channels are operated by people born after 1985 and 40% of them are born from 1990 to 1995 and the majority of writers are women (interview, April 2018). Not only restricted to the urban-based, educated population, people from Chinese rural society also see opportunities for becoming wanghong creators. In late 2017, for example, Liu Suliang and his partner Hu Yueqing launched their channel Huanong Brothers (华农兄弟) on Xigua and Bilibili, two of the most popular video platforms in China. Their videos document everyday routine life on their farm, such as feeding and petting the bamboo rats, pigs and dogs, and exploring local fruits and vegetables grown in their village. Two years later, they have managed to obtain over 5,000,000 followers on Bilibili and 3,000,000 on Xigua, becoming one of the trendiest wanghong creators in China.

As indicated by these stories, the emerging social media economy in China seems to have enabled a diverse group of individuals to become Chinese wanghong. Specifically, we can trace two forms of social mobility facilitated by the new entertainment industry. First, wanghong incorporates those professional media and cultural professionals who used to work for legacy media organisations such as television, news press and film. Before creating the *Luogic* Talkshow, Luo Zhenyu, for example, was an experienced and well-known television producer at China Central Television (CCTV). The rise of Internet and social media entertainment since 2012 motivated Luo to resign from the CCTV and to found his own company and content channel on Youku and WeChat. In this show, Luo shares his reading experiences with the audience, always in a practical and comprehensible manner. In two years, Luogic Talkshow had become the most influential online program in China providing knowledge sharing content. At the same time, as I mentioned at the beginning, traditional media have now also started creating their "wanghong style" content by inviting celebrities to create amateurish livestreaming shows and short videos tailored for wanghong platforms like Douyin and Kuaishou. Chen He, a popular actor named for his casting in the trendy television series *iPartment*, has attracted over 60,000,000 followers on Douyin, where his posted videos employ a more "amateurish", "everyday" but amusing pattern. Creators like Luo Zhenyu and Chen He come from a professional background: They received professional or higher education in colleges and have worked in or for legacy media sectors for many years. Before joining social media, they were active in Chinese screen culture and managed to establish their social network in the cultural industries. On Chinese social media, these wanghong individuals are usually regarded as "the big V" (verified), or Key Opinion Leaders (KOLs). Thanks to their career experience within the media industry, they also have a closer relationship with capital and legacy media. Their content production is sometimes grouped as PGC model (professionally generated content) and thus has a high entry threshold due to its requirement for more finance and expertise.

The other type of wanghong creators are those who often come from a more grassroots background and adopt an amateurish style in their content production. There is an immense diversity among these creators in terms of their social backgrounds and genre of content. By 2018, according to *Chinese Wanghong Economy Report 2018* (iResearch, 2018), more than half (50.1%) of wanghong creators were female and over 37% of creators were located outside of Chinese first- and second-tiered cities. Though the majority of them have higher education experience, there are over 20% of creators without the experience of studying at university. Within this second category we can thus find both urban-based, university-educated, young hipsters and rural peasants and migrant working class. We see Chinese and international multilingual creators vlogging about their cosmopolitan tastes and lifestyles on Douyin and Bilibili, but we can also find rural fishermen filming their fishing and farming skills at sea or in the forests. From platforms like WeChat, Kuaishou and Xigua to Taobao, Little Red Book and Huya, good-looking girls and boys make videos and livestreaming shows about their DIY tutorials on fashion, make-up, crafting or game play, but also their attitudes and values about relationship, marriage, career and life. Compared to the "big V" wanghong, creators in the second category often start their wanghong career with low budget and self-taught skills (photography, audio-visual editing, make-up, etc.) in content production. This amateurish style is often regarded as *user-generated content* (UGC). Wang Rui, for example, lives in a small village in Anhui, a province located in the Eastern region of the country. His future was rather uncertain, chances were high he would become one of the migrant workers in the city, most likely Shanghai. But already at a young age he developed a strong interest in computer games, and with the emergence of platforms like Douyin, he slowly started a career as an online games commentator. Based in his countryside village, he posts short videos and writes commentaries on games, a job that earns him enough money to sustain himself (interview, April 2018). Similarly, A Feng and Lao Si both live in fishing villages in south China. In 2018, they started their channels on Bilibili, making and posting fish-catching videos almost every day. By 2020, their seemingly unsophisticated personalities and exotic fishing lives have won them over 1,000,000 followers on Bilibili and each single video can obtain 300,000 views. The online traffic generates decent financial returns. Since Bilibili has a special reward system that pays 3 CNY/1000 views, without even doing advertising or e-commerce A Feng and Lao Si can easily earn 900 CNY (114 EUR)/video.

This distinction between those with a professional and grassroots background, however, is by no means comprehensive or always clear-cut. In effect, we should view these two categories as aspects or dimensions embodied in the labour process of wanghong production. Along with the growth of popularity and revenue, for example, the grassroots, amateurish production is often gradually professionalised and the UGC model can quickly transform into the PGC model. In this process, grassroots wanghong also transforms into the "big V". Before achieving her success, Zhang Dayi was an unknown model working for fashion magazines and occasionally posting selfies on Weibo. After accumulating a small number of followers, she started sharing her fashion tips and some rough-cut videos. In 2014, the MCN (Multi-Channel

Network) company Ruhn approached her and helped her to establish a professional team in charge of Taobao e-commerce and personal branding. In the following years, the professionalised operation quickly led to the exponential growth of Zhang Dayi's wanghong business. With over 12,000,000 followers (by 2020) on Weibo and the prosperous e-commerce business together with advertising, she is not only the most influential Chinese beauty blogger, but also one of the most successful wanghong entrepreneurs in China. In a similar but slightly distinctive trajectory, prior to her wanghong career Papi Jiang was a not-so-successful actress and media professional. In 2015, she started making and posting videos on Weibo. This often spoof-like video content rapidly went viral on Chinese social media. In 2016, her team received an investment of 12,000,000 CNY (1,500,000 EUR) from the production company of the Luogic Show and the professionalisation was swiftly initiated (Wei, 2016). In the same year, with another talent agency Mountain Top, she founded the MCN agency Papitube.

These cases clearly demonstrate the great diversity of wanghong creators as well as the vibrant social network the wanghong economy has fostered. Developments in information and communication technologies have empowered nonprofessional individuals to create audio-visual content at a low cost, while leaving the job of content circulation and marketing to social media platforms by means of their sophisticated algorithms, which promise to distribute this so-called user-generated content to the right "target audience". At first sight, the workspace of wanghong manages to expand beyond the urban centres: Either in some remote rural village, in the poorly decorated student dormitory, or a simple bedroom with basic lighting. Those "3Ts"—technology, talents and tolerance—defined by Florida (2005) as three fundamental characteristics of creative cities that can attract the creative class now seem unnecessary for wanghong creators: A well-established digital infrastructure, as I will explicate in the following section, provides a solid foundation for diverse social spaces and localities to become the workplace of wanghong production.

3 Infrastructure, Workplaces and Labour Relations

In a video post in April 2020, Wang Gang, a well-known wanghong food blogger located in Fushun, a remote county in west China, tells behind-the-scenes stories of his online food-making videos. After leaving his chef job in Zhuhai, an affluent city in South China where he worked for about twenty years, Gang went back to his hometown Fu Shun and rented a 40-sqm apartment. "It was not supposed to be a good location to run a restaurant, too small and isolated", he discloses in the video. But with a monthly rent of 1000 CNY (126 EUR) and some renovation costs, the place ideally served as a decent kitchen and studio for making food videos. Aside from this rented kitchen, Gang also occasionally make videos in his parents' countryside house with his old uncle. In less than three years, Gang's channels on Xigua, Bilibili and YouTube in total have obtained over 1,000,000,000 views and 17,000,000 followers (12,000,000 on Xigua, 4,400,000 on Bilibili and 1,500,000 on YouTube). The huge online traffic also creates considerable financial income. According to estimates by Chinese media, the platform advertising and his own online shop together bring Gang an annual revenue of at least 40,000,000 CNY (5,000,000 EUR).

Though not every Chinese wanghong creator can be as successful as Wang Gang, his story represents a crucial distinction of the Chinese wanghong industry as compared to the social media entertainment (Cunningham & Craig, 2019) in the global context. The well-established Internet infrastructure across China and its immense consumer market make the networked wanghong economy even more inclusive in terms of demography and geolocation. According to the official statistics, the rate of penetration of the Internet into Chinese society reached 61.2% by June 2019 and among them there are 847,000,000 mobile Internet users (CNNIC, 2019, p. 15). Although the rural-based users only constitute 26.3% of the Chinese online population, the actual number exceeds 225,000,000 (CNNIC, 2019, pp. 15–16) and the coverage rate of fibreoptic cables and 4G mobile Internet in villages have reached 95% (4G 网络覆盖率达 95% [The coverage rate of 4G internet reaches 95%], 2018). In terms of Internet speed, 91% of users now connect to the

Internet via the fastest *Fiber To The Home* (FTTH) system and 77% have access to 100 MB broadband speeds (CNNIC, 2019, p. 13). Most importantly, thanks to the state initiative "tisu jiangfei" (提速降费) to increase the speed and lower the cost launched in 2015, the Internet subscription fee has been reduced by over 90% within four years.[3]

This wide penetration of Internet infrastructure and the reduced subscription cost have enabled a maximum incorporation of the Chinese population and of spaces into the platform and the wanghong economy. The "sinking market" (下沉市场), a term frequently used by Chinese media and business organisations in the past five years to refer to the small-town and rural markets, has become a new competitive field of investment among Chinese platform companies (平台经济破解"成长烦恼", 2019). The two leading platforms Kuaishou (short video) and Pinduoduo (e-commerce) are believed to have obtained success by targeting the sinking market through rural wanghong creators and cheap consumer products. At the same time, previously urban-based platforms such as Alibaba, Tencent and Jingdong have also lined up to adjust their strategies to expand into the rural society. In 2018, for example, Jingdong, the second largest Chinese e-commerce platform, launched its Super New Star project, in which five new apps (e.g., Fenxiang and Jingxi) have been developed to target the Chinese rural market and compete against Pinduoduo (Futunn, 2019). Alibaba built a new e-commerce platform CunTaobao, still embedded in its original Taobao ecosystem, but clearly focusing on the rural market.

This rapid expansion of digital infrastructure and platform economy across Chinese society has engendered lucrative career opportunities for diverse Chinese individuals to become wanghong creators as analysed in the previous section. However, this inclusive nature of the wanghong economy does not necessarily guarantee a stable and secure life and career without risk and precarity. As noted earlier, while Chinese policy-makers have seen the wanghong and platform economy as a crucial engine for restructuring the national economy and boosting employment, the Party State also keeps a vigilant eye on the content and culture it produces. To investigate and stop practices that may "harm social morality" and social or political stability (Lin & de Kloet, 2019), Chinese authorities have accelerated their regulation and censorship of productions on various social media platforms since 2016. For example, in mid-2016, the State Administration of Press, Publication, Radio, Film and Television (SARFFT) banned female livestreamers from "erotic banana-eating" (Phillips, 2016). In 2017, a nationwide inspection of fifty major livestreaming platforms led to the shutdown of ten online platforms and around 30,000 livestreaming accounts, aiming to eliminate content that is "vulgar, obscene, violent, superstitious, concerns gambling, or harms the psychological health of underage people" (Lai, 2017). In April 2018, Kuaishou and Toutiao, the leading Chinese short video platforms, were both "interviewed" by the CAC (Cyberspace Administration of China) for their "ignorance of the law and disseminating programs that are against social moral values" (Liu, 2018). The CAC demanded that the two companies give a "comprehensive rectification", after which their websites and apps shut down thousands of user accounts that posted "unhealthy content" and set up special volumes for disseminating "positive and healthy values".

For individual creators, this stringent censorship regime forces them to meticulously self-censor their creative content and strive for a balance between expectation from the audience, state or platform and themselves. Sisdong is a beauty and fashion blogger based in Dongguan, Guangdong. After his cross-dressing video went viral on Iqiyi in 2015, he opened his Weibo and later WeChat channels, posting cross-dressing photographs and giving instructions on beauty and fashion. Sisdong described himself as a "small, local wanghong", who gains popularity only in the city where he lives. Even so, he has managed to develop multiple revenue sources including advertising (for beauty and fashion products), e-commerce and livestreaming. Being as much eye-catching as sensitive, his cross-dressing content and openly gay identity occasionally cause him trouble and to certain extent limit his popularity. Sisdong shares the following during the interview:

> They [the platform] suspended my Weibo channel last year. You cannot be too obvious as an LGBTQ member. They didn't give me the reason for suspending my account, but I guess so ... I have it but I cannot be so obvious anymore. Just use it to scroll up those message and movie stuff, I cannot post things that I want to post anymore ... if I become bigger,

maybe it would be too dangerous to keep my style … (Interview, October 2018)

Ironically, with a growing online popularity, the wanghong creator's creative career becomes rather more contingent and vulnerable. Tian You, for example, was celebrated as the most successful livestreamer in 2017. During that time, his livestreaming shows on Kuaishou attracted over 35,000,000 followers and earned him more than 2,000,000 USD a year in payments from virtual gifting and advertising. He even released his own songs and aired on Chinese state-owned television. However, in early 2018, Tian You was accused by China Central Television, the central television network controlled by the state, of talking about pornography and drugs during his livestreaming. Shortly after, Tian You was banned across all Chinese platforms (including both legacy and Internet media) and his performing career seems to have reached an end (Chen, 2018).

Aside from career uncertainty caused by censorship, wanghong's everyday production also entails an intensive involvement of affective labour, which obfuscates boundaries between life and work, personal and public. As Elane Zhao (in press) points out, "wanghong operate in a liminal space where the line between public personae and private selves is blurred" (ibid., p. 231). To navigate in this liminal space requires wanghong's effective self-management. The high interactivity and connectivity online expose creators to both praise, celebration and "public shaming, humiliation and harassment" (Zhao in press, p. 232). Anna, a former livestreamer and a production manager for the Bigo platform, reveals one of her experiences with fans:

> I have one follower who knew my Instagram. He started stalking me and my friends. He kept asking why I wasn't streaming and why I didn't reply to his messages. He started to send messages like: "I know what you did, I know who you were, you are not allowed to be with another man, I've been supporting you, you cannot go out with another man". … He started to send me things anonymously, like flowers, and when I refused to accept them, he got really angry. I tried to report it to the company even though I was no longer there. They responded with: "Don't worry

about it, you're just popular, they'll go away, there's nothing much we can do anyway, just ignore it". (Interview, July 2018)

As Anna's story demonstrates, the highly social nature of wanghong labour aims to produce intimacy between creators and followers, yet such virtual relationship can also turn into harassment and mental pressure for creators. While exploiting and monetising the online traffic brought by such virtual sociality, platform companies and MCNs have failed to provide sufficient protection to their online influencers. In less dramatic cases, the involvement in cyberspace also causes a lack of engagement with the real, private life, engendering commonly shared loneliness among many creators. According to Kiki, a female livestreamer active on Huajiao and Huoshan in 2017:

> Livestreaming is a job but it is different from nine-to-five jobs. We are also diligent. We sit for 6 hours and talk and dance and rehearse … We need to know the songs, the colour, and the clothes they like … we will have connection. … But sometimes … I feel lonely. … We do not have a private life. We post pictures to fans everyday like: "Oh I am eating breakfast at 8:00 a.m., going to gym at 9:00 a.m., and do my nails at 10:00 a.m., take a nap at noon and in the afternoon I am livestreaming", but nobody actually finds out I am doing these things all alone … We have fans to take care of, but in real life, we have little time to meet friends. We think about how to communicate with fans all day. Gradually I feel I am not living in reality. (Interview, June 2017)

Chinese Internet censorship, fierce competition and the isolation from the offline world together induce considerable uncertainty to the wanghong career. Viewing the wanghong economy and creators as crucial new engines for income generation, the Chinese state and Internet companies, however, provide few labour protections to combat the quite precarious working conditions of wanghong individuals. Confronted with these various uncertainties and precarity, what continues to motivate these creators is the prospective financial income and the self-transformation and social mobility a wanghong identity promises. Often starting as an amateur creator, as the previous section shows, wanghong calculate themselves and others (followers, business partners, the state, etc.) in terms of personality, creativity, data and cost and profits. This entrepreneurial mode of production is always premised on, following Rose (1990, p. 6), a notion of a "better self". The wanghong economy in this sense provides this imagery of a better self, compared to their pre-wanghong lives: being richer, but also more creative, popular, fashionable and/or beautiful.

4   The Unlikely Creativity

The geospatial expansion of the wanghong economy and the actual precarity of wanghong labour is juxtaposed with a kaleidoscopic wanghong culture characterised by what I term the "unlikely creativity". Shougong Geng (Handcraft Geng) is a popular wanghong channel on Bilibili and Kuaishou that posts videos of handcrafts made by Geng Shuai, a local farmer from Baoding, Hebei province. Named bizarrely as "head knocker", "gatling gun", "robotic washing machine" and "handstand hairwasher", these ingeniously designed and crafted inventions are yet mostly "useless" in our everyday life. For instance, "handstand hairwasher" allows Geng Shuai to wash his hair when doing a handstand; "smile assistant" is a device similar to a mouth opener that can "assist" those who do not like to smile; "robotic washing machine" is made of a waste gas cylinder that can automatically wash clothes with its electric mechanical arms. These sophisticated yet quirky instruments have won Geng Shuai great popularity on the Chinese Internet; he has been jokingly referred to by his fans as "the useless Thomas Edison", "the most miserable wanghong" and "the jeans lover". In the videos, Geng Shuai introduces the usage and design of his devices, often in a prudish manner and with his Hebei accent. Together with his iconic jeans overall, thick and long hair and big round eyes, these videos generate a particular sense of absurdity as well as humour, which according to Geng imitates the Mo lei tau comedy in Stephen Chow's films. At the same time, the idea of making these inventions was initially sparked by his early working experience. His average income was 900 CNY (114 EUR) during the time when he stayed in five cities experiencing all kinds of jobs: plumber, construction worker, phone seller … His dream by then was to open a fireworks factory. Geng mocks himself for having been part of "the mobile builders of Chinese cities": either working on some remote construction sites or on the way to the next job. Later on, learning from his father, Geng became a skilled welder working on the local railway. In 2016, tired of this mundane life, he decided to start his own business and transformed the backyard of his house in the village into a studio, where he would make saleable machinery. Unfortunately, this hope of entrepreneurship was in vain, until he discovered Kuaishou and Bilibili, where his "useless" inventions were incredibly welcomed and acclaimed by millions of online viewers.

As analysed in the previous section, the participatory social media platforms like Kuaishou, Douyin and livestreaming apps enable a creative labour mobility that expands Chinese popular cultural production into the more marginalised groups of the population: the forming of the "unlikely creative class" (Lin & de Kloet, 2019). Wanghong culture in that sense is not necessarily limited by terms like youth culture, urban culture or subculture. In the 1990s and early 2000s, Chinese contemporary culture was mostly written in or by cities, "especially large conurbations on the eastern seaboard were the nodes through which international and other new influences presented themselves to young Chinese" (Clark, 2012, p. 7). In contrast, the rise of the wanghong economy seems to dissolve and expand beyond such spatial segregation and the urban imagery of popular culture. It resonates with what Jenkins (2008) terms convergence culture, "where old and new media collide, where grassroots and corporate media intersect, where the power of the media producer and the power of the media consumer interact in unpredictable ways" (ibid. p. 2).

It is from this unlikely mobility of the creative class that we can observe the forming of multifarious, sometimes unlikely aesthetics. Compared with content broadcast on legacy media, the creative repertoire of wanghong absorbs the everyday experiences from disparate individual backgrounds. Evidenced by Geng Shuai's inventions, those that might be viewed as "bizarre", "useless" and "nonsensical" in the mainstream culture are celebrated by their followers as authentic, sensational and creative. In his unboxing videos, we see Xiao Xiangge using a traditional corn-popper to cook crawfish, nibbling a 3000 CNY (370 EUR) king crab, and getting stuck to a lightbulb lollipop. A Feng and Lao Si display the fishes, crabs and shrimps they have pulled from the choppy sea. In his daily livestream on Taobao, Li Jiaqi, through his queer style of performance, brags about his selected lipsticks and cosmetic products from L'Oréal, SK-II, Armani, and so forth. On Douyin, we find a divergent mixture of trendy dances, music and comical performances, while on Kuaishou we learn tricks of magic, cooking and crafting. Even high-school teachers like Li Yongle can catch attention from his 9,000,000 fans through his science lectures such as *Do aliens really exist?*, *Why is a fart so smelly?* and *Can we create a time machine?*.

These kaleidoscopic aesthetics are unlikely not because they are impossible to organise or make, but given first of all the unlikeliness of their presence in Chinese popular culture. From television to commercial cinema, for decades the production of Chinese screen culture has been dominated by state-owned television networks and film studios, in which the national discourse of "double responsibilities" (Lin, 2019)—generating revenue alongside conforming politically—makes the autonomy of creative labour within this legacy cultural system quite contingent and expects its creative workers to "be creative for the state". The participatory wanghong economy, in contrast to the legacy media industries, seems to unleash the creative impulse from below. Though sooner or later they will be territorialised into part of the capitalist logic of platform economy and are not immune to censorship and official culture, the wanghong economy operates as a platform for the vernacular creativity (Burgess, 2006) to thrive, shifting the dynamics of Chinese popular cultural production from the professional and the state to the vernacular and the individual.

More importantly, these mediated, creative representations of the local place, life and identity by no means simply replicate or extend the preexisting social, spatial and power relations. The grotesque aesthetics as shown above may not easily find a position in the offline world that has often been highly hierarchical, patriarchal and normative. The various local places serve as versatile workplaces for wanghong production, while at the same time these places are also reproduced through the labour and creativity of wanghong creators into, borrowing Castells' (2011) term a "space of flows"; local places and their identities still matter, but in wanghong culture they only exist on a surface level that can add to the performative authenticity creators attempt to claim and monetise. In this sense, the ICT infrastructure and the wanghong economy together deterritorialise the previous spatial and social relationship in which these individual creators are located, providing them with new spaces for work and creativity that may be deemed as "inadequate", "unfulfilling" and even "unacceptable" in the original space of places. For creators, wanghong creativity and subjectivity have become desirable alternatives to the tedious work and identity as cook, farmer, high-school teacher or college graduate waiting to be hired by companies. The banality of the everyday has been converted into the productive footage of their online creativity, signifying a moment when banality, creativity and career converge. The subjectivity of wanghong thus constitutes a mixed process of becoming, transcending the simple identity of either their "authentic", everyday job or the professionalised creative worker. Through the accessible digital screens and platforms, these online visual contents also create a cordial resonance with their viewers' similarly mundane lives and fills their empty time that is unavoidable and intolerable in the daily routines. As to what it does to creators, the entertaining, simple and relevant wanghong creativity promises an approachable alternative, in which the vernacular can not only watch but participate—an "authentic" alternative to both the established screen culture and the banality of everyday life in local places that to a certain extent appear more artificial and restrained.

5 Conclusion

This chapter introduces the specificities of the Chinese wanghong economy and its implications for the existing spatial relationships in Chinese contemporary society. The wanghong industry first of all fits into the Party State's agenda of restructuring the economy and boosting employment, while its mass participation and immense diversity also lead to the Party State's mixed approach of both protection and censorship. At the local level, the well-established ICT infrastructure propels the booming platform economy and facilitates a maximum incorporation of individual creativities and labour from disparate social and spatial contexts into the wanghong economy. This highly networked economy engenders a social mobility that transcends geolocational limitations and transforms individuals including those from marginal social backgrounds into wanghong creators, providing them versatile spaces for creativity and employment that they are less likely to obtain in the pre-existing social settings.

For creator individuals, however, this empowering discourse of wanghong does not necessarily promise a secure career and life. Internet censorship and the rapidly evolving social media industry demand a continuous self-governance that incorporates self-censorship, continuous learning and emotional management. Various empirical cases show that these wanghong creators are confronted with highly stressful, competitive and affectively intense working conditions, in which boundaries between life and work, personal and public are obfuscated for the aim of "a better self" (see the contributions by Calle Rosengren, Ann Bergman and Kristina Palm as well as by Dominik Klaus and Jörg Flecker in this volume): of being creative, affluent, popular, fashionable and attractive. This mixed reality of empowering and disabling contributes to a kaleidoscopic landscape of wanghong culture. My textual analysis of these popular contents shows this particular online space gives voice to the vernacular, grassroots creativities that are sometimes deemed "useless" and "grotesque" in Chinese mainstream screen culture. These vernacular aesthetics underscore the "unlikeliness" of wanghong culture, distinguishing them from the artificial and more restrained traditional screen culture by their engagement with the vernacular, grassroots and banal everyday life.

But the wanghong economy and culture also transcend the banal everyday life embedded in the local places. The network effects of the digital communication and wanghong industry transform the local space of places into "the space of flows" (Castells, 2011), in which local lives, identities and values become increasingly subject to the logic of platform capitalism and state surveillance. However, the wanghong economy and culture also deterritorialise these local spatial and social relationships, which all become potential sources for creative production and monetisation on the side of individual creators. It is for this reason that the unlikely creativity of wanghong culture becomes desirable to creators and their online communities, serving as an imagined alternative to the tedious or normative everyday work as either cook, farmer, high-school teacher or college graduate waiting to be hired by companies. Taken out of the local context, these seemingly "bizarre" and "inadequate" creativities turn out to be highly entertaining and relevant and add flavour to the banal everyday life.

Notes

1. Since 2016, the Chinese government has promoted e-commerce in rural impoverished areas to stimulate sales of agricultural products and employment of local farmers (The State Council, 2016).
2. Coined by Nye (1990), soft power has been a popular term in international diplomacy, and cultural export has been touted as its key element. This term was embraced by the Chinese government in the early 2000s and soft power became one of the prime objectives of developing the cultural economy—through the "going-out of Chinese culture" (中国文化走出去 zhongguo wenhua zouchuqu; Keane, 2013).
3. For example, according to the Chinese Ministry of Industry and Information Technology, the average cost for mobile internet per GB and month has decreased from 139 CNY (17.58 EUR) before 2017 to 8.5 CNY (1.08 EUR) in 2019 (The State Council, 2019).

References

4G 网络覆盖率达 95% (The coverage rate of 4G internet reaches 95%). (2018, October 14). *People's daily*. http://finance.people.com.cn/n1/2018/1015/c1004-30341881.html. Accessed November 30, 2020.

Burgess, J. (2006). Hearing ordinary voices: Cultural studies, vernacular creativity and digital storytelling. *Continuum, 20*, 201–214.

Cai, X. (2020). *Reality shows present slice of indoor life during epidemic*. Sixth Tone. http://www.sixthtone.com/news/1005218/reality-shows-present-slice-of-indoor-life-during-epidemic. Accessed Februvary 15, 2021.

Castells, M. (2011). *The rise of the network society* (2nd ed.). Blackwell.

Chen, X. (2018, February 13). *Live-streaming star banned over 'offensive' content*. Shine. https://www.shine.cn/news/nation/1802130400/.

China Academy of Information and Communications Technology (2019). 中国数字经济发展与就业白皮书 (White paper on Chinese digital economy and employment 2019). Resource document. China Information and Communications Research Institute. http://www.caict.ac.cn/kxyj/qwfb/bps/201904/P020190417344468720243.pdf. Accessed February 15, 2021.

China Internet Network Information Center (2019). 第44次中国互联网络发展状况统计报告 (The 44th China National Statistical Report on Internet Development). Office of the Central Cyberspace Affairs Commission. http://www.cac.gov.cn/2019zt/44/index.htm. Accessed February 15, 2021.

Clark, P. (2012). *Youth culture in China: From red guards to netizens*. Cambridge University Press.

Couldry, N., & McCarthy, A. (2004). *Mediaspace: Place, scale and culture in a media age*. Routledge.

Cunningham, S., & Craig, D. (2019). *Social media entertainment: The new intersection of Hollywood and Silicon Valley*. New York University Press.

Duan, W., & Jiayan, N. (2020). 受宅经济推动, 虎牙一季度营收同比增长近五成 (Driven by the housing economy, Tiger Tooth's first-quarter revenue grew nearly 50% year-on-year). Yicai. https://www.yicai.com/news/100637878.html. Accessed 15 Feb 2021.

Florida, R. (2005). *Cities and the creative class*. Routledge.

Futunn (2019). 2019 电商巨头攻防战: 别再只关注下沉市场了 (The war between e-commerce giants in 2019: More than the sinking market). https://news.futunn.com/post/4722481. Accessed February 15, 2021.

Hong, Y. (2017a). *Networking China: The digital transformation of the Chinese economy*. University of Illinois Press.

Hong, Y. (2017b). Pivot to internet plus: Molding China's digital economy for economic restructuring? *International Journal of Communication, 11*, 1486–1506.

iResearch (2018). 2018 年中国网红经济发展研究报告 (Chinese Internet Industry Report 2018). https://www.iresearch.com.cn/Detail/report?id=3231&isfree=0. Accessed February 15, 2021.

Jenkins, H. (2008). *Convergence culture: Where old and new media collide*. New York University Press.

Jin, D. Y. (2013). The construction of platform imperialism in the globalization era. tripleC: *Communication. Capitalism & Critique. Open Access, 11*, 145–172.

Keane, M. (2013). *Creative industries in China: Art, design and media*. Polity.

Lai, C. (2017, May 26). *Chinese live-streaming platform punished for broadcasting fake 'forbidden city' video*. Hong Kong Free Press. https://www.hongkongfp.com/2017/05/26/chinese-live-streaming-platform-punished-broadcasting-fake-forbidden-city-video/. Accessed November 30, 2020.

Lin, J. (2019). Be creative for the state: Creative workers in Chinese state-owned cultural enterprises. *International Journal of Cultural Studies, 22*, 53–69.

Lin, J., & de Kloet, J. (2019). Platformization of the unlikely creative class: Kuaishou and Chinese digital cultural production. *Social Media + Society, 5*(4). https://doi.org/10.1177/2056305119883430.

Liu, J. (2018, April 8). 快手、今日头条、火山小视频被约谈 (Kuaishou and Toutiao got interview!). *People's Daily*. http://gongyi.people.com.cn/n1/2018/0408/c151132-29910514.html. Accessed November 30, 2020.

McIntyre, D. P., & Srinivasan, A. (2017). Networks, platforms, and strategy: Emerging views and next steps. *Strategic Management Journal, 38*, 141–160.

Nieborg, D. B., & Poell, T. (2018). The platformization of cultural production: Theorizing the contingent cultural commodity. *New Media & Society, 20*, 4275–4292.

Nye, J. S. (1990). Soft power. *Foreign Policy, 80*, 153–171. https://doi.org/10.2307/1148580

Philips, T. (2016). *Gone bananas: China bans 'erotic' eating of the fruit on live streams*. Guardian News & Media Limited. https://www.theguardian.com/world/2016/may/09/gone-bananas-china-bans-erotic-eating-live-streams. Accessed November 30, 2020.

Phoenix New Media (2020). I slept twice, was watched by 18.6 million people, and earned 50,000 yuan. https://ent.ifeng.com/c/7uDIypK0uAQ. Accessed February 15, 2021.

Rose, N. (1990). *Governing the soul: The shaping of the private self*. Routledge.

Srnicek, N. (2016). *Platform capitalism*. Polity.

Sun, W. (2010). Mission impossible? Soft power, communication capacity, and the globalization of Chinese media. *International Journal of Communication, 4*, 54–72.

The State Council (2015a). 国务院关于加快构建大众 创业万众创新支撑平台的指导意见 (Instructions on constructing platforms to promote mass entrepreneurship). http://www.gov.cn/zhengce/content/2015-09/26/content_10183.htm. Accessed November 30, 2020.

The State Council (2015b). 国务院关于积极推进'互联网+'行动的指导意见 (Instructions on promoting "Internet +"). http://www.gov.cn/zhengce/content/2015-07/04/content_10002.htm. Accessed November 30, 2020.

The State Council (2016). 大力推进农产品电子商务 (Promote e-commerce for agricultural products). http://service.sh-itc.net/articleds/dianzisw/dsdsdt/dsgjdt/201610/1403892_1.html. Accessed February 15, 2021.

The State Council (2018). 关于发展数字经济稳定并扩大就业的指导意见 (Guidelines on developing digital economies and expanding employment). http://www.gov.cn/xinwen/2018-09/26/content_5325444.htm. Accessed November 30, 2020.

The State Council (2019). 网络提速降费加码，国务院常务会部署五大重点任务 (Five major tasks to increase the Internet speed and lower the cost). http://www.gov.cn/zhengce/2019-05/15/content_5391966.htm. Accessed February 15, 2021.

Van Dijck, J., Poell, T., & De Waal, M. (2018). *The platform society: Public values in a connective world*. Oxford University Press.

Wang, S., & Xiong, X. (2020). 中国深度贫困地区农产品电商报告 2020 (Reports on agricultural e-commerce in Chinese impoverished areas 2020). http://www.farmer.com.cn/2020/04/30/wap_99852276.html. Accessed February 15, 2021.

Wei, W. (2016, March 21). PAPI酱的1200万 (The 12 million of Papi Jiang). *36Kr*. https://36kr.com/p/1721054330881. Accessed 30 Nov 2020.

Xiaoyan, W. (2020). 2020 年直播电商行业市场规模及发展趋势分析 (Analysis of Chinese livestreaming e-commerce market in 2020). *Qianzhan*. https://www.qianzhan.com/analyst/detail/220/200520-e486bcbc.html. Accessed February 15, 2021.

Xu, L. (2020, May 26). 2020 年Q1净利润同比激增 742% 斗鱼直播带货瞄准直男市场 (Douyu's rapid increase of revenue in the Q1 of 2020). *NBD*. http://www.nbd.com.cn/articles/2020-05-26/1438912.html. Accessed November 30, 2020.

Youwenyouda. (2020). 新冠肺炎疫情下,网红经济的"异军突起"对我国产业结构的主动性调整有何重大影响？(How will the rise of Wanghong economy impact the restructuring of national economy during the Covid-19?). *Zhihu*. https://zhuanlan.zhihu.com/p/109357506. Accessed November 30, 2020.

Zhao, E. (in press). Wanghong: Liminal Chinese creative labor. In S. Cunningham & D. Craig (Eds.), *Creator culture: Studying the social media entertainment industry* (pp. 220–241). New York University Press.

平台经济破解"成长烦恼" (The break-through of the platform economy). *People's Daily*. (2019, October 9). http://www.xinhuanet.com/fortune/2019-10/09/c_1125080668.htm. Accessed November 30 2020.

7

Reconfiguring Workplaces in Urban and Rural Areas: A Case Study of Shibuya and Shirahama, Japan

Keita Matsushita

This chapter explores transformations in the perception of place in workplaces and workstyles, examining phenomena such as working in co-working spaces (shared workplace with a community), *workationing* (working while on vacation), based on fieldwork in Shibuya and Shirahama, Japan.

The spread of mobile media, including smartphones and tablet devices, has allowed people to work remotely (telework, remote work, nomadic work) and brought about a redesign in workstyles and workplaces. Mobile media and Wi-Fi environments have turned urban spaces such as cafés, train stations and airports into workplaces. While we can see traditional office work as a *place-based workstyle* where a workplace defines the way of working, these recent changes can be positioned as

---

K. Matsushita (✉)
Faculty of Sociology, Kansai University, Suita, Japan
e-mail: keita-m@kansai-u.ac.jp

© The Author(s), under exclusive license to Springer Nature Switzerland AG 2021
M. Will-Zocholl and C. Roth-Ebner (eds.), *Topologies of Digital Work*, Dynamics of Virtual Work,
https://doi.org/10.1007/978-3-030-80327-8_7

the emergence of *style-based workplaces* where an individual's workstyle renders their workplace to be possible anytime, anywhere.

As workplaces proliferate in different parts of the city, community formation has become a subject of interest. Community is a central theme in the study of co-working spaces and digital nomads (Avdikos & Iliopoulou, 2019; Blagoev et al., 2019; Bouncken et al., 2018; Intaratat, 2017; Orel, 2019). Among these, "communities of practice" (Lave & Wenger, 1991), which aims at networking and the exchange of skills and knowledge has attracted much attention. At the same time, however, Matsushita (2019) has pointed out that we can also observe *community of style*, which aims at empathy for work and lifestyles.

How are workplaces reconfigured from the viewpoints of style-based workplaces and a community of style? To find out, we conducted fieldwork, which included interviews with managers and users of co-working spaces in Shibuya, the centre of co-working, and Shirahama, an excellent place for working vacations in Japan.

This section is followed by an overview of the emergence of style-based workplaces and transformation from urban space to workplaces in Japan. The third section introduces co-working research with a focus on community, and community of style. The fourth section contains the results of fieldwork in Shibuya and Shirahama. The fifth section consists of a conclusion and discussion based on results.

1 From Place-Based Workstyles to Style-Based Workplaces

We watch most disasters and sporting events, like soccer and baseball, on television or through other forms of relay broadcasting. *Doubling of place* is the term used by Scannell (1996) to describe the simultaneous occurrence of an event in two places when we watch or listen to something through mass-media channels like TV or radio: The first place is where the event is physically happening and the second is where we are watching or listening to it. Since the 2000s, *doubling of place* has started to occur through smartphones and mobile PCs or devices in addition to mass-media channels, a phenomenon that Moores (2012) labels the "instantaneous pluralisation of place" (ibid., p. 16). How has the instantaneous pluralisation of place by using mobile media transformed workplaces and workstyles? To put it briefly, it has triggered a transformation from *place-based workstyles* to *style-based workplaces*.

1.1 The Rise of Style-Based Workplaces

So far, workstyles have originated in places such as factories and offices, which have directed the way in which we work. However, in recent years, we have seen more attention given to designing places *for* a given workstyle, as in *activity-based workplaces* (ABW) (Arundell et al., 2018; Candido et al., 2019; Skogland, 2017). This preference for designing workplaces around workstyles has gone beyond factories, offices and other conventional workplaces, spreading to urban spaces as well.

One of the backgrounds of this trend is the spread of telework and remote work. In the Japanese context, according to the Urban Environment Policy Office (2020) in the Ministry of Land, Infrastructure, Transport and Tourism's (MLIT) *Survey of Teleworkers' Demographics*, they define teleworkers as individuals who work at places that are not their usual places of work, and as of 2019, teleworkers are 14.8 per cent (16.6 per cent in 2018) of employees and 20.5 per cent of self-employed workers (24.5 per cent in 2018), which is roughly the same proportion as in 2016. By gender, 19.8 per cent of male and 8.9 per cent of female employees were teleworkers. Among self-employed workers, 22.4 per cent of men and 17.1per cent of women were teleworkers. When asked where they conducted their telework, 56.9 per cent of the respondents used a satellite office (office space away from the headquarters or branch), 48.2 per cent were at home and 48.2 per cent were mobile (multiple responses possible). The average number of hours worked per day by location was 4 hrs at the satellite office, 3.5 hrs at home and 2.2 hrs on mobile devices. The introduction of telework and remote work has been promoted as a response to chronic traffic congestion, as well as to disasters such as typhoons, earthquakes and infectious diseases like Covid-19 in 2020.

The Japan Telework Association (2017) has proposed the concept of *third workplace*, which includes "decompressing spaces" (*sukima kūkan*) like karaoke boxes and cars, to describe workplaces other than one's home and office. They explain that "telecommuting is not a special workstyle", and by turning spaces besides offices into activity-based workplaces, "the only difference is that the most appropriate place to facilitate one's work tasks is outside the office. That is, it will become natural for telecommuting to cease to be something that special people do, and instead be something everyone does in order to improve productivity at work" (ibid. p. 9).

For example, Tokyo Metro collaborated with Fuji Xerox in June 2018 to launch a proof-of-concept for the use of satellite offices by installing individual workbooths in subway stations. Japan Railways (JR) East also launched a service called "station work" in 2019, which consists of shared booth-style offices that have been installed inside stations in Tokyo. While train and subway stations are a frequently-used hub for commuting, travelling and other forms of mobility, they are also places where people often end up waiting for appointments or transfers. This is also true for airports, highways, hotels and shopping malls, which have been positioned as Urry's (2007) "intermediate spaces" created by mobility; or Augé's (2008) "non-places", which have been abstracted by media and communication technologies.

1.2 Officisation: Making a Workplace from Urban Space

In this chapter, *officisation* is defined as treating a non-office space as an office by utilising mobile media. We are arguably now at a point where mobile work will see further officisation of such intermediate spaces and non-places in Japan's crowded major cities, where many people commute and move around by train and subway. Tuan (1977) distinguishes space and place thus: Space corresponds to freedom and yearning; place corresponds to safety and attachment. When we have experiences and spend time in a space, meaning is attached to it and the space becomes a place. Attachment arises and transforms a space into someone's home or place as a function of experience. In this sense, we can say that these movements of mobile work are transforming urban *spaces* into work*places*.

This trend indicates that the density of work (tasks and communication) will increase further for individual workers, occupying even the time they spend moving from place to place, while at the same time the density of cities has also increased, with their free spaces and free moments being filled by work.

This is also arguably a trend that will "officise" increasing amounts of "alone-space" (*hitori kūkan*), or spaces where one can be alone in cities (Nango, 2018). Alone-space is facilitated by a constant connection to mobile media, which is simultaneously both a medium for communication that connects us to others and a "territory machine" (Fujimoto, 2006) by which users create a space that is just for them. Mobile media has thus officised all possible urban space by not only facilitating everyday communication between users, friends and family, but also by connecting the individual to work.

The process by which the decompressing spaces in cities become officised can also be viewed as part of the sharing economy. However, it would be more accurate to regard this as a superimposition on time and space rather than simply a transformation of it. These services and ways of using space arguably make it possible to replace one space with another, giving rise to a time and space that is used in parallel, or superimposed, with another use. What is happening in these style-based workplaces is a shift in perspective from *What workstyles are possible at this place?* to *How will I use spaces (including non-offices) to suit my workstyle?*. This is due to the increase in flexible workstyles like freelancing and flexible forms of commuting such as remote work and telecommuting.

2 *Community of Style* in Co-Working Spaces

Co-working spaces are arguably a symbol of style-based workplaces. A pioneering example of co-working space is C-base, a hacker space established in Berlin in 1995. In modern terms, the first co-working space was

Spiral Muse, a facility where engineers in San Francisco got together to work in 2005. Since then, San Francisco has been home to a number of co-working spaces, such as Hat Factory and Citizen Space, where freelancers, mainly in the IT industry, work. This trend has spread across the United States, as seen in New York's New Work City and Seattle's Office Nomads. Furthermore, co-working spaces have been also increasing in Europe and Asia. In Japan also, co-working spaces have been spreading around urban areas with the establishment of Cahootz in Kobe, PAX Co-working in Tokyo, and Juso Co-working in Osaka from around 2010. According to coworking.com (Tsukumo Network, 2020), which lists co-working facilities in Japan, there were 1301 registered co-working facilities in Japan as of October 2020, of which 414 (32 per cent) were in Tokyo, and 122 (9 per cent) were in Osaka. As of May 2015, there were 300 registered, of which 132 (44 per cent) were in Tokyo, and 32 (11 per cent) were in Osaka. This shows that the number of co-working spaces in Japan increased more than fourfold between 2015 and 2020, and looking at the ratio, the number of local co-working spaces increased, not just in urban areas like Tokyo and Osaka.

The global trend of increasing of co-working spaces has been accompanied by a wealth of research in fields such as management studies, sociology and architecture with regard to how co-working spaces are used, and their value in urban areas (Akhavan & Mariotti, 2018; Akhavan et al., 2019; Intaratat, 2017; Jamal, 2018; Mariotti et al., 2017; van Winden & Carvalho, 2016) or connected to sharing economy (Bouncken & Reuschl, 2018; Durante & Turvani, 2018). The central interest in these studies is collaboration and the formation of community in co-working spaces (Avdikos & Iliopoulou, 2019; Blagoev et al., 2019; Bouncken et al., 2018; Intaratat, 2017; Merkel, 2015, 2019).

Kwiatkowski and Buczynski's (2014) relatively early study positions co-working as a "space catalyst" discussing how the community created by co-working spaces supports freelancers and remote workers physically, emotionally and psychologically. Based on Engeström's activity theory-based analysis, Spinuzzi (2012) describes co-working as "working alone, together", and positions co-working space as "a superclass that encompasses the good-neighbours and good-partners configurations as well as other possible configurations that similarly attempt to network activities within a given space" (ibid. p. 433).

2.1 Focusing on Community in Co-Working Spaces

The community in such co-working spaces is not monolithic; rather, co-working spaces can be categorised into several types based on their function. For example, Capdevila (2014) categorises co-working spaces into "Convenience Sharing" and "Community Building" types. Convenience Sharing spaces incorporate a dimension of knowledge-sharing, and supporting a collective action for effective planning and execution, while Community Building spaces incorporate a dimension of expanding individual action to the wider collective and broadening creative fields (Castilho & Quandt, 2017). Facilitating collaboration and knowledge-sharing in such a co-working space requires the *co-presence* of co-workers—that is, their coincidental presence—in that space (Parrino, 2015).

How then, do the members of a co-working space come to have a sense of community? According to Garrett et al. (2017), they follow three pathways to gaining a sense of community: *espousing*, *learning* and *enacting*. Espousing refers to experiencing community by mutually having the goal of building a community; learning refers to experiencing community based on that community's shared psychological image; and enacting refers to experiencing community by following behaviours appropriate to that specific community.

2.2 Community of Practice and Community of Style

The afore-mentioned perspectives on communities in co-working spaces are mainly based on studies of urban co-working spaces. In contrast, Matsushita (2019) has discovered from his research on co-working spaces that, particularly in resorts, there is another type of community besides "Convenience Sharing" and "Community Building" as mentioned above (Capdevila, 2014); this type is the ephemeral or "pop-up" community, which is based on temporary, loose connections for exchanging information about navigating daily life, and to overcome inconveniences whenever they arise. This type of community is characterised by workers' act of sharing, affirming and reinforcing a type of digital nomad workstyle or lifestyle, which involves working while traveling, through an ephemeral or pop-up community. That is to say, it is a community whose goal is for people to share their individual workstyles, lifestyles and mindsets, for the purpose of running or starting a business or for profiting in any specific way.

This community should also be called a *community of style*. Originally, Pihl (2014) used this term to refer to a fashion blogger community and described it as a platform where consumers create, discuss and reveal how they perceive brands, and how they can be combined to create favourable expressions of style that are in line with current trends. We can find communities of style not only among fashion bloggers but also among workers in co-working spaces. Communities of style, where workers in co-working spaces share and enforce their lifestyles or workstyles, is contrasted with *communities of practice* (Lave & Wenger, 1991) in workplaces.

If we suppose that communities of practice, which include "Convenience Sharing" and "Community Building", are *instrumental* for sharing knowledge, skills and networks that lead to starting and running a business, then this would position communities of style as *consummatory*. This means that they are formed in an ephemeral, ad hoc fashion and facilitate the affirmation and sharing of members' workstyles and lifestyles, which is in itself the objective of such communities (see Table 1). Of course, these two are not mutually exclusive, and it is often the case that one includes elements of the other.

3   Case Study in Shibuya and Shirahama

With the proliferation of mobile media, we have increasingly seen urban spaces as workplaces. Such emerging workplaces can be called style-based workplaces. Additionally, communities of style, where workers can share their workstyles and lifestyles have emerged in co-working spaces in

Table 1 Comparison of community of practice and community of style in co-working spaces

Category	Community	
	Of practice	Of style
Nature	Convenience Sharing and Community Building	Ephemeral/pop-up
Objective	Instrumental	Consummatory
What is shared	Business knowledge, skills, networks, and so forth	Workstyles/lifestyles

resort areas. What impact do style-based workplaces and the communities of style have on the redesign of workplaces in urban and rural areas? To illustrate this, we will discuss a case study that was conducted in Shibuya (Tokyo) and Shirahama (Wakayama Prefecture)—urban and rural examples, respectively.

3.1 Overview of the Study

We carried out field research by visiting two co-working spaces in Shibuya (urban area of Japan) and two satellite offices in Shirahama (rural area of Japan) as participant observations. We observed the design of the places, the users and their communication. We also collected relevant information on community, locales, workstyles and business models through short interviews with users, planners and managers of the facilities.

Moreover, we conducted two in-depth group interviews. One was conducted in February 2020 at a co-working space in Shibuya. The interviewees were a planner and a project manager of the co-working space. The other took place in July 2019 at a satellite office in Shirahama. The interviewees were the local government leader, a project manager and a person in charge of the company occupying the satellite office. These interviews lasted around one hour and were transcribed. Three topics were covered, including the concept of the place, workstyle of the members and connection to locales. These interviews were fully transcribed, and coded for themes based on research topics such as space or place recognition, design concepts or workstyles. Based on the topics developed from these interviews, the transcripts were reviewed again to see the relevances for each topic and the range of mentions and experiences. The interviews were conducted in Japanese; quotations from the interviews in the following chapter were translated by the author.

3.2 Co-Working Spaces: Shibuya

Shibuya is one of the busiest areas in Tokyo, with a population of about 200,000. Shibuya is the "mecca" of pop culture and subcultures such as music and fashion among young people. In recent years, the number of offices in the area has increased due to large-scale redevelopment, and it has become a business area mainly for IT companies. In the mid-1990s, it was called "Bit Valley" and many IT firms subsequently based themselves there. Recent years have seen it being redeveloped. In addition to the offices that Google and other relatively large-scale IT companies such as CyberAgent and GMO Internet have there, the number of startups based there has also increased. Besides startups, many co-working spaces for individual programmers and designers have also been built in Shibuya, giving it a different feel compared to cities like Otemachi, Marunouchi and Shinjuku, where existing companies of other industries have their offices. Shibuya has also come to be known as the city for exploring workstyles, as typified by the TWDW (Tokyo Work Design Week), which has been held there since 2013.

The *co-ba-network*, which is the subject of this case study, started in 2011 with the construction of *co-ba shibuya*. A total of twenty-two centres have since opened around the country. In the Shibuya area, *co-ba jinnan* was opened in October 2018 in an area not far from *co-ba shibuya*, and *co-ba ebisu* was opened in December 2019. Jinnan is an area close to Shibuya Station with many small fashion stores, while Ebisu is the next station to Shibuya Station and is known for its high culture.

Takahiro Ogino, who planned and launched the two new centres, says in an interview that we are now in a time where one's office itself is portable thanks to the proliferation of mobile PCs, Wi-Fi-friendly environments and cloud services. Within this context, he further declares: "It is important to create something that is unique to that place when designing workplaces and urban or rural spaces" (interview, February 2020).

Unlike ordinary co-working spaces, *co-ba jinnan* has no reception counter and is furnished with a dining space called *co-dining*. Candidates for its name initially included *co-fighting* space and *Shibuya East*, as it was heavily geared towards supporting startups. However, it was deliberately named *jinnan* because of a desire to both connect the concept of supporting startups with "Jinnan-ness", and for its members to also play a part in the space's "Jinnan-ness". Even within Shibuya, the Jinnan area is known for being an underground youth fashion and culture hotspot, with small "indie" shops rather than large chain stores, and by rereading, or redesigning, the core elements of past fashion and culture in the context of startups, rather than creating the same thing, *co-ba jinnan* tries to preserve this "localness".

Co-ba ebisu was opened with the aspiration of being a workstyle liberation zone where workers, rather than companies, could choose their workstyle freely, and of their own initiative. The area of Ebisu itself has developed out of what was a black market and alleyways after World War II, but today, it is known as a fashionable area, and a popular place to live. Though it is not particularly thought of as a place to work, it is full of the headquarters of major firms, such as the beverage company Sapporo Holdings, and many more relatively small companies. According to Ogino, *co-ba ebisu* incorporates these characteristics of the area into its interior design as a metaphor. The balance between not being overdone and applying designs characterises the co-working space on the ground floor. While the interior is not "finished" per se—it does not have individual spaces with variable walls, its air conditioner ducts are exposed, and there are no curtains—this flexibility makes the place easily adaptable. In addition to serving as co-working space, the first floor is a residence floor with twenty rooms. Residents can go back to their room and, at the same time, access their workplace directly. Unlike *co-ba jinnan*, which is focused on startups, *co-ba ebisu*, with its expanded frontage, looks forward to welcoming people with a variety of workstyles to its workstyle liberation zone. The people who work there range from freelancers such as designers and programmers to corporate employees. And they range from individuals to groups such as startups.

We can see them communicating with each other and planning events for the exchange of their workstyles and lifestyles.

Many of its members signed contracts to use *co-ba ebisu*, even while it was still under construction. Ogino also says in the interview that "for them, the deciding factor was not the interior, convenience, or any functional considerations; instead, they resonated with the story about creating a place and a community from scratch". In that sense, the "perpetually under construction" interior encourages the commitment of its participating members.

According to Ogino, *wazawaza* (going through the trouble of doing something) and *tamatama* (happenstance) are key concepts in designing and running co-working spaces. It is important to incorporate this happenstance, or serendipity, so to speak, into the spatial and experiential design of co-working spaces in order to build a community there and to transform the co-ba from space to place.

3.3 Workationing: Shirahama

Shirahama (Wakayama Prefecture) is located in the Kansai region, a two-hour drive or train ride from Osaka or a seventy-five-minute flight from Tokyo. The town and its neighbouring areas are known as a resort area, rich in touristic resources, including a beautiful coastline, hot springs and the Kumano Kodō pilgrimage routes (a UNESCO World Heritage site). Though Shirahama receives many tourists even today, it is a pioneer in bringing workationing to Japan, having developed bespoke facilities since 2015, in order to attract visitors.

The word *workation* was coined to describe working while on vacation and/or a workstyle of staying in a resort area for several days or weeks. This[1] might involve working at a co-working space in the morning and enjoying one's hobbies in the afternoon, for example. Workation has emerged for digital nomads or companies that require only a computer and Internet connection to work. In Japan, more and more companies have been trying to introduce workationing as a system to collect paid leave or as part of a "workstyle reform". For example, in July 2017, Japan

Airlines (JAL) announced the introduction of workationing. The press release of Japan Airlines (2017) explains it as follows:

> *Workation* is a portmanteau of "work" and "vacation", which refers to telecommuting from domestic or international resort spots, from one's hometown outside the city, or in the countryside in general. The aim of this new workstyle of working from one's vacation (travel) destination is to leave mornings and nights free for employees to spend as they wish so that they have more energy for work. Workationing is also expected to increase opportunities for employees to travel and spend time with their families. It will also contribute to community revitalisation in the countryside by encouraging employees to participate in events held there.

As this indicates, the goals of workationing are to (a) increase energy for work, (b) increase time spent with family, and (c) revitalise rural communities. Along with company-led initiatives like this, there is also a significant number of locales whose tourism industry aims to attract workationers. In 2019, the Workation Forum was held in Tokyo, where sixty-five local governments across Japan, mainly from Wakayama and Nagano Prefectures, formed the Workation Alliance Japan (WAJ). Local governments actively welcoming workationing for the purpose of community revitalisation is probably a particularly Japanese phenomenon.

Shirahama has converted the initially existing facilities, such as park management offices and company sanatoriums, as facilities for workationing. They are not co-working spaces for individual workers, but satellite offices for companies. There are two satellite offices in the town. When we visited and observed these facilities during field research, we found that the interior itself was similar to a modern office in an urban area, while the offices were designed to offer a beautiful view of the coast and forest from the windows.

One of them is the "Shirahama-chō IT Business Office", which was converted from the old sanatorium of a life insurance company in 2004. Even though it is located at a distance of approximately five minutes by car from both the local airport and downtown Shirahama, and the sea and the beach are visible from inside, its offices remained vacant for years. Salesforce set up its Shirahama satellite office there as part of the Ministry of Internal Affairs and Communications (MIC) 2015 *Regional*

Pilot Project to Promote Hometown Teleworking which prompted other IT companies such as NEC Solution Innovators and V Cube to do the same. They conduct a portion of their operations from there.

The Shirahama-chō IT Business Office eventually became full; so a second branch was opened in an area not far from the first, where there was a park management office. The office's first floor was rebuilt as a new park management office and park rest area that doubles as a co-working space, while the second floor contains four public-use meeting rooms that are offered as rental offices. Shirahama-chō IT Business Office #2 makes the town's business strategy explicit in its membership requirements, which specifically relates to IT-related companies. In 2018, Mitsubishi Jisho Sekkei entered this market, opening a workation office called *WORK × ation Site Nanki–Shirahama* in Shirahama-chō Business Office #2. Mitsubishi positions this as an initiative to leverage remote work to enable employees to stay in a resort area or other favourable environments and combine work or training with vacations. The company plans to open similar facilities elsewhere in Japan in the future.

In addition to building workation facilities, Shirahama local government has also requested that Japan Airlines introduce larger aircrafts for flights from Tokyo, increased Wi-Fi-friendly environments, and promoted collaboration between local industry and workationers.

Like Salesforce, NEC Solution Innovators was chosen for the MIC's campaign (Ministry of Internal Affairs and Communications) to promote hometown teleworking in 2016, upon which it set up its satellite office at the Shirahama-chō IT Business Office. Its activities there are broadly categorised into "company work" and "community relations". There is a mix of employees comprised of those who have migrated and those who stay for a certain period as a workation. By setting up an environment where work can be coordinated remotely with company workflows and systems, employees are able to work the same way as in the city. It also allows them to spend their free time in a way that they would not be able to in the city. For example, one of the resident telecommuters says:

> I enjoy visiting hot springs in my free time, so on weekends I visit the nearby hot springs. I was never really able do that when I was working in

Tokyo, but since I started living here, I have been able to visit more than 20 in a year. (Interview, July 2019)

Another employee states:

I can do most of my management work online. I only go on occasional business trips, but the rest of the time I can work with a beautiful view of the ocean from this office, so it's a great environment. (Interview, July 2019)

Community relations, meanwhile, might involve engaging in problem-solving with local business owners, or developing "ideathons" and other co-creation activities that include universities. A manager says: "We are fostering interaction with the local community and giving back to it by incorporating business elements such as holding 'ideathons' with our NEC's technologies and local tourism unions" (interview, July 2019).

In this sense, the workation phenomenon in Japan has been led by the government or businesses rather than being popularised by individual workers choosing it as a workstyle for themselves. One might even go as far as to say that a "workation industry" is being formed. We can see increasing participation not only from local governments hoping to attract visitors and private companies that want to introduce workationing, but also from the IT industry, real estate, railroads and airlines, and hotels and the tourism industry.

In the face of limited mobility due to Covid-19, telework has been encouraged, and vacancies in urban offices and co-working spaces have become noticeable. Meanwhile, following the government's announcement in May 2020 that it would support the promotion of workation, local governments, hotels and co-working spaces have also begun to create an environment for workation in order to promote the tourism industry. The number of local governments participating in the WAJ also exceeded 150 in November 2020.

4   Conclusion and Discussion

Both co-working spaces in Shibuya and workationing in Shirahama are arguably examples of style-based workplaces in urban and rural areas, respectively. These examples reflect two different perspectives on the trend of redesigning urban and rural workplaces into style-based workplaces: *deofficisation/officisation* and *delocalisation/localisation*.

What is *deofficisation/officisation*? As described earlier, officisation means that non-office spaces in cities are being used as workplaces, in an office-like way, due to the use of mobile media. Conversely, recent years have seen creative offices being set up with kitchens, spaces for relaxing, comfortable furniture and convenient amenities, which mark a break with former concepts of "office-ness". This trend of rejecting what used to constitute office-ness is deofficisation.

Moving on, what is *delocalisation/localisation*? With the spread of style-based workplaces, there is a trend to set up facilities and environments so people can work in the same way wherever they are, be that in the city or the country. That is delocalisation. In Japan, people continue to flock to overcrowded Tokyo in droves. For this reason, it is of the utmost importance for rural areas to enable people to work in the same way as they can in cities like Tokyo and Osaka, so that they can have workers stay there or attract them as new residents. In contrast, localisation refers to the trend of discovering and leveraging the uniqueness of a city or rural area in order to differentiate it from others amid the spread of delocalisation. Discovering what that uniqueness is and using it to foster a sense of civic pride makes places more attractive, be they urban or rural, and provides a source of competitive power to attract talented workers.

From field research, Shibuya's *co-ba jinnan* and *co-ba ebisu* are deofficisation-oriented, in the sense that the intention was to create a place that is different from conventional offices, by being a place for startups and a metaphor for the city. Typically, these premises are equipped with kitchens, and offer their users space for relaxation and comfortable furniture as well as convenient amenities, and often these areas are guided by metaphors such as bar, park and café. Furthermore, the interview with the planner indicates that for these places, "Jinnan-ness" and "Ebisuness" is a matter not just of spatial design but also of place-making, which is indicative of the trend of co-working spaces contributing to local uniqueness. That is, they are localisation-oriented, in the sense that they combine the uniqueness of the area with the concept of a co-working space while also defining what it means to be located in that area. Thus, in Shibuya, we can observe the trends of deofficisation and localisation through *co-ba's* co-working spaces.

Meanwhile, the workation-related developments in Shirahama are at present focused mainly on the construction of satellite offices to enable remote work, and are thus officisation-oriented, in the sense that such developments involve renovating existing facilities and repurposing them into satellite offices. Interviews with workers and managers show that workers living there can work while simultaneously enjoying their rural life and workationers can enjoy their stay as a vacation while also being able to work in the same way as in the city despite being elsewhere. In that sense, it can be said that workplaces in Shirahama are oriented towards delocalisation. That is, the workplaces set up for workationing in Shirahama at present consist of satellite offices more so than co-working spaces, which indicates the trends of officisation and delocalisation.

In conclusion, as style-based workplaces are spreading, we have seen deofficisation and localisation in urban co-working spaces, and officisation and delocalisation in the regional orientation. What is interesting is that when locals consider workation as an approach to community revitalisation, we expected workation facilities to reflect deofficisation and localisation because it leverages local uniqueness. However, field research shows that they instead reflect officisation and delocalisation by emphasising the capability to work in the same way as in the city. Almost no community of style could be found among the employees gathered at the spaces in Shirahama. However, it is possible to see a community in the interactions between the employees on workation and the residents. As Matsushita (2019) found from one example of workationing overseas, workers form a community of style among themselves, but a community of style that includes residents is not common. In that sense, this is in contrast to the Japanese case, and it is not unrelated to the fact that workationing in Japan is less an individual workstyle choice, and more often tends to be part of initiatives for community revitalisation by local governments in rural areas or a system introduced by companies. Longitudinal studies of single regions and international comparative studies will be necessary in this field going forward.

As we saw in the case of Shibuya, co-working spaces in urban areas, on the other hand, actually reflected the trends of deofficisation and localisation, which we expected in local areas. The reason for this was that in the Greater Tokyo Area, Shibuya needed to show its uniqueness in order to compete with the established office cities of Marunouchi, Otemachi, Ikebukuro and Shinjuku. That is, there is competition among the cities in the Greater Tokyo Area, but the approach to localisation in urban areas is different than that in rural areas. As we observed in field research, localisation as workplace in urban areas calls for a workplace's story to overlap with the story of the area and update it, for which it is important to have communities of style. Of course, communities of practice, where members can share knowledge, skills and networks for launching startups, as observed in *co-ba jinnan*, are also important. However, if it is the case that *co-ba ebisu* and also *co-ba jinnan* need to juxtapose and update stories in order to be what they are and define what it means to be in that place, then sharing knowledge, skills and networks becomes less important than sharing lifestyles and workstyles. In that sense, communities of style, as far as workplaces are concerned, are *more* than just communities of workers among themselves. Rather, they are an important element in preserving and shaping what makes an area unique.

In future research, it will be essential to explore how communities and places should be constructed in working environments such as offices, co-working spaces and homes as teleworkers expand under the influence of Covid-19. For this purpose, in addition to the interviews with designers and managers discussed in this paper, interviews with workers should be analysed using qualitative content analysis to analyse how they perceive and construct their workplaces and communities, and to clarify their behaviour and activities concerning community building and work through participatory observation.

Note

1. "Workcation" is often used in English-speaking countries, but "workation" is used more often in Japan. In this paper, unless it is a proper noun, we use "workation".

References

Akhavan, M., Mariotti, I., Astolfi, L., & Canevari, A. (2019). Coworking spaces and new social relations: A focus on the social streets in Italy. *Urban Science, 3*(1), 2. https://doi.org/10.3390/urbansci3010002.

Akhavan, M., & Mariotti, I. (2018). The effects of coworking spaces on local communities in the Italian context. *Territorio, 87*, 85–92. https://doi.org/10.3280/TR2018-087014.

Arundell, L., Sudholz, B., Teychenne, M., Salmon, J., Hayward, B., Healy, G. N., & Timperio, A. (2018). The impact of activity based working (ABW) on workplace activity, eating behaviours, productivity, and satisfaction. *International Journal of Environmental Research and Public Health, 15*(5), 1005. https://doi.org/10.3390/ijerph15051005.

Augé, M. (2008). *Non-places*. Verso.

Avdikos, V., & Iliopoulou, E. (2019). Community-led coworking spaces: From co-location to collaboration and collectivization. In R. Gill, A. C. Pratt, & T. E. Virani (Eds.), *Creative hubs in question* (pp. 111–129). Palgrave Macmillan.

Blagoev, B., Costas, J., & Kärreman, D. (2019). 'We are all herd animals': Community and organizationality in coworking spaces. *Organization, 26*, 894–916. https://doi.org/10.1177/1350508418821008.

Bouncken, R. B., Laudien, S. M., Fredrich, V., & Görmar, L. (2018). Coopetition in coworking-spaces: Value creation and appropriation tensions in an entrepreneurial space. *Review of Managerial Science, 12*, 385–410. https://doi.org/10.1007/s11846-017-0267-7.

Bouncken, R. B., & Reuschl, A. J. (2018). Coworking-spaces: How a phenomenon of the sharing economy builds a novel trend for the workplace and for entrepreneurship. *Review of Managerial Science, 12*, 317–334. https://doi.org/10.1007/s11846-016-0215-y.

Candido, C., Thomas, L., Haddad, S., Zhang, F., Mackey, M., & Ye, W. (2019). Designing activity-based workspaces: Satisfaction, productivity and physical activity. *Building Research and Information, 47*, 275–289. https://doi.org/10.1080/09613218.2018.1476372.

Capdevila, I. (2014). *Different entrepreneurial approaches in localized spaces of collaborative innovation*. https://ssrn.com/abstract=2533448. Accessed 15 February 2021.

Castilho, M. F., & Quandt, C. O. (2017). Collaborative capability in coworking spaces: Convenience sharing or community building? *Technology Innovation Management Review, 7*(12), 32–42. https://doi.org/10.22215/timreview/1126.

Durante, G., & Turvani, M. (2018). Coworking, the sharing economy, and the city: Which role for the 'coworking entrepreneur'? *Urban Science, 2*(3), 83. https://doi.org/10.3390/urbansci2030083.

Fujimoto, K. (2006). The anti-ubiquitous "territory machine": The third period paradigm: From "girls' pager revolution" to "mobile aesthetics." In M. Ito, D. Okabe, & M. Matsuda (Eds.), *Personal, portable, pedestrian: Mobile phones in Japanese life* (pp. 77–101). MIT.

Garrett, L. E., Spreitzer, G. M., & Bacevice, P. A. (2017). Co-constructing a sense of community at work: The emergence of community in coworking spaces. *Organization Studies, 38*, 821–842. https://doi.org/10.1177/0170840616685354.

Intaratat, K. (2017). Community coworking spaces: The community new learning space in Thailand. In S. F. Tang & S. E. Cheah (Eds.), *Redesigning learning for greater social impact: Taylor's 9th teaching and learning conference 2016 proceedings* (pp. 345–354). Springer.

Jamal, A. C. (2018). Coworking spaces in mid-sized cities: A partner in downtown economic development. *Environment and Planning a: Economy and Space, 50*, 773–788. https://doi.org/10.1177/0308518X18760857.

Japan Airlines. (2017). JALは、テレワークを推進し、働き方改革を進めます (JAL is promoting telework and work style reforms) [Press release]. https://press.jal.co.jp/ja/release/201707/004350.html. Accessed 15 February 2021.

Japan Telework Association. (2017). *The possibility of using the third workplace for workstyle innovation.* Resource document. http://www.japan-telework.or.jp/pdf/report2017-02.pdf. Accessed 15 February 2021.

Kwiatkowski, A., & Buczynski, B. (2014). *Coworking: Building community as a space catalyst.* Cohere Coworking.

Lave, J., & Wenger, E. (1991). *Situated learning: Legitimate peripheral participation.* Cambridge University Press.

Mariotti, I., Pacchi, C., & Di Vita, S. (2017). Co-working spaces in Milan: Location patterns and urban effects. *Journal of Urban Technology, 24*(3), 47–66. https://doi.org/10.1080/10630732.2017.1311556.

Matsushita, K. (2019). *Mobile media jidai no hatarakikata* (Workstyles in mobile media age). Keiso Shobou.

Merkel, J. (2015). Coworking in the city. *Ephemera: Theory & Politics in Organization, 15,* 121–139.
Merkel, J. (2019). 'Freelance isn't free'. Co-working as a critical urban practice to cope with informality in creative labour markets. *Urban Studies, 56,* 526–547. https://doi.org/10.1177/0042098018782374.
Moores, S. (2012). *Media, place and mobility.* Palgrave Macmillan.
Nango, Y. (2018). *Hitori kuukan no toshiron* (Urbanism of alone space). Chikuma Shobou.
Orel, M. (2019). Coworking environments and digital nomadism: Balancing work and leisure whilst on the move. *World Leisure Journal, 61,* 215–227.
Parrino, L. (2015). Coworking: Assessing the role of proximity in knowledge exchange. *Knowledge Management Research & Practice, 13,* 261–271. https://doi.org/10.1057/kmrp.2013.47.
Pihl, C. (2014). Brands, community and style–exploring linking value in fashion blogging. *Journal of Fashion Marketing and Management, 18,* 3–19.
Scannell, P. (1996). *Radio, television and modern life.* Blackwell.
Skogland, M. A. C. (2017). The mindset of activity-based working. *Journal of Facilities Management, 15,* 62–75. https://doi.org/10.1108/JFM-05-2016-0016.
Spinuzzi, C. (2012). Working alone together. *Journal of Business and Technical Communication, 26,* 399–441. https://doi.org/10.1177/1050651912444070.
Tsukumo Network. (2020). *Coworking.com.* https://co-work-ing.com. Accessed 30 November 2020.
Tuan, Y.-F. (1977). *Space and place: The perspective of experience.* University of Minnesota Press.
Urban Environment Policy Office. (2020). *Survey of teleworkers' demographics.* Resource document. Ministry of Land, Infrastructure, Transport and Tourism. https://www.mlit.go.jp/report/press/content/001338554.pdf. Accessed 15 February 2021.
Urry, J. (2007). *Mobilities.* Polity.
van Winden, W., & Carvalho, L. (2016). Urbanize or perish? Assessing the urbanization of knowledge locations in Europe. *Journal of Urban Technology, 23*(1), 53–70.

Part III

Virtual Working Spaces

8

ICT Enforced Boundary Work: Availability as a Sociomaterial Practice

Calle Rosengren, Ann Bergman, and Kristina Palm

Following in the trail of new technology and the digitalisation of society, the previously clearly defined spatial and temporal boundaries between work and private life are weakening (Allvin et al., 2011; Berkowsky, 2013; Bittman et al., 2009). This is because access to Information and Communication Technology (ICT) functions (e.g., email, text and voice messages) enables employees to continue working after leaving the office for the day, and to stay in connection with family and friends when at the office. An individual can, for example, coordinate the family schedule via snapchat or text messages while working on a project report at the office during office hours. And conversely, that same person can coordinate the next day's schedule with colleagues and clients in a video meeting

C. Rosengren (✉)
Faculty of Engineering, Lund University, Lund, Sweden
e-mail: calle.rosengren@design.lth.se

A. Bergman · K. Palm
Karlstads University, Karlstad, Sweden

at home in the evening after dinner with the family. In this sense, a larger part of the day becomes potential working time and an increasing number of physical locations become potential working places. ICT together with a decreased regulation of the temporal and spatial aspects of work makes new combinations of previously distinct temporal and spatial zones possible (see the contribution by Christian Oggolder in this volume), as well as new ways of combining work and family (Brannen, 2005).

One's ability to make autonomous decisions about how to meet and interact with the demands from both the work and non-work domains implies an increased feeling of the employee being in control (Anderson & Kelliher, 2011). In relation to workplace health promotion, the increased opportunity to control and influence work is generally considered a positive factor in the prevention of negative stress and psychosocial ill health (Karasek & Theorell, 1990). However, this also poses new challenges to employees to balance the expectations from different spheres in their lives and to allocate their time to different actors (such as colleagues, managers, clients, friends and family members). This has potential positive and negative effects for achieving a work–life balance (Bäcklander et al., 2018; Lehdonvirta, 2018). Barley and Kunda (2004) and Bourne and Forman (2014) argue that when given increased autonomy regarding when and where to work, people tend to prioritise work over non-work obligations and even put in longer working hours than before. Several reasons behind this have been put forward. For example, it could be explained by the sense of fulfilment and satisfaction employees receive from their jobs, increased expectations from managers or difficulties to separate work and non-work time. In fact, work conducted in the domestic area is not even always recognised as work since it is sometimes conducted while doing other things such as "sipping wine in one hand and filing papers with the other" (Bourne & Forman, 2014, p. 77).

Bergman and Gardiner's (2007) concept of "availability" was developed to capture how individuals use and distribute their time, energy, capacity and commitment along temporal and spatial dimensions. They define the concept as follows: "Available is to be accessible in time and space and responsive to the needs and wants of others, for example one's employer or family. Availability is both a disposition and a capacity, emphasising both structural conditioning and action" (Bergman & Gardiner, 2007, p. 401). Hence, the concept accounts for individual choice and motivation—agency—as well as social structures and objective conditions (Bergman & Gardiner, 2007; Bergman & Gustafson, 2008; Holth et al., 2017). The concept was developed to capture men and women's temporal and spatial availability patterns regarding work and family before the increased use of ICT. Today, the demands and possibilities to be multi-available with ICT in various spheres of life in time and space are shedding new light on the concept.

The digitalisation of work poses a growing challenge both for individuals and organisations to find a level of availability that supports both work productivity and personal well-being (Dery et al., 2014). That is why it is important to gain knowledge on how digital technology affects the relationship between the spheres of work and private life, and the consequences this has on employee well-being. This chapter explores how this process takes place with a focus on how ICT is actively used by employees to manage their availability to the different spheres of work and private life. The process of either separating or integrating work and non-work to different times and places is referred to as *boundary work*, an area that is receiving increasing attention from scholars in the field of organisational studies (Fleck et al., 2015; Golden & Geisler, 2007; Kossek, 2016; Kreiner et al., 2009; Mellner, 2018). Little attention, however, has been directed towards how ICT specifically is used in boundary work. Throughout the chapter, we argue that availability should not be seen only as technological possibilities or organisational demands, but as a sociomaterial practice (Feldman & Orlikowski, 2011) that takes different shapes and forms through the interaction of the employees with one another and with their digital infrastructure. This sociomaterial practice is hereinafter described as *ICT boundary work* (Kreiner et al., 2009). The aim of this chapter is to further the understanding of how ICT is actively used to manage one's availability to the spheres of work and private life.

We begin the chapter by sketching previous research around boundaries: boundary theory, ICT and boundary work, and boundary control. Next, we outline the study design, a practice-based approach and the qualitative data collection method used. We then present the results in three parts, focusing on how employees leave work at work, how employees are available for work at home and for private life at work, and finally how special places can be banned from work. Finally, we discuss our results through the lens of availability as a sociomaterial practice.

1 Boundary Theory

Integration and *segmentation* are two basic concepts in boundary theory, and describe two different ways to manage the spheres of work and private life. Depending on personal preferences and contextual factors, employees can be placed on what Nippert-Eng (1995) refers to as the "integration–separation continuum". At one end there is the person who tries to hold work and private life apart at all costs (segmentor). That person shows a low flexibility in his or her ability to attend to matters in the other sphere. Consequently, there is a low level of permeability of the domain boundaries. At the other end of the continuum there is the person who blends the spheres and integrates them into everyday life (integrator). This person is more likely to work from home or make himself or herself available to personal matters while at work, and there is a high level of permeability of the domain boundaries (Nippert-Eng, 1995). It is important to note from a spatio-temporal perspective that the blending of spheres can relate to both *where* and *when* work is conducted (Bergman et al., 2020). Anderson and Kelliher (2011) define only one type of segmentor, and that is a person who "chooses to stay late in the office to complete a piece of work, rather than completing it later when at home" (ibid. p. 305). This is a person who likes to keep the domestic area free from work-related activities, but may still integrate work into the evenings. In our research we define this kind of strategy as a place separator, that is, the boundary of space is important, but this does not apply to time (Bergman et al., 2020).

The practice of integration or segmentation can be related to one's preference for mentally disconnecting from work, one's identification with roles related to different spheres and or external demands. As mentioned, this process is referred to as *boundary work* (Kreiner et al., 2009). It is the process of either segmenting work and non-work to different times and places and thereby keeping the work and personal life separate, or integrating the two. The latter can imply, for example, that one works at weekends in order to be able to manage and compensate for dealing with personal matters during office hours. What this process looks like and how much effort it takes can differ between people and over the course of a lifetime. Mellner (2018) argues that everyday boundary work is much more complex for working parents than for those living on their own. Also, external factors such as the situation under Covid-19 and the challenges when schools and childcare were closed can come into play. Kossek (2016) describes how there can be hybrid forms of integration and separation in the sense that over the course of one week, one month or one year, a person can exhibit different patterns. This can be related to marital status (e.g., a divorced parent with child custody every other week) or seasonal variance in work pressure.

1.1 ICT and Boundary Work

With few exceptions, there is little research into how using technology in different ways can enforce boundary work. Kreiner et al. (2009) use the concept of *leveraging technology* to describe how technology is used to facilitate boundary work. This includes the need to consider the active use of behavioural strategies (or *tactics*) in the use of technology. In a similar vein, Fleck et al. (2015) describe the tactic of consistently dividing different spheres across different technological devices (e.g., using separate devices for home and work). Battard and Mangematin (2013) use the concept *sedentarisation* to describe the practice of only using certain technological devices in certain locations (e.g., leaving the laptop and work phone at the workplace), and also to show how boundaries between different spheres can be *integrated into the technology* (e.g., by using different email accounts and ringtones). According to Fleck et al. (2015), these features of the technology can help people manage boundaries because they enable them to decide when to interact with different spheres and to avoid being subject to work demands at inappropriate times. By using these different behavioural strategies, individuals in practice shape their own spatio-temporal patterns by deciding when and in what way they want to interact with the surrounding community. In this process of boundary constructing, they are trying to uphold boundary control. However, managerial and organisational expectations also play a role in the individuals' possibilities to shape their own boundary patterns. Studies show, for example, that there are strong links between how the work is organised, the specific characteristics of different professions and the conditions of accessibility for work and family (Bergman & Gardiner, 2007; Lindsay & Maher, 2013). Where organisations have adopted family-friendly policies and working time arrangements, research indicates that this leads to increased job satisfaction, increased performance, reduced sick leave and work–life balance among employees (Kossek & Ozeki, 1999). At the same time, there is research showing that there is a mismatch between what employers consider to be promoting work–life balance and the breathing experiences of these (Warhurst et al., 2008) and that much of the work–life balance discussion is conditional on the employer's interests and that flexible working conditions rather tend to generate conflicts between home and family (Brannen, 2005; Healy, 2004). Furthermore, research suggests that organisations and management reward employees who are multi-available and tend to reduce any problems to individual concerns and not organisational issues (Bergman & Gustafson, 2008).

1.2 Boundary Control

As presented, there are a number of boundary behaviour styles. According to Fleck et al. (2015), what is central for well-being is not so much the type of strategy that is implemented, but the perceived sense of boundary control (Fleck et al., 2015). An example of low boundary control is the case of a person who prefers to keep evenings free from work and perceives an inability to do so (due to the work phone ringing or push emails). A sense of being in control is a generally accepted theoretical foundation for explaining work-related stress, or conversely well-being and motivation. One of the most widespread theories relating job design to stress and illness, from a psychosocial perspective, is Karasek and Theorell's (1990) demand/control model. The model is based on the assumption that a hazardous work environment comes from a high level of demands combined with low decision latitude. On the other hand, a high level of demands in combination with high decision latitude leads to active jobs associated with learning and a high level of motivation. This illustrates how a high level of demands does not in itself necessarily pose a risk to employee health because it can either result in activity and learning or stress and illness. This all depends on one's level of control.

It could be assumed that the discretion to choose location (work from home or at the office) and or scheduling could increase an employee's perceived control and in turn alleviate stress, which would have a positive effect on the overall well-being of the employee. However, as colleagues, customers and managers work and communicate around the clock, the work conditions can change (for example, meetings can be changed or rescheduled, new tasks can be added). This in turn can contribute to a feeling of not being in control (in the sense of a perceived ability to manage workflows and plan the work week ahead). Similarly, the pressure of being expected to be online during personal time is related to a lack of boundary control (Kossek, 2016). Parasuraman and Simmers (2001) also argue that the absence of a clearly defined work schedule not only can be a source of stress, but can also generate work–family conflict. Elvin-Nowak (1998) argues that not being able to be there for work and family can generate feelings of failure and guilt. Kossek (2016) argues that low levels of boundary control, for example, always being "on call", may force employees into work–life integration against their will. Control in relation to this is something that is not only given but also taken. The employee, though, is not a passive receptor of contextual factors. On the contrary, we view the individual as an agent who actively takes part in the everyday construction of work, using what is at hand to conform life to his or her wishes. We are interested in furthering the understanding of how employees with a high level of discretion as to when and where to perform work define and structure their working day with the active use of technology.

2   Study Design and Method

The goal of the study was to capture how ICT was actively used by employees to manage their availability to the spheres of work and private life. A qualitative methodology was used in which the respondents' thoughts and experiences were analysed. Data were collected from the pen-and-paper time diaries and semi-structured interviews of thirty-eight employees from three companies. Data collection took place in Sweden between 2017 and 2019 at three different industrial companies: one Swedish site in a global science-led biopharmaceutical business, one Swedish site in a global developer and supplier of technologies, automation and services for the pulp, paper and energy industries, and one site in a Swedish forest and pulp production organisation. The companies were chosen because of their interest in the posed research questions.

A practice-based approach (Barley & Kunda, 2004; Feldman & Orlikowski, 2011) to boundary work was applied when we designed the empirical study on which this article is based. Such an approach to working life implies that people's "everyday doings" are central to this research. Schatzki et al. (2001) defines practices as "materially mediated arrays of human activity centrally organised around shared practical understanding" (ibid. p. 11). The empirical research is made up of three multinational industrial companies at three different sites in Sweden. In close collaboration with these companies, we conducted an explorative time diary and interview study with employees on how they managed their digital working life. The focus was on the boundaries between work and private life. Studying boundary work from a practice-based theoretical perspective thus implies that our starting point will be the concrete practices relating to how boundaries are placed, removed, transcended, thinned or thickened to suit one's practices (Nippert-Eng, 1995). This approach requires research methods that are sensitive to complexity and ambiguity because it means engaging with the everyday realities of life. A practice-based approach means that we do not look at the technology, the employee and the organisational setting as separate entities but rather as co-constituents (Feldman & Orlikowski, 2011). This means we consider the intertwinement of technology, personal preferences, social structures and organisational context to gain a broader understanding.

2.1 Participants

The participants were strategically, but still randomly, chosen by the research team from a contact list provided by the Human Resources (HR) division in each company. Of the thirty-eight respondents, thirty-four were white collar employees and four were blue collar workers representing various occupational roles. The emphasis on white collar workers in the selection can be explained by the fact that being able to work part- or full-time from home was one of the preconditions to be included in the study. All were working full-time and on permanent contracts. Twenty-two were women and sixteen were men. Nine were between 23 and 34 years, ten between 35 and 44 years, sixteen between 45 and 54 years and three between 55 and 67 years. Twenty-one had children under 18 years of age. Individual ten-minute meetings were booked with the participants at their workplace. In these meetings, we talked the participants through the time diary and showed them how to fill it in. They were instructed to keep the diary for seven consecutive days. They were also asked to send or turn-in the diaries to the researcher as soon as they could after completion.

2.2 Time Diaries

The time diary method involves the collection of entries that are written by participants over time (Cohen et al., 2006). Over a seven-day period, the respondents made written entries in their diaries when they carried out (a) privately related activities during normal office hours (such as talking on the phone with their partner or child, or booking a doctor's appointment), and (b) working task related activities outside of normal office hours (such as reading and answering emails on the phone or preparing for a meeting on the computer). The diary entry included the nature of the task, the technology that was used, how long it took, when and where it was performed, who else was in the room and how the participant felt about it. Each day in the diary was divided into seven time slots including day and night hours. The respondents summarised each slot by indicating their general emotional state(s), and could also add a comment to the slot in the form of a free text answer.

2.3 Semi-Structured Interviews

Three to six months after completion of the time diaries, the participants were asked to participate in a follow-up interview. Of the thirty-eight participants, all but one took part in the interviews. The interviews were semi-structured with a fixed set of areas and questions. They also included specific follow-up questions related to the entries in each person's diary, as well as questions related to the relevant themes emerging in the interview. The interviews lasted from forty to sixty minutes, were carried out on Skype or at the respondents' offices, and were recorded and transcribed verbatim. The interviews could be categorised as open-ended (Yin, 2003), which allowed room for the interviewees' reflections.

2.4 Analysis and Coding of Data

The time diaries were copied and the originals were returned to the participants. The diary data were transcribed by the authors into a Word file according to a common structure. All three authors first independently analysed all the transcriptions using an explorative content analysis to identify individual patterns of practices in the diaries by devising codes and relationships between them (cf. Maxwell, 2012; Saldaña, 2015). In the coding process, we emphasised the agency of the respondent and the ICT boundary work was interpreted as a means to achieve boundary control. In order to guarantee anonymity, the participants' responses are not presented with age, gender and organisational position. In the instances where the family situation is central in the analysis this will be highlighted. Quotes from the interviews presented in the result section have been translated from Swedish to English by the authors.

3 Results

The results suggest that there is a wide variety between different practices of managing work and private life. These practices seem to be related in part to personal preferences (to integrate or separate the spheres of work and private life) and in part to contextual variables such as workload, technological affordances and the practices of colleagues and family members.

3.1 Leaving Work Technology at Work or Bringing Work Technology Home?

It was of interest to hear the respondents' reflections in the interviews on their perceptions of what work actually is in a context that is fluid. Or rather how it was framed in everyday working life at the intersection of working tasks, time, space and technology. Sometimes work was defined in terms of a given physical location. As one respondent stated: "You go to work, and at work, you do your work." In this case, work is equivalent to a certain place you go to. Work was also defined in terms of place *and* technology, or as a merging of the two into one: "It's really that way. I leave all work-related technology [phone and laptop] at work. So, I don't bring it home; I leave work at work." When work, in this sense, is defined by technology, it is easy to understand that a person who wants to separate the spheres of work and private life will leave the work-related technology at the office. "Leaving work at work" in this instance served as a way to uphold spatial boundaries between the spheres of workplace and home. As already mentioned, the practice of dedicating certain technological devices to certain places is also referred to as *sedentarisation* (Battard & Mangematin, 2013). This is how one respondent reasoned about leaving work-related technology at work:

> Yes, I usually never bring my computer home with me. … I try to avoid doing this any way I can because I don't want it in my house. … I want to know that when I walk out [of the office] and close the door I'm free, and I really like that sensation. Kind of "Well, that's it; now it's over".

> But I'm really happy about working hard and long hours at work, but I don't want to do it from home. (Interview, own research)

In this case, longer days at the office are preferred over working from home. The compromise made is less in terms of the spatial dispersion of work at the cost of more temporal dispersion; that is, letting work spill over into the evenings. Freedom (from work) is defined by "closing the door". What time of the day it is seems less important. For those who are willing and able to leave their work-related technology at work, it seems like a good strategy to mentally detach from work.

For others, taking work-related technology home seems to alleviate stress. This is because it helps to avoid the necessity of going to the workplace at weekends or being able to leave the office early to work from home in the evening.

> Personally, for me, it has definitely helped to alleviate stress. If I have a lot to do I can simply take out my laptop and work for 1 hour or 2 at home at the weekend, rather than having to go into the office. (Interview, own research)

So in these two cases, the different ways of using ICT to enforce boundary work seem to alleviate stress depending on personal preferences and contextual factors. However, an important conclusion from this study is that bringing work-related technology home does *not* mean that *all* times and places are available for work. On the contrary. In the next section we will show a variation in how work actually is introduced and circumvented in the domestic sphere.

… and being selectively available for work while at home (microsedentarisation). *Microsedentarisation* refers to the practice of bringing technology home that enables work but at the same time leveraging technology in a way that allows for controlled exposure to work. This thereby upholds a person's ability to be in charge of when to interact with colleagues, clients and managers. Our interpretation of the practice of microsedentarisation is that an employee purposely places the work mobile phone out of sight and out of sound at home in order to maintain mental and physical distance and to stay in control over if and when he or she wants to interact with work. One respondent takes home the work mobile phone, which has an email client that pushes work emails and alerts the user with a beep when a new email arrives. However, the phone is kept in a bag that (purposely) makes the sound hard to detect.

> So, if I hear it, I hear it [the phone]. It's not like I look ... check who it is and don't respond. It can stay in the bag for example. And then I don't hear when it makes a sound. (Interview, own research)

Another respondent had a specific, dedicated place for the work phone at home: "So it's not 'carried around' at all, period! It's dedicated to the kitchen. And if I happen to notice that someone is trying to contact me, I may pick it up. Otherwise, it can stay there" (interview, own research).

This is similar to another respondent who brings the work phone home (because the boss wants it that way), but then turns off the sound so he or she can decide when to "check in" and see if a call was missed or if there is any mail. In this way, the respondent is able to be *both* "available", but still in control of when to interact with work: "Yes, I'm always available on the mobile phone. I turn off the sound but can still see the display if anyone has called. Then I check what it is" (interview, own research).

This practice, of course, means that you do not always notice if someone is trying to reach you:

> Yes ... I keep it on mute. So it's only the vibration I react to ... if I notice it at all. I've told everybody that it's not 100% sure that I actually will answer if you call after office hours. So they take a chance and call ... and if I answer, I answer. Or I don't answer. But if there is a small beep, text message or something like that. Then it goes unnoticed. (Interview, own research)

Alternatively, a distinction is made in relation to what makes a sound (mail, text or ring signal): "The mobile phone ring signal is on; however with emails and stuff like that, it does not make any sound at all. No, it doesn't!" (interview, own research).

Or the sound is turned off at all times but emails are pushed so they can be seen on the display:

> I turn the push notifications feature on so I can see on the display if I got an email. So there is no sound that I need to pay attention to. But it's visible if I pick up the phone. I have to actively check. (Interview, own research)

Once again, the respondent can make a decision beforehand to either "check in" or not hear the phone ring or signal. The interpretation of this practice is that it makes the respondent feel in control of when and what work needs his or her attention. Another way of limiting availability for work-related communication while at home or on the commute is to avoid certain programmes on the phone. In the following case, not having Skype installed on the phone seems to alleviate the pressure of having to make a decision to interact with colleagues or not:

> I have had colleagues try to get in touch with me on Skype, via my phone, when they know I'm on my way home. "And we can't have that, can we?" So, I decided to not have that technology installed on my phone. This means that I don't need to make an active decision whether to interact or not. (Interview, own research)

One conclusion, based on these examples, is that being available does not mean one thing. Rather availability, seen as a sociomaterial practice constituted at the intersection of intention, expectations and technology, is a phenomenon that takes different shapes and varies in degrees.

3.2 Being Available for Family While at Work: Blood is Often Thicker Than Water

Some of the contextual factors are easier to foresee and to handle than others and thus easier to counter in the ICT boundary work.

> For example, if I know that I have a deadline at work on Monday, I'll bring the computer home with me on Friday. It's a pre-planned activity. This in relation to the unforeseen event of receiving a call from the preschool saying that my child is sick. (Interview, own research)

The preschool scenario is not only harder to foresee, but also to manage. It may be all right to use ICT in a way that makes it hard for others, like colleagues and managers, to get in touch with you while you are at home and in the evenings, but perhaps not so for your children's ability to contact you while at work. Consequently, family to work expectations not only seem harder to foresee but also pose a greater threat to perceived boundary control:

> It bothers me much more when domestic issues call for my attention while I'm at work … rather than when it's something [work-related] that I am doing at home in the evening. Because then it's preplanned; I'm in control … when I'm doing anything work-related at home. (Interview, own research)

What causes frustration in this case is not the communication in itself, but the feeling of not being in control. This is even more obvious in the following excerpt from one of the respondents' time diary:

Place: At work
Time: 9:00 to 12:00 a.m. General feeling: frustrated

- Speaking on the telephone with daughter, 2 min, smartphone (work), not content
- On the telephone with daughter, 1 min, smartphone (work), not content
- On the telephone with daughter, 2 min, smartphone (work), not content
- Texting with son, 2 min, smartphone (work), content

Comment: My daughter "chased" me—bad test results + dentist appointment. It bothers me a lot when I have to switch roles between being a mom and being a boss; when I'm not in control. My son was at home, feeling unwell—it felt good to check in with him and see that he was OK. (Diary entry, own research)

Specific strategies are also developed in order to stay connected with the kids without disturbing meetings. This can look like:

> Yes, of course. I always carry my private phone with me ... on mute. So I can see if it's lit up. I'm available to the kids, so to speak. If there is anything they want, I guess I can see that. (Interview, own research)

Many times, being available at work has been preceded by a discussion between the parent and child on the kind of matters that qualify for contacting the parent at work: "And if they call, it's usually important, and then I have to take it. It's a well-established routine, so to speak" (interview, own research).

However, it is worth noting that this participant does not see it as "necessary" to answer work-related phone calls while at home: "Contrary to work-related calls, if I already have left for home, I screen them out if I don't find it convenient to answer" (interview, own research).

In a similar fashion, one respondent describes this in terms of dropping everything work-related when contacted from someone in the family sphere:

> I have three grown-up daughters and two grandchildren. One of the daughters sends quite a lot of pictures [of the grandchild], which I look at during working hours. As soon as the phone beeps I drop everything, look at the pictures, read the message and answer. (Interview, own research)

But while at home: "When my daughter comes with my grandchild who is 2 years old, I would never in my life even consider checking the phone for mail or answering when it rings. I would never do that" (interview, own research).

Being available for family at work not only relates to children but can also be for elderly parents:

> I mean, I'm available on my private phone [while at work] if anything were to occur. My parents are retired; if anything happens, of course they call me. I may not answer the phone right away, but I can get back to them. So in that sense I'm available during office hours. (Interview, own research)

Here we see in our data a clear difference in those respondents that do not have children living at home. They are more likely to limit communication with people from their private life while at work in order to focus on work and reduce interruptions: "Yes, well private life. I just felt I can't be bothered with a lot of private stuff that calls for my attention on my phone while I'm at work" (interview, own research).

In a similar fashion: "When I'm at work I don't use my private phone. Don't bring it to meetings and such" (interview, own research).

The study results indicate that permeability is unevenly distributed in the sense that the ICT boundary work of the respondents (especially those with children still living at home) makes them available to a higher degree for the private sphere than the work sphere. Even if the ring signal is turned off, availability to some degree is achieved via visual cues on the phone. We did not, however, find any difference between respondents with children and those who did not have children related to being available for work at home.

3.3 This Far, but No Further: No Go Zones and No Go Times for Work

According to our data, the practice of integrating or separating work from private life not only follows a strict daily or weekly pattern, nor is restricted to the domestic area. Rather, it seems that there are gaps of "no-go zones" scattered over both times and places. These times and places are no-go zones for work-related activities and where the availability as a result is very low. This could be a summer house, a stable or a part of the home such as the bedroom. Even though the diary did not ask for times and places that did not include boundary crossing activities, some of the respondents reported these times and places. We understand this, as these times and places were very important in their boundary management strategies and we therefore include them here. Sometimes this practice of blocking certain physical locations appears to be a very conscious decision, as illustrated by the following respondent who decided to ban work-related technology from the stable. Note from a time diary:

> Place: In the stable
> Time: 5:00 to 8:00 p.m. General emotions: feeling engaged and spirited
> Comment: The stable is my mobile free zone. I bring my mobile phone with me, but leave it in the saddle room. (Diary entry, own research).

Sometimes lack of availability for work seems related to external circumstances like no Internet and is experienced as a nonpreferred disconnection from work. Note from a time diary:

> Place: Vacation house
> Time: Saturday (the whole day)
> Comment: No boundary crossing activities on Saturday. This is partly related to the fact that I've been at my vacation house which lacks Internet reception. (Diary entry, own research)

Similarly, this respondent is unavailable at night and in the bedroom. Due to a lack of reception: "No, I'm not available at night. I live out in the country and there is no Internet in the bedroom because it's located in the basement" (interview, own research).

No-go zones can be related to physical places, but they can also be related to specific times of the year. For example, one respondent goes so far as to lock away the work computer in a closed cabinet over the Christmas holidays to prevent himself or herself from working:

> I didn't work at all [between Christmas and New Year's Eve] because I was super determined not to. So I put my computer in a cabinet and told the others: "If you see me getting close the cabinet, lock it, because now I want to relax!" (Interview, own research)

4   Discussion: Taking Control of Boundaries Using ICT

The starting point of this chapter was to show how ICT was used by employees to manage temporal and spatial availability for work and private matters. This sociomaterial practice is described in terms of ICT boundary work. First, when looking at different practices it becomes evident that availability—or what it means to be accessible in time and space and responsive to the needs and wants of others—cannot be seen as a dichotomous outcome, that is, being available or not. Rather, availability should be seen as a dynamic process of ongoing interactions between personal preferences, technological infrastructure and contextual factors (such as expectations for availability from family, colleagues and or clients). From our results we can conclude that the active use of ICT contributes to creating spaces for work and or leisure in various spatial locations and in different temporal zones. From this perspective, a working space emerges through action and can thus not be seen as separate from human action and interaction. This means that working spaces can basically be created anywhere and anytime, as long as there is Wi-Fi and one's mobile ICT devices are at hand, making it possible to conduct work and be available for colleagues, managers and or clients.

However, by tweaking the technology (e.g., turning off the sound, stopping push mail) and by microsedentarisation (dedicating technology to certain places within the domestic area), people can control when and where to interact. In this way, spatio-temporal spaces for rest and recuperation are safeguarded within the domestic sphere of the home. To some extent the result presented in this chapter counters the findings by Barley and Kunda (2004) and Bourne and Forman (2014). Specifically, when endowed with increased autonomy regarding when and where to work we saw that permeability was unevenly distributed in the sense that the ICT boundary work of the respondents (especially those with children still living at home) made them available to a higher degree for the private sphere than the work sphere. When talking about prioritising one sphere over another a distinction needs to be made in relation to availability practices and actual time dedicated to one activity over the other.

One of the central mechanisms in this context is perceived control. ICT is a double-edged sword. Because it is not restricted in time and space it means that people can be connected to work and family almost anytime and anywhere. In some cases, this fact can alleviate stress and increase perceptions of being on top of things; such as being able to check in with your children during the day to see if they are alright, and them being available to contact you if anything happens. In relation to work—this means being able to screen the mailbox and the calendar on Sunday, and thus know what awaits you on Monday. Increased spatial and temporal fluidity of the location of work signifies autonomy, but it can also become a problem. Too much availability for family matters can prevent you from focusing on your work by, for example, being forced to switch roles from being a "boss" to being a mother. Unlimited availability can also create the problem of not mentally detaching from work. Our focus on employee agency and the active use of technology shows different practices that limit availability both spatially and temporally. An example of this is the work mobile phone that is purposely placed out of sight and sound in order to maintain some audio-visual, and thus mental distance, and to stay in control over when or if one wants to engage in work. Through this lens we see employees' ingenuity of finding ways to use ICT to make themselves available and unavailable and the shades between these two poles. Our results indicate that despite being constantly on call, employees may yet manage the technology in ways that allow separation when it is wanted. Similar to Lehdonvirta (2018), we found that employees use technology in order to alter the rules of the game. This use of technology is not restricted to professional workers, but can be found in all areas of society and working life (Rosengren, 2018).

In terms of employee well-being the results from this study suggest that more attention should be focused towards employees' feelings of boundary control. Or, in other words, to what extent there is a fit between preferred and actual boundaries between work and private life. This rather than trying to determine whether a specific type of boundary behaviour style (integration or segmentation) generates stress or well-being. We have seen that depending on personal preferences, for some taking the work computer home with them alleviates stress and for others leaving the computer at the office has the same effect, depending on preferences for integration or segmentation. For those with preference for segmentation, we saw that bringing work-related technology devices to the home did not mean that all times and places became available for work. On the contrary, we saw a great variation in how work actually was introduced and circumvented in the domestic sphere.

This study's contribution to boundary theory is that it highlights the need to focus more firmly on the intertwinement of ICT, personal preferences, social structures and organisational context in the analysis. As pointed out, the very same technology that contributes to the blurring of boundaries can help employees to facilitate their boundary work. In terms of implication for practitioners we can conclude that since employees have different availability preferences of boundary work, organisations need to offer their employees enough freedom to implement them. In order to achieve this, one important aspect is a continuous dialogue at the workplace level, taking the working conditions and the preferences of the employees into account. A shared understanding and a deeper knowledge of how employees prefer to manage their work and life is a fundament for building an organisational climate that allows a diversity in availability patterns, but at the same time has the capacity to create working conditions where individual boundary control is a central component.

References

Allvin, M., Aronsson, G., Hagström, T., Johansson, G., & Lundberg, U. (2011). *Work without boundaries: Psychological perspectives on the new working life*. Wiley.

Anderson, D., & Kelliher, C. (2011). Spatial aspects of professionals' work–life integration. In S. Kaiser, M. Ringlstetter, D. R. Eikhof, & M. Pina e Cunha (Eds.), *Creating balance?: International perspectives on the work–life-integration of professionals* (pp. 303–315). Springer.

Bäcklander, G., Rosengren, C., & Kaulio, M. (2018). Managing intensity in knowledge work: Self-Leadership practices among Danish management consultants. *Journal of Management and Organization, 25*, 1–19. https://doi.org/10.1017/jmo.2018.64.

Barley, S. R., & Kunda, G. (2004). *Gurus, hired guns, and warm bodies: Itinerant experts in a knowledge economy*. Princeton University Press.

Battard, N., & Mangematin, V. (2013). Idiosyncratic distances: Impact of mobile technology practices on role segmentation and integration. *Technological Forecasting and Social Change, 80*, 231–242.

Bergman, A., & Gardiner, J. (2007). Employee availability for work and family: Three Swedish case studies. *Employee Relations, 29*, 400–414.

Bergman, A., & Gustafson, P. (2008). Travel, availability and work–life balance. In D. Hislop (Ed.), *Mobility and technology in the workplace* (pp. 192–208). Routledge.

Bergman, A., Rosengren, C., & Palm, K. (2020). Gränshanteringsstrategier och digitalisering: Utmaningar för organisation och person (Boundary management strategies and digitalisation: Challanges for organisations and employees). In B.-I. Keisu (Ed.), *Att arbeta för lika villkor: Ett maktperspektiv på arbete och organisation* (Working for equal conditions—A power perspective on work and organisation). Studentlitteratur.

Berkowsky, R. W. (2013). When you just cannot get away: Exploring the use of information and communication technologies in facilitating negative work/home spillover. *Information, Communication & Society, 16*, 519–541.

Bittman, M., Brown, J. E., & Wajcman, J. (2009). The mobile phone, perpetual contact and time pressure. *Work, Employment and Society, 23*, 673–691.

Bourne, K. A., & Forman, P. J. (2014). Living in a culture of overwork: An ethnographic study of flexibility. *Journal of Management Inquiry, 23*, 68–79.

Brannen, J. (2005). Time and the negotiation of work—Family boundaries: Autonomy or illusion? *Time & Society, 14*, 113–131.

Cohen, D. J., Leviton, L. C., Isaacson, N., Tallia, A. F., & Crabtree, B. F. (2006). Online diaries for qualitative evaluation: Gaining real-time insights. *American Journal of Evaluation, 27*, 163–184.

Dery, K., Kolb, D., & MacCormick, J. (2014). Working with connective flow: How smartphone use is evolving in practice. *European Journal of Information Systems, 23*, 558–570.

Elvin-Nowak, Y. (1998). *Flexibilitetens baksida: Om balans, kontroll och skuld i yrkesarbetande mödrars vardagsliv* (The flip side of flexibility: On balance, control and guilt in the everyday lives of employed mothers) (Report No. 101). Stockholm University, Department of Psychology.

Feldman, M. S., & Orlikowski, W. J. (2011). Theorizing practice and practicing theory. *Organization Science, 22*, 1240–1253.

Fleck, R., Cox, A. L., & Robison, R. A. V. (2015). Balancing boundaries: Using multiple devices to manage work–life balance. In *Proceedings of the 33rd*

Annual ACM Conference on Human Factors in Computing Systems, Republic of Korea, 15, 3985–3988. https://doi.org/10.1145/2702123.2702386.

Golden, A. G., & Geisler, C. (2007). Work–life boundary management and the personal digital assistant. *Human Relations, 60*, 519–551.

Healy, G. (2004). Work–life balance and family friendly policies—In whose interest? *Work, Employment and Society, 18*, 219–223.

Holth, L., Bergman, A., & MacKenzie, R. (2017). Gender, availability and dual emancipation in the Swedish ICT sector. *Work, Employment and Society, 31*, 230–247.

Karasek, R., & Theorell, T. (1990). *Healthy work: Stress, productivity, and the reconstruction of working life*. Basic Books.

Kossek, E. E. (2016). Managing work–life boundaries in the digital age. *Organizational Dynamics, 45*, 258–270.

Kossek, E. E., & Ozeki, C. (1999). Bridging the work–family policy and productivity gap: A literature review. *Community, Work & Family, 2*, 7–32.

Kreiner, G. E., Hollensbe, E. C., & Sheep, M. L. (2009). Balancing borders and bridges: Negotiating the work–home interface via boundary work tactics. *Academy of Management Journal, 52*, 704–730.

Lehdonvirta, V. (2018). Flexibility in the gig economy: Managing time on three online piecework platforms. *New Technology, Work and Employment, 33*, 13–29.

Lindsay, J., & Maher, J. (2013). The intersections of work time and care time: Nurses' and builders' family time economies. *Work, Employment and Society, 28*, 189–205.

Maxwell, J. A. (2012). *A realist approach for qualitative research*. Sage.

Mellner, C. (2018). Strategier, gränskontroll och ledarskap i gränslöst arbete (Strategies, boundary control and leadership in boundaryless work). In G. Aronsson (Ed.), *Gränslöst arbete: En forskarantologi om arbetsmiljöutmaningar i anknytning till ett gränslöst arbetsliv (Boundaryless work: A research anthology on work environment related challanges in a boundaryless working life)* (pp. 37–46). Arbetsmiljöverket.

Nippert-Eng, C. E. (1995). *Home and work: Negotiating boundaries through everyday life*. University of Chicago Press.

Parasuraman, S., & Simmers, C. A. (2001). Type of employment, work–family conflict and well-being: A comparative study. *Journal of Organizational Behaviour, 22*, 551–568.

Rosengren, C. (2018). Adapting reality to the matrix: Digital technology in social home care. In S. Schaefer, M. Andersson, E. Bjarnason, & K.

Hansson (Eds.), *Working and organizing in the digital age* (pp. 43–49). Lund University.
Saldaña, J. (2015). *The coding manual for qualitative researchers*. Sage.
Schatzki, T. R., Knorr-Cetina, K., & von Savigny, E. (Eds.). (2001). *The practice turn in contemporary theory* (Vol. 44). Routledge.
Warhurst, C., Eikhof, D. R., & Haunschild, A. (2008). *Work less, live more?: Critical analyses of the work–life boundary (Critical perspectives on work and organisation)*. Palgrave Macmillan.
Yin, R. K. (2003). *Case study research and applications* (6th ed.). Sage.

9

Virtual Spaces, Intermediate Places: Doing Identity in ICT-Enabled Work

Dominik Klaus and Jörg Flecker

Since the early days of telework, the use of information and communication technology (ICT) has increasingly contributed to the blurring of boundaries between work and private life. In recent years, the development has reached a new quality as portable devices like smartphones act as work-extending technologies (Towers et al., 2006) providing an "omnipresent connectivity" (Holtgrewe, 2014) where many types of work are usually just a click away. Following Messenger and Gschwind's (2016) classification of generations of telework, the possibilities to work outside the office have expanded from the traditional telework at home to working on the move using laptops. Nowadays, the most recent third generation has extended the possibility of work to intermediate spaces, such as the train on the way to work or the cafeteria during lunch. The possibility of occasional work in intermediate places pushes the blurring

---

D. Klaus (✉) · J. Flecker
Department of Sociology, University of Vienna, Vienna, Austria
e-mail: dominik.klaus@univie.ac.at

of work boundaries to a new level. This development is fostered by an array of new developments in the field of ICT, closely related to a steady mobile Internet and Wi-Fi connections. As devices such as smartphones are always carried on the body, their use is not always a conscious decision but may become a routine. In this situation, it is very hard to define working time. The boundary-blurring effect is not limited to communication patterns and the question of availability of workers to answer emails or telephone calls. In addition, core tasks in clerical, managerial, research and other "knowledge" work are often carried out away from the office. The blurring of boundaries has thus reached a new quality and quantity.

In addition, the "New New ICTs" (Holtgrewe, 2014) have been used for a series of other changes such as algorithmic management, GPS control, real-time recording and cloud computing. As Messenger and Gschwind (2016) state, the new technologies alter not only the traditional workplace, "but also working time policies, work schedules, and, consequently, work–life balance" (ibid., p. 202). The use of ICT and the design of work organisation are intertwined with an organisation's approach to control labour and enhance work-discipline in order to maintain value realisation and the production of surplus value (Thompson & Smith, 2010). Thus, the experience of work and the power relations within the employment relationship have changed as well as the preconditions for labour agency (Hall, 2010). What is part of paid work and where does paid work end not only becomes blurred, it may turn into part of the contested terrain of labour utilisation. Yet, making this contest visible becomes difficult in relation to jobs with "flexibility through empowerment" (Allvin et al., 2011) where workers tend to have "positive attachments to work and work identity" (Thompson & Briken, 2017, p. 258). Therefore, it is crucial to understand how workers themselves draw the line between work they get paid for and additional unpaid supportive tasks. Workers' identity thus becomes part of the equation and needs to be considered when analysing both boundary blurring and its consequences.

Against this background, this contribution addresses the interrelation of blurring work boundaries and identity work. In doing so, it focuses on spatial aspects and in particular on the separation of physical and geographic space on the one hand and social, organisational and work relationships on the other. The physical workplace, the office and the co-presence of people in it impact on identity work. The same holds for dispersed workplaces, home office, work in third places, lack of co-presence and so forth. In what way do both identity-supporting and identity-threatening factors change in a process of ICT-enabled blurring of work boundaries? Sect. 9.1 will conceptualise identity work in the context of ICT-enabled boundaryless work. Section 9.2 will address the spatial aspects of the blurring boundaries and their consequences. Section 9.3 will present interim results of an empirical study on business consulting and virtual assistance that illustrate influencers of identity work at the levels of the organisation and the interaction. In Sect. 9.4, we will provide conclusions on the interrelation between boundary blurring and identity work.

1 Conceptualising Identity Work

The term *identity* is heavily used in research about work and employment, yet often serves as a placeholder for the residual factors of relatedness and individualism. As its theoretical foundation can differ widely, it is important to clarify one's understanding of the term. Grasping the impacts of work upon identity at full scale requires a concept of identity that pays tribute to the features of reflexivity and temporality of identities (Dejours et al., 2018). It needs to allow for dynamic aspects, as subjective life has to be sustained via the integration of complex internal processes related to external challenges and resources, while also containing normative aspects to decide what is to be considered a success. Despite claims that work might have lost its importance as a source of identity in postmodernity (e.g., Bauman, 2005), we think of it as a central battleground for a positive self. Following Dejours et al. (2018), we understand identity "as something that is vulnerable to various forms of challenge and that must struggle to maintain itself in the midst of those challenges" (ibid., p. 80). We conceptualise identity work (Keupp & Höfer, 1997) in the context of gainful employment as a subjective process which aims at constructing and maintaining work-related identities (e.g., based on an occupation, professionalism or an organisational membership) as well as a coherent story of life (Hürtgen & Voswinkel, 2012). To be successful, this requires certain skills and resources (Ahbe, 1997) in the sense of constructing a positive and coherent self while avoiding harmful experiences and stigmatisation (Goffman, 1975). Building on Mead's (1973) groundbreaking work on the intersubjective character of identity, Honneth (1994) points to social recognition as the most vital resource in this process. As we focus on the context of paid work, the work of Stephan Voswinkel (e.g., 2000, 2013) is of particular interest and proves that recognition is a helpful perspective to address work-related issues of identity. Voswinkel (2013) has carved out various institutions of recognition, which are subject to transformation processes. These institutions or sources of recognition provide a suitable concept for the analysis of changes regarding the resources of identity work in the fields of blurred work. As these sources are located on different levels (such as the level of direct interaction, the level of the organisation, and the level of society), they allow for a systematic examination and comparison with various scopes.

On the *macro level of society*, the negotiation of legitimate claims for recognition has consolidated in various institutions. While these institutions represent resources for successful identity work, they are constantly challenged and changed by contemporary developments of the labour market (Voswinkel, 2013):

- Occupations are defined by a specific bundle of competences. In the sense of a traditional occupational profile, they enable a worker to identify with a certain professional group, often backed up by an occupational association. As Sennett (1998) famously stated, traditional occupations tend to erode in the processes of taylorisation and rationalisation.
- Organisational membership is closely linked to feelings of belongingness and reciprocal relationships inside the organisation ensure a stable ground for one's identity, independent of occupational structures.
- The merit principle is another institution for societal recognition and a common battleground of discourse. Various definitions of merits or performances are at the core of the debate. Under the constraints of

capitalist wage labour, income tends to be a universal legitimation, regardless of its origins. However, new debates about meaningful work (Rosso et al., 2010) and bullshit jobs (Graeber 2018) challenge the societal value as well as the valuation of performance.

On the *level of the organisation* (be it a company, a project or a platform), the interests of the employers have led to a series of artificial sources of recognition, in the attempts of exerting control (Alvesson & Willmott, 2002). Traditional measures (e.g., the employee of the month) are followed by a series of new valuations and rating systems, enabled by new technologies. More fundamentally, the office of a corporation as social space is a place of communication with colleagues and associates. As a place of daily life and profound social practices (Merrifield, 1993), the workplace in a traditional office once provided for means of self-identification, social support and solidarity. Nowadays, as virtual work in the online space is decoupled from a traditional physical workplace (Koslowski, 2016), the virtual workers are in need of compensation. Social media offers some of these new spaces (e.g., Facebook groups for virtual assistants). They provide new ways of acquiring sources of recognition and contribute to the process of subjectification (Roth-Ebner, 2016).

On the *micro level*, the most basic source of appreciation is social interaction. Daily interactions with customers and colleagues are crucial for the work-related conception of oneself. On this level, the major potential for distance by the intense utilisation of ICT is significant (Lehdonvirta & Mezier, 2013). Regarding the relationship between virtual workers and their colleagues in a company, the perceived proximity is also influenced by the identificatory potential of the organisation and the strength of communication (Wilson et al., 2008). With the loss of spontaneous communications in traditional meetup places, communication with mobile or virtual workers requires a lot more planning (Hislop & Axtell, 2007). On the other side, new technologies like social media and messenger services have enabled new ways of communication that can be used for compensation. Still, these communication channels need active management, especially as boundaries between private and business-related relationships tend to erode (Archer-Brown et al., 2018). The nature of the task is another important factor to take into account, for instance, within the scope of meaningful work (Rosso et al., 2010).

The developments of late capitalism (e.g., individualisation) tend to complicate the adoption of these institutions and traditional sources of recognition. Thus, identity work has become harder to handle (Keupp, 2008). Overall, the increasing importance of mediatised communication, that is, the use of digital communication tools and channels, and the loss of importance of face-to-face communication are changing the processes of the communicative construction of reality (Krotz & Hepp, 2012) as well as the construction of identity. As the "mediatization of everyday life" (Kaun & Fast, 2014) continues, more and more activities become bound to technologically mediated flows of information (Markham, 2013) and increasingly take place over the Internet (Turkle, 1995).

Thus, the relocation of work to virtual spaces and intermediate places affects identity work in a threefold way. First of all, traditional institutions and resources for recognition (Voswinkel, 2013), such as the organisation, dress codes and the physical office are losing importance or are being transformed. Second, virtual spaces offer new opportunities for identity work, partly used by employers and platforms aiming to shape work-related identities in their own interest (Alvesson & Willmott, 2002). Third, identity work is realised by practice, which nevertheless largely happens in a specific space/place setting (Pink, 2012). Within this approach, the focus of this contribution lies on the sources of appreciation and their specific space/place setting. The subjective appropriation of these sources is subject to ongoing research.

2 Consequences of ICT-Enabled Blurring of Boundaries

We define the blurring of spatial boundaries as a separation of physical and geographic space and place from social, organisational and work-related spaces (Flecker & Schönauer, 2016; Will-Zocholl et al., 2019). This means that people cooperate and communicate even though they are not co-present in a particular place such as an office. Working from home or from third places, using ICT for communication or as collaborative tools, having access to databases or shared files provides opportunities to extend the cooperative space beyond the joint workplace. This relates to companies with dispersed workplaces, to teleworking of various types and to virtual teams and employees in transnational organisations or networks of firms. In the following, we include various workplaces, such as co-working spaces, hot-desking offices, train compartments, hostel rooms or the kitchen table at home. The blurring of spatial boundaries affects the ways in which people relate to their work and identify with aspects of their jobs. The "fixed" workplace, e.g., the office and the office building, impacts on the individual and his or her identity work in several ways: The worker is subject to supervision and disciplining efforts, involved in work-related or non-work-related interaction and communication, equipped with a desk or another private space of work and his or her presence clearly counts as working hours. Places, spaces, distances, furniture and equipment may be functional or dysfunctional for the tasks to be performed. But they also serve a symbolic function as the individual office or the desk in an open-plan office signify organisational membership and a particular status within the organisation. Recognition in wage labour is always graded (Voswinkel, 2000) and therefore also the spatial arrangements may act both as "identity pillars" and "identity threats", that is, affect individuals' identity work positively or negatively.

Additionally, the way people relate to their jobs affects their boundary management: People who see themselves as professional knowledge workers want to be available for their customers, self-employers want to advertise their services constantly, hoping to attract new customers. They contribute to the blurring and tend to broaden their availability (Gold & Mustafa, 2013), extending their working hours as well as the places of work (e.g., by reading emails on the train) (see the contribution by Calle Rosengren, Ann Bergman and Kristina Palm in this volume).

When it comes to blurring boundaries, spatial aspects are usually addressed in a negative way in the sense of a lack of something. Many aspects of social relations in work are linked to the spatiality of work: the spatial closeness as a basis of solidarity, opportunities for unplanned interaction and communication, offices as status symbols, entering and leaving the office as structuring the day and limiting working hours, and so forth. ICT-enabled telework, it is often assumed, does not provide such opportunities or provides them to a lesser extent and thus lacks many self-evident facts of paid work (e.g., Hislop & Axtell, 2007; Ojala et al., 2014).

The consequences are manifold: Teleworkers may lack opportunities of interaction and thus miss recognition, they can rely on status symbols to a lesser extent, or they may develop a weaker sense of belonging to the work group. There is usually a much greater need for mobile workers or home workers to structure their working day. In general, in order to handle increased work autonomy effectively a higher demand for self-governance or self-control is required (Allvin et al., 2013). More flexible working conditions often lead to depleted individual resources, strain and negative effects on the individual well-being, indicated by increased emotional exhaustion (Sonnentag & Fritz, 2007) and increased emotional and cognitive irritation (Mohr et al., 2006). As the results of the European Working Conditions Survey (EWCS) 2015 show, workers with high utilisation of ICT-enabled mobility report the highest level of work-related stress and negative health effects (International Labour Organisation and the European Foundation for the Improvement of Living and Working Conditions, 2017). The spatial and temporal arrangements impact on the ability to detach and recover and, under the conditions of blurring boundaries, need to be compensated for.

But this interrelationship between the blurring of boundaries and identity work is not without ambiguities: The presence in the office, for example, may not only provide "identity pillars" in the form of recognition during interaction with colleagues but also "identity threats" in the form of mobbing or abuse by superiors or colleagues. Workers may thus welcome the opportunities to work from home or from a third place, allowing them to avoid unpleasant encounters. Aspects like organisational membership or the presence in the office might support identity, but they can be Janus-faced as well. For each condition which can serve as an identity pillar we can also think of a potential threat to somebody's identity. Martina Sproll (2016) gives the example of call-centre workers in the Brazilian banking sector: Compared to the core bank workers, working in a call-centre does not provide full organisational membership and comes with worse terms and condition. However, it is much easier for members of minority groups and coloured people to get a job in a call-centre and there is no need to dress smartly.

Physical boundaries and distances have separated the different spheres of life, e.g., the realms of work and private life, ever since labour started to be expended outside the farm and the artisan's home (see the contribution by Christian Oggolder in this volume). This separation is partly or fully overcome when ICT is used, for example, to work from home. Under the condition of boundaryless work, it is often up to the individual to structure time and space and to fend off greedy employers and demanding colleagues and customers. This may imply the reproduction of spatial boundaries (the study in the home), the drawing of time lines or constantly switching between the different spheres, that is, practicing "micro role transitions" (Fonner & Stache, 2012). ICT provide functions that may support individuals' structuring of time and space—not least a button to go off-line or to turn them off. Yet, ICT use is embedded in a complex interplay of interests and power relations (Wajcman, 2015). Not least, the indirect forms of control over workers (Peters & Sauer, 2005; Sturdy et al., 2010) instigate them to stretch work over spatial and temporal boundaries. At the same time, management may use ICT to exert more or less subtle forms of control regardless of the place where workers actually do the work or may benefit from workers' additional effort which they exert in return for the flexibility they have gained (Kelliher & Anderson, 2010).

3 Occupational Case Studies: Fields of Blurred Work

In order to investigate the changes of both identity-supporting and identity-threatening factors in a process of ICT-enabled blurring of work boundaries, we conducted two occupational case studies in the area of knowledge-intensive business services (Miles et al., 2018). As widely autonomous work settings with a high possibility of ICT utilisation, these fields often rely on forms of indirect control (Peters & Sauer, 2005) and forms of subjectivation of work (Moldaschl & Voß, 2002). A crucial aspect of this kind of work is that large parts of it have no natural end—they are never clearly finished: It is up to the worker to decide when a presentation is good enough, when he or she has put enough effort into acquisition or research. In these fields, working hours may always be extended to improve quality or self-marketing. At the same time, productivity or compliance with the process of work are hard to measure and control directly.

In order to grasp the subjective perspective, coping strategies and agency of highly mobile knowledge workers, this contribution builds on qualitative research from two occupational case studies: Business Consulting and Virtual Assistance. Our empirical research builds on a total of twenty-eight qualitative interviews, whereof seventeen were conducted with business consultants in various employment situations, such as a big consulting enterprise, a medium consulting enterprise and a couple of self-employed consultants. Eleven interviewees work as virtual assistants with varying set working hours, whereby most of them are self-employed. The majority of the interviews were conducted face-to-face, yet in some cases we made use of Skype, as some of our interviewees were currently abroad or in remote places. Using a semi-structured guideline that allows for extended narrations on whatever the interviewees deem noteworthy, the length of the interviews varied between 1.0 hours and 2.5 hours. Following a circular research process, several sessions of in-depth group interpretations were held before finishing the inquiry. Thus, we were able to follow a sampling strategy that allows for a wide difference regarding interesting characteristics. In this contribution, we present the first results after the inquiry and the in-depth interpretation sessions. As the interviews were conducted in German, the following quotes were translated into English.

Contrasting these cases, our research aims to discover general strategies as to how workers deal with the blurring of boundaries, changing spatial resources and preconditions for identity work. As our study shows, employees are able to deal with these changes in various ways, aiming at a suitable boundary management and relationship to work. In conclusion, the results show both obstacles to, and resources for, identity work in ICT-enabled boundaryless work. Next to the fundamental aspects of the physical workplace and the social space in which it is embedded, we address issues of identity with regard to forms of control, recognition and signalisation of experience and willingness, as well as the ways in which people interact with each other.

3.1 Occupational Case Study A: Business Consultants

Business consulting is a traditionally blurred field of work, with a high degree of mobility and excessive working hours. For this research project, we conducted interviews with several members of a joint consultancy project in the field of human resources. Whereas framework and target were the same for the involved consultants, they had various employment situations, including a large company, a smaller one and several self-employment arrangements. Highly mobile knowledge work such as this implies high levels of autonomy and self-responsibility as the employees have to organise their work mainly by themselves. This regards the acquisition of customers, the process of consulting, its preparations and scheduling, as well as the communication with customers. As there are very heterogeneous approaches to consulting, it is hard to present a clear picture of the work as a consultant in order to maintain an occupational identity.

Physical Workplace(s): Business consultants tend to have several workplaces, as they need to be highly mobile and often have to visit the customers' premises. The different employment situations induce various places of work: While some of the interviewees are often on business trips, oscillating between customers' premises, a hot-desking office and intermediate places, others are self-employed and make use of co-working spaces and shared offices. Some of them are part of a smaller company with a traditional office, whereas others work for a rather big company which utilises a hot-desking principle where only a few employees on the higher ranks have a permanent individual office or desk. A third group of business consultants are self-employed, making use of co-working spaces or shared offices.

Concerning identity work, having multiple workplaces can be a resource or a burden. In some cases, consultants make use of more than one office: They have their own office at home and still use the office at a company as a second workplace. Self-employed consultants make use of co-working spaces, as it comes cheaper than a single office and provides a social surrounding while they work. In other cases, combinations of co-working spaces and home offices are used. In one outstanding case, the consultant even uses three distinct co-working spaces: a prestigious one with a beautiful meeting room in the city centre, a second one shared with business colleagues, and a third rather quiet one for work that requires more concentration. Depending on the available income, it can make sense to spend money on workplace infrastructure and even to use more than one office. On the other side, there are times in which employees do not have a single workplace available. As a younger consultant from a large company with hot-desking noted, he would prefer to work from home on some days, because all the desks at the office might be in use or the noise level is simply too high to stay focused and get things done.

Social Space and Relations: The traditional office was a place of togetherness, where a steady exchange with colleagues helped to establish a feeling of relatedness and to socially construct a certain occupational identity, professionalism or corporate identity. In the realms of spatially blurred work, this has become increasingly difficult. Meetings with colleagues are unlikely to happen spontaneously, when employees spend most of their time outside the office or—as with the case of hot-desking—if they don't have a permanent workplace at all. The majority of the business consultants work on their own most of the time. Not being part of a team with regular occasions to meet reduces the chances of unplanned communication and makes it difficult to get into contact with colleagues spontaneously. Instead, social events (e.g., having lunch together) need to be actively initiated. In order to do so, employees rely on electronic communication devices. This reduces the opportunities for recognition in direct interaction and makes it more difficult to develop and experience a feeling of affiliation and belonging.

However, having colleagues is not necessarily a perk and the need to work together in an office can also have its downsides. After bad experiences of contempt or even mobbing, some respondents would rather work from home than being in a continuous struggle at the office. Thus, being in constant contact with colleagues at work is not always welcome. It requires appreciative and respectful relations, a certain level of bonding and solidarity. Especially in a competitive work environment, this cannot be taken for granted. In cases that lack appreciative relations, the mobility tends to be used to avoid negative effects, protecting a positive self. However, the escape from the office comes with the cost of having to provide one's own infrastructure.

Autonomy and Self-Control: Within a traditional workplace, employees would often have their day and working time structured by institutional settings and forms of direct control. As work leaves the physical place of the office, workers need to make more efforts to structure work. The company only demands a minimum amount of accountable working time, leaving the organisation and acquisition of customers to the employees. Often enough, this leads to significantly more work, especially for those starting out in the job. In this period, workers are eager to prove their worth to the company which leads to high motivation and long working hours. This is even more the case if work stretches beyond the borders of the office. As a young consultant states:

> Sometimes, when I am unwell or I feel dizzy, but I don't want to stop working, I take a break, I drive home, maybe eat something, and then I continue working. What a great possibility! If you can't work from home, it would be over when you leave the office. (Interview, business consultant)

By the means of indirect control or neo-normative control, the employer puts the employee in a so-called position of autonomy and tries to foster a strong job identification. Highly qualified youngsters without any family obligations are predestined for this strategy, but it is not limited to the young. Professionalism and a strong career orientation are often found within knowledge work. This is also because it is hard to manage this kind of work by issuing direct orders. Under the ideas of management by objectives, performance agreements have become more common, especially in fields of subjectified labour (Moldaschl & Voß, 2002). This bears the potential of experiencing contempt, as well as feelings of rivalry and competition. While the results are the only thing to be recognised, the efforts expended become less visible. As we will show in the next section, the lack of physical presence at the workplace has changed these mechanisms as well.

Presenteeism and Availability: Having a lot of customers and thus generating income, is not fully in the hands of the employees. It depends on the customers' choice. Also, the efforts are not always visible to the others. Back in the days of the traditional office, the commitment to work was indicated by being present in the office, which was called presenteeism (Cooper & Lu, 2018). Presenteeism required the others to perceive and acknowledge the physical presence of an employee. In a flexible office with hot-desking, flexible working hours, external work and home office, it is not possible to know where an employee should be at any given time. This could cause a decline of presenteeism and a new way of signalling commitment: Instead of being there, employees would be available via ICT, wherever they are. No matter where they sit, they are available for the needs of customers and colleagues. As several respondents have stated, being available for the customers as well as for the colleagues at work is key to showing a professional service orientation.

This indicates that a new "availabilityism" could supersede the presenteeism in traditional work settings, but it could also be a new source of stress. As one interviewee indicates:

> For me personally, always having a laptop and a smartphone with me seems to be a very good working style. When I am able to work everywhere, I feel less stressed because I don't have to think about what I could have missed. ... Last weekend, however, was very hard, because the Internet connection did not work, I had no access to emails and so on. This is more stressful to me than knowing I can do everything at any time I want. (Interview, business consultant)

Availability is, however, a double-edged sword. As Cavazotte et al. (2014) point out, the use of smartphones by professionals makes them feel more autonomous and flexible, while they simultaneously suffer from being at the beck and call of the company outside working time (e.g., calls outside of working hours, emails at the weekend).

The importance of availability is accompanied by a second signal to indicate commitment: "I am fine". Regardless of the actual emotional condition, the constant signalling of being fine seems to be of great importance in the field of consultancy work. Emotional work (Hochschild, 2012) is not only a known requirement of interactive service work (Böhle et al., 2015; Holtgrewe, 2003) but is also strongly linked to the self and the relation to work itself (Wharton, 1999).

3.2 Occupational Case Study B: Virtual Assistants

Virtual assistance is an emerging field of gendered work, enabled by new technologies and the emerging platform economy. Being self-employed, the virtual assistants in our sample provide a wide range of services for other online professionals or smaller companies. Jobs may include regular service tasks (e.g., providing bills for accounting, answering calls or sorting emails), but also tasks that rather qualify as knowledge-intense work (e.g., e-commerce and social media marketing) or creative work (e.g., designing logos, websites and presentations). As this variety shows, virtual assistance is not limited to a certain level of qualification or complexity—despite the term *assistance*. As the term and the provided services are not well known, virtual assistants sometimes take the lead when it comes to decisions on the work process or the used tools:

> A lot of customers are not experienced in the collaboration with virtual assistants. I have the impression that they like to lie back and tell me: "Okay, you decide on this", or: "Please guide me, take me by the hand".
> (Interview, virtual assistant)

This allows them to act more like professionals, not just assistants. This is also backed by setting up their own websites and advertisements. Though most of the virtual assistants tried mediating platforms at the very beginning, they soon left the platforms and focused their marketing activities on their own websites and social media channels. which however imply different demands than usual, because claims for flexibility and availability increase. Maintaining a high quality of service essentially demands communication and social skills that compensate for the lack of face-to-face interaction. In order to ensure a longer-term engagement, virtual assistants need to put a lot of effort into forging trusting business relations with a personal attachment. Taking place in a virtual space, this requires new ways of performing as a service provider and building trust and relatedness.

Physical Workplace and Digital Nomads: Within the fields of highly mobile work, employees have lost the office as an important resource and place of community and practices of identity. The virtual assistants in our case study work anywhere: at their kitchen table, in a library, in a co-working space, even at a hostel while on vacation (see the remarks on work while on vacation by Keita Matsushita in this volume). As it is typical for knowledge-intense services, the work of a virtual assistant comes with a relatively low entry barrier regarding the necessary infrastructure. As one of the interviewees states: "All you need to get started is a laptop and Wi-Fi." Nevertheless, this seemingly placeless work (Flecker & Schönauer, 2016) is performed in a physical place. Of course, these places come with a different set of resources, regarding actual work as well as identity work.

Interviewees have shown a number of different reasons for appreciating the spatial mobility. For virtual assistants, the possibility to work from anywhere is one of the prime motivations to engage in this emerging field of work. Reasons vary from the wish to spend more time on travel (e.g., to southern countries, holiday destinations, at the beach), to the wish to spend more time at home. Preferences to stay at home can be fostered by long commuting times as well as care obligations. In these cases, preferences for places of work are closely related to non-work identities.

From a general point of view, the possibility to work completely over the Internet has also led to a new social milieu of digital nomads

(Makimoto & Manners, 1997; Reichenberger, 2018). Young and well-educated people use their skills to earn their income over the Internet while living abroad or travelling. Among the interviewees, some of the younger ones have indicated that being able to travel or to spend the winter in Brazil is the prime motivation for engaging in this kind of work. Generating enough income to live in countries with lower costs of living with only around ten hours of work/week has proved possible for some. This is a fair motivation to do that job, as it provides a lot of freedom and allows for gaining experiences. While being a rather instrumental approach to work, it implies a praised mode of working on holidays which, in turn, is a potential source of recognition. Being able to live "in paradise" for so long, being self-employed, free to work only a quarter of a traditional employment contract, is recognised as a good way of life. However, the presentation of this lifestyle requires new forms of communication provided by social media (e.g., Instagram, Facebook). As our research shows, longer social relations are primarily maintained by these channels and new relations on the site are mostly short term. Successful cases amongst the interviewees have shown the possibility to follow this pattern of work, yet it should be noted that it requires additional resources.

Social Space and Online Communities: While virtual assistants are not part of an organisation in a traditional sense, most of them are part of an emerging online community, where they connect with each other and share experiences and tips about their work. Next to aspects of emotional support, these communities contribute to form an occupational identity, which helps to decide what is part of the job and what is not. These communities may partly substitute for an organisation or association of professionals. It is noteworthy that the group of engaged assistants is quite heterogeneous and they pursue a wide variety of tasks.

While all of them benefit from a network of knowledge, some of them have started to make commercial use of this: Offers for Virtual Assistant Camps in Egypt or Portugal promise not only the knowledge and skills to enter this sought-after field of seemingly placeless work, but also advertise a lifestyle which is focused on the place of living (and not the work content and career).

Another aspect of social space are the physically present people at the workplace. Despite lacking a social working environment in the common sense, our respondents reported that they are never alone. Often enough, virtual assistants find themselves working in the presence of others, be it other guests at a hostel in South America, flatmates, family members or other workers at a co-working space. In all of these cases, social interaction is likely to happen during work. Recognising the assistant's activity at the laptop as work and thus having consideration for it, helps to avoid disturbances and to maintain a workplace infrastructure. Be it the kitchen table or a desk at the hostel, work needs to be recognised as such, which is not always the case. A lack of recognition results not only in the interruption of work, but also in the experience of disrespect.

Self-Employment and Self-Control: The step from assistant to virtual assistant means not to work in the same office as the people one assists and at the same time it means to become self-employed. The spatial aspect and the legal situation are closely intertwined. Self-employed people need to constantly motivate themselves to get up and get work done. This is a certain skill as well as a constant struggle and should be emphasised as a major part of structuring their working day. The successful solution of this problem is a central challenge in doing work in the form of self-employment. It can be helped with good scheduling and agreements with the customers, regular feedback and communication about the work process itself. However, there are cases where people were not successful with this. They quit after several months (or even years) because they were not able to attract customers or could not get enough work done. In the absence of the office, this seems to depend entirely on them. Though the absence of disciplinary aspects of the office can be challenging, being your own boss is a new strong source of recognition. Furthermore, this is fostered by the discourses on entrepreneurial self on a macro level. In everyday life, people generally experience the (physical) absence of a boss and the responsibility for their own working results as freedom.

The wish to be self-employed can be fostered by negative experiences within traditional forms of employment. It is noteworthy that every virtual assistant reported previous experiences as an employee in a traditional office. Most of them worked as an assistant before, stating that their work was not appreciated back then. Rather, it was taken for granted. As one of the interviewees stated:

> When customers say: "Oh my, thank you for helping me and fixing this", and they even recommend me to others, that is a huge appreciation. It is way more than I experienced as an employee. Because as an employee, I worked a lot and I got a lot done, but you don't get recognised. Nobody says: "Thank you", they rather ask. "Why have you worked overtime?" (Interview, virtual assistant)

This lack of appreciation in direct interactions causes discontent. Another negative experience is the feeling of being stuck, lacking opportunities and job prospects. Assistants were asking themselves: "Is this it?" before they quit their jobs and started to travel or became self-employed. If we point out the lack of recognition in interactions for virtual assistants because of the relatively isolated type of work, we thus also have to take into consideration the lack of recognition experienced by assistants working in an office.

Social Interaction, Professionalism and Availability: Virtual assistants may work for a customer without ever meeting him or her face-to-face (Koslowski, 2016). This, of course, has a huge influence on the employment relationship as well as on the demands towards the virtual assistant. Assistants often try to establish a more personal relationship with their customers, utilising software like Skype for initial meetings. Though this is helpful in the beginning, it cannot replace the daily talks a traditional workplace offers. Whenever workers feel the need to talk, it requires additional efforts to be able to do so.

Another difficulty in the work of virtual assistants is the presentation of work experience and thus professionalism. Not only is the relationship with customers largely limited to virtual communication, and the occupation not well known, also the presentation of experience is challenging, as customers prefer to stay anonymous. They generally don't tend to write recommendations, which could be used as references in advertisements. Thus, the invisibility of work, which is often mentioned as a problem for identity work, stresses the need for presenting experiences.

A major question on the level of direct interaction is the opportunity to get into contact. The need for constant availability is one of the most famous burdens of blurred working time arrangements. While the actual preferences regarding boundary management (Kossek, 2016) may vary and include preferences for more fluent boundaries (Sayah, 2013), the power of control over it is a central point for contention (see the contribution by Calle Rosengren, Ann Bergman and Kristina Palm in this volume).

In the interviews, variations reach from harassing calls on Sundays to very sympathetic customers who take account of familial responsibilities, recognising the virtual assistant as a "real person". Thus, clients do not always use assistants as some kind of "post-it", as the case study by Koslowski (2016) suggested. It depends on the relationship the assistant is able to build with the customers, as well as the ability to simply drop unfavourable clients. It is important to mention that in the case of Koslowski (2016), the virtual assistant works for a single customer. In our cases, virtual assistants always had several customers, usually around four.

In most cases, the respondents managed to establish a respectful relationship with their customers, enabling them to express the virtual assistants' own restrictions regarding availability (e.g., taking care of children at home). In these cases, the acknowledgement of limited availability adds up to the recognition by the customers. However, a lack of understanding from the customer can be a burden for identity work, as assistants feel reduced to their function and remain invisible as a person.

4 Conclusion

In this contribution, we have focused on the interrelation between ICT-enabled blurring of boundaries and identity work in knowledge-intensive occupations. We have argued that space, place and physical aspects of workplaces do have meaning for workers' identities in various ways as they allow for recognition in face-to-face interactions, signify organisational membership or provide graded status symbols. Therefore, moving work from the company's office to virtual spaces, to the home or to third places does have consequences for identity work. We have stressed that these consequences can be negative or positive insofar as characteristics of workplaces and the interactions within them may constitute both pillars and threats to identity work.

Two occupational groups were studied to shed light on the relation between teleworking and identity work: business consultants and virtual assistants. Their experiences with remote work and blurred boundaries showed both commonalities and differences. As far as the commonalities are concerned, a higher level of alienation may result from increasingly working over ICT and decreasing face-to-face communication. A lot of sources for identification are lost in the process of blurring boundaries, such as spatial status symbols in the office (e.g., owning a desk), contact and belonging to peer groups in the office, infrastructure such as an IT help-desk, workshops and trainings, and social interaction.

Another commonality relates to changes in the ways in which workers deal with alienation and excessive working hours. Under the right circumstances, availability seems to make up for presenteeism in one case while it can be limited to suit an assistant's needs in the other. This is important to note, since it enables us to look at the possibilities to resist the demands and to develop strategies of resilience and resistance. Despite the overwhelming influence of capital interest, the sources and criteria of recognition are socially constructed. There is always a margin for relevance and a recombination of values and meanings, enabling resistance and reinterpretation (Holtgrewe, 2003).

In both occupational groups, the boundary of a fixed workplace had several functions for the individual and their ability to detach and recover. Now that it has blurred, the individuals must take care of the tedious balancing of rivalling needs all by themselves. An increasing demand for self-governance or self-control can be observed; it is necessary to handle the increased work autonomy effectively (Allvin et al., 2013; Voß & Pongratz, 1998). Both business consultants and virtual assistants face the fact that neither their work nor its outcome is directly visible, nor is it known to most people. Working in these rather abstract fields requires other sources of recognition as a compensation. Business consultants seem to make it up with the "glittering picture" of the industry itself, as well as being part of a prestigious company (in the sense of organisational membership). Virtual assistants are not part of an organisation and the majority has no office or co-working space to be part of. Instead, the placelessness of the task allows some of them to work from remote places or holiday destinations, which gives them a certain feeling of freedom and self-reliance. Of course, this is a short-term way of life, suitable during a younger age with no other obligations. Leaving traditional workplace settings and lifestyles of central Europe behind, they pursue a new style of life, apart from the ordinary employment biography.

Bauman (2005) stated that in postmodernity work has lost its importance as a source of identity, whereas leisure and consumerism have gained prominence. In contrast to this, we see that the quest for a positive self in the sense of successful identity work is still to be fought in the realm of employment. Yet, some virtual assistants have indicated that the prime motivation to engage in this field is to be found outside work itself. In contrast to business consultants, they might have rather instrumental work orientations, seeing their job as enabling a different lifestyle rather than providing a source of identity itself. Apart from the prestige of being self-employed, spatial independence allows for self-realisation in other areas of life.

To conclude this contribution, ICT-enabled boundaryless work lacks some of the pillars of identity work related to work in a company's office and the co-presence of colleagues. Some workers benefit from avoiding threats to their identity stemming from experiences of disrespect or mobbing. Technology plays a role not only in making remote work possible but also by providing tools that may be helpful in compensating the loss of identity pillars, e.g., by allowing for networking with fellow virtual assistants. However, this function of technology is of comparatively little importance. The findings show that the question as to how remote work impacts on identity can only partly be answered in a general way. Various forms of inequality both between the two occupational groups and within them result in a diversity of outcomes. What may be experienced as a pillar of identity for some, poses a threat to others. Similarly, while some may compensate for the loss of identity-supporting aspects of office work, others find it hard to cope with social isolation, invisibility and inappropriate physical working conditions. Nevertheless, for most, work seems to remain a crucial source for their identity construction.

References

Ahbe, T. (1997). Ressourcen—Transformation—Identität. In H. Keupp & R. Höfer (Eds.), *Identitätsarbeit heute: Klassische und aktuelle Perspektiven der Identitätsforschung* (1st ed., pp. 207–226). Suhrkamp Taschenbuch Wissenschaft.

Allvin, M., Aronsson, G., Hagström, T., Johansson, G., & Lundberg, U. (2011). *Work without boundaries: Psychological perspectives on the new working life*. Wiley.

Allvin, M., Mellner, C., Movitz, F., & Aronsson, G. (2013). The diffusion of flexibility: Estimating the incidence of low-regulated working conditions. *Nordic Journal of Working Life Studies, 3*(3), 99–116.

Alvesson, M., & Willmott, H. (2002). Identity regulation as organizational control: Producing the appropriate individual. *Journal of Management Studies, 39*, 619–644. https://doi.org/10.1111/1467-6486.00305

Archer-Brown, C., Marder, B., Calvard, T., & Kowalski, T. (2018). Hybrid social media: Employees' use of a boundary-spanning technology. *New Technology, Work and Employment, 33*, 74–93. https://doi.org/10.1111/ntwe.12103

Bauman, Z. (2005). *Work, consumerism and the new poor* (2nd ed.). Oxford University Press.

Böhle, F., Stöger, U., & Weihrich, M. (2015). *Interaktionsarbeit gestalten: Vorschläge und Perspektiven für humane Dienstleistungsarbeit*. edition sigma.

Cavazotte, F., da Costa Lemos, A. H., & Villadsen, K. (2014). Corporate smart phones: Professionals' conscious engagement in escalating work connectivity. *New Technology, Work and Employment, 29*, 72–87.

Cooper, C. L., & Lu, L. (2018). *Presenteeism at work*. Cambridge University Press.

Dejours, C., Deranty, J.-P., Renault, E., & Smith, N. H. (2018). *The return of work in critical theory: Self, society, politics*. Cambridge University Press.

Flecker, L., & Schönauer, A. (2016). The production of 'placelessness': Digital service work in global value chains. In J. Flecker (Ed.), *Space, place and global digital work* (pp. 11–30). Palgrave Macmillan.

Fonner, K. L., & Stache, L. C. (2012). All in a day's work, at home: Teleworkers' management of micro role transitions and the work–home boundary. *New Technology, Work and Employment, 27*, 242–257.

Goffman, E. (1975). *Stigma: Über Techniken der Bewältigung beschädigter Identität*. Suhrkamp.

Gold, M., & Mustafa, M. (2013). 'Work always wins': Client colonisation, time management and the anxieties of connected freelancers. *New Technology, Work and Employment, 28*, 197–211.

Graeber, D. (2018). *Bullshit jobs: A theory*. Penguin.

Hall, R. (2010). Renewing and revising the engagement between labour process theory and technology. In P. Thompson & C. Smith (Eds.), *Working life: Renewing labour process analysis* (pp. 159–181). Palgrave Macmillan.

Hislop, D., & Axtell, C. (2007). The neglect of spatial mobility in contemporary studies of work: The case of telework. *New Technology, Work and Employment, 22*, 34–51. https://doi.org/10.1111/j.1468-005X.2007.00182.x

Hochschild, A. R. (2012). *The managed heart: Commercialization of human feeling* (updated with a new preface). University of Central Punjab.

Holtgrewe, U. (2003). Anerkennung und Arbeit in der Dienst-Leistungs-Gesellschaft. Eine identitätstheoretische Perspektive. In M. Moldaschl & G. G. Voß (Eds.), *Subjektivierung von Arbeit* (2nd ed., pp. 211–233). Reiner Hampp.

Holtgrewe, U. (2014). New new technologies: The future and the present of work in information and communication technology. *New technology, work and employment, 29*, 9–24.

Honneth, A. (1994). *Kampf um Anerkennung. Zur moralischen Grammatik sozialer Konflikte*. Suhrkamp.

Hürtgen, S., & Voswinkel, S. (2012). Subjektivierung der Biographie. Lebensorientierungen und Anspruchshaltungen. *Österreichische Zeitschrift für Soziologie, 37*, 347–365. https://doi.org/10.1007/s11614-012-0060-4

International Labour Organization, & the European Foundation for the Improvement of Living and Working Conditions (ILO Eurofound). (2017). *Working anytime, anywhere: The effects on the world of work* (Joint ILO-Eurofound report). Author.

Kaun, A., & Fast, K. (2014). *Mediatization of culture and everyday life*. Södertörn Högskola. http://urn.kb.se/resolve?urn=urn:nbn:se:sh:diva-22485. Accessed 23 February 2021.

Kelliher, C., & Anderson, D. (2010). Doing more with less? Flexible working practices and the intensification of work. *Human Relations, 63*, 83–106.

Keupp, H. (2008). Identitätskonstruktionen in der spätmodernen Gesellschaft: Riskante Chancen bei prekären Ressourcen. *Zeitschrift für Psychodrama und Soziometrie, 7*, 291–308. https://doi.org/10.1007/s11620-008-0026-5

Keupp, H., & Höfer, R. (Eds.). (1997). *Identitätsarbeit heute: Klassische und aktuelle Perspektiven der Identitätsforschung*. Suhrkamp.

Koslowski, N. C. (2016). 'My company is invisible'—Generating trust in the context of placelessness, precarity and invisibility in virtual work. In J. Flecker (Ed.), *Space, place and global digital work* (pp. 171–199). Palgrave Macmillan.

Kossek, E. E. (2016). Managing work–life boundaries in the digital age. *Organizational Dynamics, 45*, 258–270. https://doi.org/10.1016/j.orgdyn.2016.07.010

Krotz, F., & Hepp, A. (Eds.). (2012). *Mediatisierte Welten*. VS Verlag für Sozialwissenschaften.

Lehdonvirta, V., & Mezier, P. (2013). *Identity and self-organization in unstructured work* [Working paper]. European Co-operation in Science and Technology (COST).

Makimoto, T., & Manners, D. (1997). *Digital nomad*. Wiley.

Markham, A. (2013). Remix cultures, remix methods: Reframing qualitative inquiry for social media contexts. In N. K. Denzin, & M. D. Giardina (Eds.), *Global dimensions of qualitative inquiry* (pp. 63–81). Left Coast.

Mead, G. H. (1973). *Geist, Identität und Gesellschaft: Aus der Sicht des Sozialbehaviorismus*. Suhrkamp.

Merrifield, A. (1993). Place and space: A Lefebvrian reconciliation. *Transactions of the Institute of British Geographers, 18*, 516–531. https://doi.org/10.2307/622564

Messenger, J. C., & Gschwind, L. (2016). Three generations of telework: New ICTs and the (r) evolution from home office to virtual office. *New Technology, Work and Employment, 31*, 195–208.

Miles, I. D., Belousova, V., & Chichkanov, N. (2018). Knowledge intensive business services: Ambiguities and continuities. *Foresight, 20*, 1–26. https://doi.org/10.1108/FS-10-2017-0058

Mohr, G., Müller, A., Rigotti, T., Aycan, Z., & Tschan, F. (2006). The assessment of psychological strain in work contexts. *European Journal of*

Psychological Assessment, 22, 198–206. https://doi.org/10.1027/1015-5759.22.3.198

Moldaschl, M., & Voß, G. G. (Eds.). (2002). *Subjektivierung von Arbeit* (Vol. 2). Rainer Hampp.

Ojala, S., Nätti, J., & Anttila, T. (2014). Informal overtime at home instead of telework: Increase in negative work–family interface. *International Journal of Sociology and Social Policy, 34*, 69–87. https://doi.org/10.1108/IJSSP-03-2013-0037

Peters, K., & Sauer, D. (2005). Indirekte Steuerung—eine neue Herrschaftsform. Zur revolutionären Qualität des gegenwärtigen Umbruchprozesses. In H. Wagner (Ed.), *„Rentier' ich mich noch?": Neue Steuerungskonzepte im Betrieb* (pp. 23–58). VSA.

Pink, S. (2012). *Situating everyday life: Practices and places.* SAGE.

Reichenberger, I. (2018). Digital nomads—A quest for holistic freedom in work and leisure. *Annals of Leisure Research, 21*, 364–380. https://doi.org/10.1080/11745398.2017.1358098.

Rosso, B. D., Dekas, K. H., & Wrzesniewski, A. (2010). On the meaning of work: A theoretical integration and review. *Research in Organizational Behavior, 30*, 91–127. https://doi.org/10.1016/j.riob.2010.09.001

Roth-Ebner, C. (2016). Spatial phenomena of mediatised work. In J. Flecker (Ed.), *Space, place and global digital work* (pp. 227–245). Palgrave Macmillan.

Sayah, S. (2013). Managing work–life boundaries with information and communication technologies: The case of independent contractors. *New Technology, Work and Employment, 28*, 179–196.

Sennett, R. (1998). *Der flexible Mensch: Die Kultur des neuen Kapitalismus.* Berlin.

Sonnentag, S., & Fritz, C. (2007). The recovery experience questionnaire: Development and validation of a measure for assessing recuperation and unwinding from work. *Journal of Occupational Health Psychology, 12*, 204–221. https://doi.org/10.1037/1076-8998.12.3.204

Sproll, M. (2016). Missing links in service value chain analysis—Space, identity and inequality in Brazilian call centres. In J. Flecker (Ed.), *Space, place and global digital work* (pp. 105–125). Palgrave Macmillan.

Sturdy, A., Fleming, P., & Delbridge, R. (2010). Normative control and beyond in contemporary capitalism. In P. Thompson & C. Smith (Eds.), *Working life: Renewing labour process analysis* (pp. 113–135). Palgrave Macmillan.

Thompson, P., & Briken, K. (2017). Actually existing capitalism: Some digital delusions. In K. Briken, S. Chillas, M. Krzywdzinski & A.Marks (Eds.),

The new digital workplace: How new technologies revolutionise work (Critical perspectives on work and employment, pp. 241–263). Red Globe.

Thompson, P., & Smith, C. (Eds.). (2010). *Working life: Renewing labour process analysis*. Palgrave Macmillan.

Towers, I., Duxbury, L., Higgins, C., & Thomas, J. (2006). Time thieves and space invaders: Technology, work and the organization. *Journal of Organizational Change Management, 19*, 593–618. https://doi.org/10.1108/09534810610686076

Turkle, S. (1995). *Life on the screen: Identity in the age of the internet*. Simon & Schuster.

Voß, G. G., & Pongratz, H. J. (1998). Der Arbeitskraftunternehmer: Eine neue Grundform der Ware Arbeitskraft? *Kölner Zeitschrift für Soziologie und Sozialpsychologie, 50*, 131–158.

Voswinkel, S. (2000). Die Anerkennung der Arbeit im Wandel. Zwischen Würdigung und Bewunderung. In U. Holtgrewe, S. Voswinkel, & G. Wagner (Eds.), *Anerkennung und Arbeit* (pp. 39–61). UVK.

Voswinkel, S. (2013). Anerkennung und Identität im Wandel der Arbeitswelt. In L. Billmann & J. Held (Eds.), *Solidarität in der Krise* (pp. 211–235). Springer VS.

Wajcman, J. (2015). *Pressed for time: The acceleration of life in digital capitalism.* UCP.

Wharton, A. S. (1999). The psychosocial consequences of emotional labor. In D. M. Figart & R. J. Steinberg (Eds.), *Emotional labor in the service economy* (pp. 158–176). Sage.

Will-Zocholl, M., Flecker, J., & Schörpf, P. (2019). Zur realen Virtualität von Arbeit: Raumbezüge digitalisierter Wissensarbeit. *AIS-Studien, 12*(1), 36–54. https://doi.org/10.21241/ssoar.64882

Wilson, J. M., Boyer O'Leary, M., Metiu, A., & Jett, Q. R. (2008). Perceived proximity in virtual work: Explaining the paradox of far-but-close. *Organization Studies, 29*, 979–1002. https://doi.org/10.1177/0170840607083105

10

The Duality of the Physical and Virtual Worlds of Work

Ingrid Nappi and Gisele de Campos Ribeiro

Offices are places supplied by the organisation, specially conceived to support workers' individual and group contributions to the organisational missions and goals, providing both functional capabilities and multiple levels of meaningful interaction and feedback for the people who work in them (McCoy, 2002). The effective management of the workplace should ensure that every company building square meter must be paid for by the business, and the area occupied by the staff must be directly linked to the requirements of the work process and the tasks performed by the employee (Then, 2012). Therefore, the effective use

I. Nappi
ESSEC Business School, Cergy, France
e-mail: nappi@essec.edu

G. de C. Ribeiro (✉)
Paris School of Business, Paris, France
e-mail: g.decamposribeiro@psbedu.paris

© The Author(s), under exclusive license to Springer Nature Switzerland AG 2021
M. Will-Zocholl and C. Roth-Ebner (eds.), *Topologies of Digital Work*, Dynamics of Virtual Work,
https://doi.org/10.1007/978-3-030-80327-8_10

of the organisation's resources lies not in fitting the staff to the workplace but in recognising that there will be a transaction between the staff and the workplace (Moser & Uzzell, 2003). However, the pressure to improve business competitiveness has resulted in the scrutiny of two aspects related to the physical workplace: the amount of built area occupied by the business and its utilisation (Parker, 2016; Then, 2012).

The advances in information and communication technologies have made it possible to work anytime anywhere. The concept of new ways of working (NWW) makes reference to a work arrangement in which employees can control the timing and place of their work while being supported by information technology (laptop, smartphones, connected through wireless network out of thin air) (Demerouti et al., 2014; van Meel, 2011). This gave many companies the opportunity to rethink the utilisation of their office settings, and more specifically, their occupancy costs (Helms & Raiszadeh, 2002; Karia & Asaari, 2016; Messenger & Gschwind, 2016; Parker, 2016).

Many organisations have adopted the NWW and adapted their workplaces to office arrangements such as activity-based offices, flexible offices, new offices or non-territorial offices (Brunia et al., 2016). These types of workplace arrangements are based on desk sharing or non-assigned workstations. The employee arrives at the office; puts his or her computer in a free workstation and works. As knowledge workers do not need to go to the office every day to do their jobs, they can work from their homes, coffee shops, and all sorts of places at any time, and thus many organisations had optimised their premises use by increasing workplace density and utilisation through desk sharing (Harris, 2015). Generally, office arrangements based on non-assigned workstations, such as flexible offices and activity-based offices are combined with teleworking or virtual office practices (Harris, 2015).

Even though teleworking or the virtual office is not a new phenomenon (van Meel, 2011), and in many situations triggered by occupancy cost reduction (Karia & Asaari, 2016), its past adoption has been restricted to a minority of workers and certain companies. In 2017, only 3% of French workers regularly teleworked. Besides, the majority of the teleworkers were knowledge workers and white-collar employees mostly working in information and telecommunication departments in big companies and public companies. Regarding their frequency of telework, 45% teleworked one day/week, 26% two days/week, and 29% three days/week or more (Hallépée & Mauroux, 2019). However, the 2020 health crisis changed this situation substantially. The rapid spread of the Covid-19 virus forced governments around the world to impose strict lockdowns in order to counter the virus spread and protect their populations. In France, the first lockdown lasted nearly two months, from 17 March to 11 May 2020, and profoundly changed the telework figures: 34% of employed people teleworked during the lockdown. Besides, during the first lockdown, teleworking was associated with the social category of the employee: 58% of managers and highly skilled professionals teleworked, compared to 20% of clerical workers and 2% of blue-collar workers (Albouy & Legleye, 2020).

Many organisations around the world were forced to adopt virtual office practices as a strategy to protect their employees, to respect the government's lockdown restrictions, and to save their business. However, this unprecedented growth of teleworking practices has the potential to change the office employees' relationship with their workplace. The duality of the employee interaction with the physical and virtual worlds of work will be examined in this study. Thus, to examine the relationship that the employee can develop with the physical and virtual workplaces, the following research questions (RQ) were established:

RQ 1: "How do office employees evaluate the duality between the work done in the physical and virtual office settings?"

RQ 2: "Will the virtual office replace employees' need or desire for the physical office or not?"

The article is organised as follows: First, we present the literature review concerning the main aspects related to physical and virtual workplaces. This is followed by a discussion about communication issues in virtual office arrangements, and virtual office as a component of a organisational crisis management plan. Finally, we present the results of two web surveys with office employees' work experience in the virtual office during the 2020 Covid-19 pandemic and a conclusion.

1 The Physical and the Virtual World of Work

This section focuses on the functions of the physical office as a facilitator of employees' social interaction, cooperation, productivity, and a source of meaning in the employees' professional life, as well as a discussion about how these dynamics play out in the virtual office.

1.1 The Physical World of Work

Environmental psychology focuses on both the effects of office environmental conditions on individual employee behaviour and on how he or she perceives and acts in this environment. The point of departure of analysis is often the physical characteristics of the office environment (e.g., noise, pollution, planning and office layout) acting directly on the individual or mediated by social variables in the environment (e.g., crowding, population heterogeneity). Indeed, many studies examine the impact of sound, light, furniture layout and office design on employees' performance and job satisfaction (Moser & Uzzell, 2003). However, the office is not only a place where people go to work but also a place to socialise and to be socialised into the organisation's culture (Helms & Raiszadeh, 2002). An important function of the physical workplace is to favour the employees' collaboration. A workplace is a form of a hub that brings colleagues together for networking, knowledge sharing, mentoring and collaboration (Harris, 2015). Close personal relationships are formed between people working together and businesses often benefit from these close relationships (Inalhan & Finch, 2012).

The physical office encourages employees' informal meetings and social interaction. After sharing the same office day after day, employees develop relationships, learn about one another, and gain a perspective of the other's personal interests (Inalhan & Finch, 2012). These face-to-face communications are important occasions to enhance employee collaboration. In the workplace environment, the most valuable form of communication is face-to-face (Pentland, 2012). When the employees do not see one another, everyday socialisation or relationship-building communications ties can be lost (Helms & Raiszadeh, 2002). Indeed, a recent literature review concerning the Internet of Things (IoT) applications in office settings highlighted research showing the importance of employees' face-to-face communications (Nappi & de Campos Ribeiro, 2020). According to this literature review, the amount of employee face-to-face communication levels is positively correlated with self-reported measures of productivity and job satisfaction, and this was also verified when employees' productivity was evaluated through objective measures.

An important asset of the physical workplace is its potential to stimulate spontaneous informal communications between office workers. These kinds of unplanned face-to-face interactions contribute largely to build interpersonal relationships, trust and collaboration between co-workers, and they receive inputs from two other processes taking place in the physical environment: workspace awareness and non-verbal communication.

Workspace awareness is the up-to-the-moment understanding of another persons' interaction with a shared workplace, and it involves knowledge about where others are working, what they are doing and what they are going to do next (Gutwin et al., 1996). In the physical office, this information is useful for many activities related to the collaboration process (for coordinating actions, managing coupling, talking about the task, anticipating others' actions and finding opportunities to assist one another). Besides, research has shown that around 70 to 90% of the entire communication spectrum is non-verbal (Mehrabian, 1972; Strengers, 2015).

In a physical office, people who engage in face-to-face communication are exposed to elements of non-verbal communication (such as personal appearance, facial expression, body language, gestures, proximity, etc.) that influence the way a message is interpreted. Thus, in addition to promoting face-to-face communication, presence in the physical office nourishes employees with two important aspects of the communication spectrum: workspace awareness and non-verbal communication. Both aspects have an important role in establishing a fluid communication process in office settings and contribute to favouring the development of trust and collaboration between office workers.

In the workplace, in addition to the exposure to non-verbal communication, office employees are affected by the presence of other co-workers. Social facilitation theory (first proposed by the psychologist Norman Triplett in 1898) has brought to light the tendency that people are better able to perform simple or well-learned tasks when others are present (Myers et al., 2014). In the workplace, the concept of social facilitation relates to the tendency that the mere presence of other people in the workplace improves an office employee's performance on a task. However, some researchers have found that the presence of others sometimes facilitates performance and sometimes hinders it. Zajonc (1965) solved this mystery, as he found that when performing well-practised tasks that come naturally, the mere presence of others improves employee performance (in other words, social facilitation works for simple tasks), and for complex tasks, the mere presence of others impairs employee performance (Myers et al., 2014). Thus, for complex activities it is better for the office employee to work in a place without other people present.

In addition to providing functional capabilities and physical resources, the office environment is also a source of meaning and security in its occupant's life (McCoy, 2002). Security is the perceived freedom from risk or danger on a physical and or psychological level within the space. It includes familiarity with the physical office, a sense of community support, a sense of belonging and a feeling of permanence (Inalhan & Finch, 2004). Therefore, when the physical office provides resources for goal attainment (security, face-to-face interaction, etc.), and when the use of these resources is frequent, workplace attachment occurs (Inalhan & Finch, 2004; Stokols & Shumaker, 1981).

Environmental psychology research concerns the relationship between human behaviour and the physical environment (Stokols & Shumaker, 1981). The theory of place attachment (Fried, 1963) is a central concept in environmental psychology and has its roots in the study of the psychological effects triggered by the forced dislocation of the population of a Boston suburb. In general, people are unaware of their bonds to certain places, and this becomes apparent only in times of loss or when considering the idea of possible separation from the place (Inalhan & Finch, 2012).

10 The Duality of the Physical and Virtual Worlds of Work

In the workplace domain, place attachment deals with the affective bond resulting from the dynamic interaction between the employees and their environment (Rioux, 2006; Scannell & Gifford, 2010), and its importance rests on three aspects. First, place attachment fosters a sense of community by supporting the integration of groups in the organisation. Second, it favours the retention of key staff, and finally, it helps to reflect and reinforce the organisational culture (Inalhan & Finch, 2012).

Workplace attachment is also an important aspect contributing to the quality of work–life. Employees attached to their workplace have higher indices of the quality of work–life indicators such as job satisfaction, well-being and performance (Dinç, 2010).

However, two phenomena are changing the relationship between the employees and their workplaces. The evolution of information and communication technologies (allows us to work anytime and anywhere) and the increasing adoption of flexible workplace design and management by organisations. Many companies around the world have adopted these office arrangements in conjunction with home-working (Harris, 2015) to avoid having more employees than the number of workstations on their premises. In specific situations in addition to the corporate office and home office, external co-working can also be used by companies as an alternative work scenario (Josef & Back, 2018). This might be occasional, for certain people or teams, only during a limited period or for a specific situation.

Thus, the evolution of information communication technology has made the dissociation between the employee and the workplace possible. Due to the virtual office, the employee does not need to be present on the company premises to perform his or her job.

In this paper, we use the terms telework, teleworking and home office to refer to work performed outside the companies' premises, more specifically the work done at the employees' homes. The terms mobile office and virtual office are used interchangeably and they refer to work performed outside the company premises (at home, on the clients' premises, on the train, etc.).

1.2 The Virtual World of Work

In the workplace life, the conception of time, place and proximity has been transformed by the possibility of working electronically using the Internet and other information and communication technologies (Larsen & McInerney, 2002). Virtual offices are those work arrangements in which employees operate remotely from each other and from managers. Work situations—and therefore teleworking—are always the result of combinations of typical measures on different organisational dimensions, such as work organisation, production and human resources (Depickere, 1999).

Teleworking is an evolutionary process that had its beginning in the 1970s and 1980s. At this time, the focus was to relocate office work into employees' homes or nearby using stationary computers, fixed telephones and fax machines. Technology, location and the organisation constitute the core of the teleworking evolutionary process. Since its beginning, three generations of teleworking have seen the day: home office, mobile office and virtual office (Messenger & Gschwind, 2016).

- ***Home office***: The first generation of telework was based on old information and communication technologies (ICTs) such as stationary computers and fixed telephone lines with a work relocation entirely or partially outside of the company setting (employer's premises), generally to the employee's home. This arrangement made it possible for employees to avoid long hours of commuting between home and work.
- ***Mobile office:*** The technological advances characterise this generation of telework. Small wireless devices such as laptops and smartphones enabled to not only work at home, but also anywhere the employee needs to work (train, clients' premises, cafés, etc.). Work became detached from specific fixed places such as the home and the employer's premises, and it could be performed anywhere and anytime.
- ***Virtual office:*** The advances on the ICTs and the Internet allow the information to be stored in clouds and virtual networks and the employee only needs a tiny device to access it, enabling him or her

10 The Duality of the Physical and Virtual Worlds of Work

to work (checking emails, recent trades, messages, etc.) anytime and anywhere.

Despite the evolution of the virtual work arrangements, these days the three generations of teleworking still coexist. The same pattern applies to workers' utilisation of virtual office applications. Some categories of workers usually make intensive use of the virtual office or the digital technology and infrastructures designed to support work activities anytime from any place. Concerning the teleworkers mobility level, Helms and Raiszadeh (2002) proposed the following classification:

- Telecommuting is the most common virtual arrangement. In this arrangement, the worker has a fixed workplace or office at the company and occasionally works from home. This provides flexibility and increasing productivity with minimal cost savings to the company.
- Hotelling virtual arrangement: Hotel-based workers may come into the office frequently, but as they are not always physically present, they have no physical office. They must reserve a cubicle "hotel room" at the company. The benefits include freed-up office areas that can reduce office size and real estate costs.
- Homeworkers: This arrangement depends upon the worker's home; the office may be an extra room or even the dining room table. The benefits are reduced real estate cost, flexibility and commuting avoidance for the employee. However, this arrangement may be difficult for those living in small spaces, for parents of small children or for those with at-home spouses. In addition, work at home may make personal issues assume greater importance during the workday.
- Fully mobile: these employees do not have an office either at home or at the company facilities. They are expected to be on the road or at the company customer sites on all of their working days. However, research has shown that the constant change of physical locations can lead the full mobile worker to remain a social outsider in all the environments he or she works in, including the main office (Koroma et al., 2014).

As seen before, the three generations of teleworking have made the separation between work and place possible. Since this evolution, where and when the work is done is less important, as work is mainly something people do and no longer a place where they go (Helms & Raiszadeh, 2002). This paradigm change has also influenced employees' mobility levels. The above classification reflects two stages of the teleworking evolution. Telecommuting and home workers reflect the first stage of the teleworking evolution where the work must be performed in a specific place (at home or the office). As hotelling virtual arrangements and fully mobile workers are detached from the place (they do not have a specific place to work), these workers' categories reflect the two last stages of the teleworking evolution: mobile office and virtual office.

Business reasons for developing virtual offices are to increase productivity, higher profits, improve customer service, access to global markets, expand work opportunities (for disabled individuals, single parents, and women), to reduce real estate expenses, and environmental benefits through the reduction of commuting, traffic congestion and pollution (Allen et al., 2015; Baruch, 2000; Cascio, 2000; Pérez et al., 2004). Virtual offices are also an opportunity to improve employees' satisfaction with organisational communication. A case study found that virtual office workers were more satisfied with organisational communication than traditional office workers (Akkirman & Harris, 2004).

The adoption of virtual office practices generally leads to a flatter hierarchical structure, more customer-oriented processes, and more responsibility on the lowest level of the organisation. Traditional control principles such as direct supervision or behavioural control become impossible to exert in the context of virtual offices (Depickere, 1999).

There are several good reasons for employers to introduce or extend teleworking. However, cost-effectiveness serves as the main impetus, and the reduction of overhead costs seems to be a primary motivation (Baruch, 2000; Helms & Raiszadeh, 2002; Karia & Asaari, 2016; Messenger & Gschwind, 2016; Parker, 2016). The potential disadvantages of teleworking are setup and maintenance costs, loss of cost efficiencies, cultural issues, employees' feelings of isolation and lack of trust (Cascio, 2000). Regarding cost-effectiveness, in some cases, the company adoption of teleworking just shifts certain costs onto the

10 The Duality of the Physical and Virtual Worlds of Work

employee (i.e., electricity and Internet connection bills, etc.) (Baruch, 2000); or, in other cases, teleworking can cause losses of cost efficiencies, for example, when expensive equipment or services are concentrated in one location where multiple users can access them, but when they are distributed across several locations this is not possible anymore (Cascio, 2000).

However, the most obvious change associated with the adoption of teleworking is the reorganisation of the office design, in cases where most of the time teleworking is combined with desk-sharing office arrangements (Depickere, 1999). These days, it has become common practice to have fewer workstations than the number of workers in the office. Many organisations plan their offices at around eight desks/ten workers, with substantially higher rates in certain parts of their businesses (e.g., where there are large consulting teams who spend much of their time on clients' premises) (Harris, 2015).

Due to the adoption of virtual offices, in 2000 IBM saved 40–60% in real estate expenses by eliminating offices for all employees except those who truly needed them, and IBM's internal studies showed productivity gains of 15–40% (Cascio, 2000). By 2009, around 40% of IBM's 386,000 global employees already worked at home (the company noted that it had reduced its physical offices by 78,000,000 sq ft and saved about 100,000,000 USD in the US annually as a result) (Kessler, 2017). However, after their massive telework plan starded in 1998, IBM finally backed down twenty years later, as it noticed a creativity decrease in relation to its 386,000 remote employees (40% of teams) (Simons, 2017). As this case shows, telework is not appropriate to companies for which innovation is an essential part of their business.

Teleworking is also not appropriate for all jobs, nor for all employees. Job characteristics that seem to be most relevant to favour virtual work are lower levels of interdependence, autonomy and empowerment (task significance) (Makarius & Larson, 2017). Besides, teleworking is unsuitable for new employees who need a period of immersion in the organisational culture and socialisation where they will learn to adapt to the company, its environment, a new manager and co-workers (Cascio, 2000).

Some aspects must be present to enable effective teleworking: the job (the nature of work and fit of technology for the specific work-role), the organisation (how supportive is the business culture to home-working arrangements, including management trust in teleworkers), the home or work interface (from the quality of family relations to place and facilities available at home); and the employee fit to teleworking (personal attitude, values, norms, qualities, and needs); (Baruch, 2000; Baruch & Nicholson, 1997).

Structural and relational factors predict the employee's adaptability to virtual work. Work independence (the ability to perform tasks without having to engage in continual interaction with other colleagues), clarity of evaluation criteria (clear expectancy concerning efforts and rewards), interpersonal trust (supervisor and colleagues), and organisational connectedness (career plans, opportunities, and sense of being part of the company community) are factors predicting employee adaptability to virtual work (Raghuram et al., 2001). Besides, employee characteristics such as age (old workers show higher levels of work independence and adjustment), gender (men show more organisational connectedness and virtual work adjustment) and previous virtual work experience (those with more experience in virtual office practices show higher interpersonal trust and virtual work adjustment) moderate the relationship between structural and relational factors and the employee's adaptability to virtual work (Raghuram et al., 2001).

A successful virtual office starts with providing the company's employees with effective hardware (laptop, mobile phone, etc.) and software infrastructure (Wi-Fi connection, etc.), and technical support. A transition period to prepare the office workers and the management is also necessary. The transition period includes essential training in the use of information technology applications (schedule meetings, videoconferences, etc.), reorganisation of the company's process workflow (for instance, moving to a process-based structure and a management-by-results rewards system), establishment of more formalised communications channels to inform and engage the office workers, implementation of informal communication strategies to keep the virtual workers in the communication loop (virtual cafés, chat rooms, etc.) and finally, regularly bringing the virtual office workers to the office for meetings and social events (Akkirman & Harris, 2004). Besides, these days, before implementing virtual office arrangements companies must consider countries' legal issues regulating virtual work arrangements (Kelly & Kalev, 2006), for instance, in France, the employee right to disconnect (Secunda, 2019).

Therefore, virtual office practice success depends on several aspects, some of them are under the control of the company, and others depend on the employees' characteristics. However, the most important aspect to consider is communication in virtual settings.

1.2.1 Communication in Virtual Office Settings

Virtual teams are a group of individuals who work together in different locations on interdependent tasks and share the responsibility for outcomes while relying on technology to provide most of their communication (de Guinea et al., 2012).

The degree of the virtuality of a team includes three dimensions: the proportion of team tasks that are performed virtually, the degree to which team members are dispersed or collocated and the geographic distance between team members (Dirks & Ferrin, 2001). Teams with higher degrees of virtuality are associated with perceived decreases in the quality of team interactions and performance (Schweitzer & Duxbury, 2010). More virtual teams exhibit higher task conflict and lower communication frequency, knowledge sharing, performance and satisfaction. However, these results are not generalised to all types of virtual teams, since these negative effects were verified only for short-term virtual teams, while in long-term virtual teams these effects are weak or have even disappeared (de Guinea et al., 2012).

Workspace awareness is obtained from information that is produced from workplace artifacts, and conversation and gestures produced by colleagues' bodies in the workplace. In the physical office, workspace awareness of one another is relatively easy to maintain, and the mechanisms of collaboration are natural, spontaneous and unforced. Being able to stay aware of colleagues plays an important role in the fluidity and naturalness of office workers' collaboration (Gutwin & Greenberg, 2002).

In the virtual office, workspace awareness is replaced by real-time distributed groupware that allows two or more geographically separated people to work together at the same time through a computerised environment. These systems typically support a group's ability to manipulate their artifacts (documents) through a shared space (Gutwin & Greenberg, 2002). Thus, dispersed teams interact by using email, telephone, teleconferencing, chatting, etc.; moreover, they must learn to trust each other and to rely on colleagues that they may never see face-to-face (Larsen & McInerney, 2002).

In organisational life, trust is defined as a "psychological state comprising the intention to accept vulnerability based upon positive expectations of the intentions or behaviors of another" (Rousseau et al., 1998, p. 395). Trust provides the conditions under which outcomes such as cooperation and performance are likely to occur (Dirks & Ferrin, 2001). However, virtual office collaboration platforms generate only a fraction of the information that is available in the physical workplace. In the virtual office, any information about where the other person is working or what he or she is doing is mostly gathered through verbal (telephone, video conference, etc.) or written communication (email, chat, etc.) (Gutwin & Greenberg, 2002). Therefore, in the virtual office, the employees' communication process does not have the same inputs that those performed in the physical office do (workspace awareness and signals of non-verbal communication), and trust does not follow the same pattern as in the physical office, and it is more difficult to generate. For instance, research with university students concerning the dynamics of dispersed virtual teams has shown that students from universities geographically separated found it difficult to trust and collaborate with students from other universities that they never met physically (Crisp & Jarvenpaa, 2013; Larsen & McInerney, 2002).

The adoption of virtual offices could also affect employees' interaction and communication in physical office settings. Golden's (2007) study evaluated how a company teleworking program influenced the employees that remained in the office. More specifically, the study evaluated the office employees' satisfaction with their teleworker colleagues. The results showed that the proportion of teleworkers was negatively associated with employee satisfaction and that this relationship was influenced by the hours the colleagues teleworked during the week, the extent of face-to-face interaction and job autonomy.

In the organisational life, the frequency of employees' face-to-face interactions plays a central role in facilitating norms of reciprocity and trust in both, collocated and dispersed teams. However, the effects of online interaction vary according to the geographical situation of virtual team workers. In dispersed teams, the frequency of online interaction leads to norms of reciprocity, trust, and outcome expectations, but this is not true for the collocated teams (Suh & Shin, 2010). Besides that, in collocated teams, norms of reciprocity and trust are positively associated with knowledge sharing (shared information that is helpful, accurate, relevant, timely and complete), but in dispersed teams only trust is associated with knowledge sharing (Suh & Shin, 2010).

Trust is vital to knowledge sharing among dispersed team members, thus, it is an essential element to ensure virtual teams' performance (Crisp & Jarvenpaa, 2013). Therefore, companies should encourage online social interaction among team workers to promote trust between virtual team members.

In conclusion, even though virtual office arrangements give more employee mobility and autonomy to choose where and when to work, and technology can back the construction of key team dynamics to permit trust and collaboration to occur in virtual settings, virtual office arrangements still do not replace some essential functions of the physical office such as workspace awareness, the positive dynamics of employee face-to-face interactions and employees' feelings of workplace attachment.

Companies have many reasons to adopt virtual office practices (Cascio, 2000; Depickere, 1999; Harris, 2015), however, in some cases, the adoption of virtual office practices is not a company choice, but the only way to keep their business running in a period of crisis. In the next section, we discuss another way through which teleworking may offer societal benefits. It can assure business continuity in periods of weather events, influenza outbreaks, health crises and other extreme situations that can disrupt business operations (Allen et al., 2015).

1.2.2 The Virtual Office as a Component of the Organisational Crisis Management Plan

An organisational crisis is a low-probability, high-impact event that threatens the viability and goals of the organisation and is characterised by ambiguity of cause, effect and means of resolution, as well as by a belief that decisions must be made swiftly (Pearson & Clair, 1998).

Crises are often defined as unexpected, abnormal events that disrupt the developmental trajectory of an organisation at a specific time in a specific place (Pearson & Clair, 1998), and if not managed in a timely way, can escalate and cause significant damage to the organisation (Simola, 2005).

Crises expose organisations to extreme situations that often force cultural changes, while simultaneously having the power to stimulate progress and change in response to opportunities and threats (Roux-Dufort, 2007; Simola, 2005). It is difficult to prepare for a crisis until indicators of potential risk are present. Organisational crisis management requires the ability to think broadly, from multiple and diverse perspectives (Simola, 2005).

Even though the inception of mobile and virtual working practices had its beginnings in the 1960s and 1970s (van Meel, 2011), the adoption of these new ways of working by a large number of companies was not automatic. In France in 2017, the practice of the virtual office was restricted to a small group of white-collar employees (Hallépée & Mauroux, 2019). This situation was not much different in other countries. In 2019 in the USA, according to the National Compensation Survey (NCS) realised by the federal Bureau of Labor Statistics, only 7% of civilian workers (private industry workers and local government workers combined) had access to telework. Besides, telework was a benefit offered mainly to managers and other white-collar employees. Around 24% of white-collar workers from management, business and financial occupations had access to a flexible workplace or telework (U.S. Bureau of Labor Statistics, 2019).

The worldwide rise of the virtual office practice was triggered by a crisis. A crisis reveals a stage of development beyond which the organisation can no longer operate on the same basis as before (Roux-Dufort,

2007). The 2020 Covid-19 crisis and the subsequent lockdown forced organisations around the world to adopt telework as a way to pursue their activities, protect their employees and their business. Many office employees around the world experienced teleworking for the first time during the Covid-19 crisis in 2020. This situation has expanded the employee categories initiated into virtual office practices. Therefore, to understand how office employees evaluate the duality between the work done in physical and in virtual office settings (RQ 1) and to explore the question whether the virtual office could replace the employee's need or desire for the physical office (RQ 2), we will present data from two online surveys carried out as part of the authors' ongoing research project.

Both studies were conducted in France and had the objective of evaluating how a long period of teleworking could affect the relationship the office employees have with their workplace. The data showed here represent an extract of both studies. Even though this article presents data collected during the Covid-19 crisis, its main focus is the impact that a long period of virtual office practices (or teleworking) had on the employees' relationship with the physical and virtual worlds of work. The Covid-19 is only the trigger of virtual office adoption, not the main object of study.

2 Methodology

Two independent online surveys were carried out via a partnership with a panel company. Two different questionnaires were developed, and their respective links sent to the panellists that matched our target population: office employees working in France. Both studies have anonymous data sets and the two samples are independent. The first study was realised four weeks after the beginning of the first lockdown,[1] and the second four months after the end of the first lockdown.

The first study focuses on the impact that the transfer from the physical office to a virtual office, due to the pandemic crisis and the lockdown, had on the office workers' personal and professional needs. It examined the adequacy of their usual workplaces to these needs, and their wish to return to their physical offices. We also evaluated whether they would like to continue the telework experience after the end of the lockdown, and their respective wishes to return to their physical offices.

The first study was conducted in a period when the study participants did not know how things would turn out, how and when they could return to their physical offices, how the office social life would be, and finally, which measures their companies would take to protect them from the current health crisis. Thus, the first study was conducted in a stressful period full of doubts.

The second study was conducted four months after the end of the first lockdown. At this time, the majority of companies had resumed their activities in their usual premises and teleworking was practiced alternately with employees' presence in the companies' physical offices. This study evaluated if the virtual office experience has changed participants' professional needs, their wish to pursue virtual office practices and what would be the ideal distribution of their working time between the company's premises, home and third places. In short, the second survey focuses on trends in the workplace post-lockdown.

2.1 Study 1 Results (During the First Lockdown)

Study 1 has a sample size of 802 white-collar employees. Among them, 63% were female and 37% male; their average age was 42 (the youngest is 18 and the oldest 66 years old, the median age is 43). Regarding the office type that the participants used to work in before the lockdown, 20% worked in individual enclosed offices, 34% in shared enclosed offices (two to six people), 25% in open-plan offices, 9% in flexible offices (hot-desking), 3% performed telework and 7% worked in other types of offices arrangements (co-working, etc.) most of the time.

The study with 802 office employees in France during the lockdown showed that 77% of them did not have the habit of teleworking before the lockdown, and among the remaining 23% of employees used to teleworking, 46% did it on a from-time-to-time basis, and only 8% on a five-days/week basis. Besides, the teleworking habitude varied according to the office type occupied before the pandemic. Among those working in flexible offices, around 53% had the habitude of teleworking, and

10 The Duality of the Physical and Virtual Worlds of Work

of those working in enclosed offices (individual or shared) and those working in open-plan offices only 21% were used to teleworking before the pandemic.

To evaluate if the telework practice during the lockdown has affected the participants' relationship with their workplaces we ask them about their future personal and professional needs. During the online survey, the study participants saw the following message: "The questions below serve to identify your post-lockdown needs and require you to project yourself onto your workplace upon returning to the office." Following this message, we asked them the following question: "Post-lockdown, do you think your personal and or professional needs will change?" Around 53% of the participants answered yes. For those, the online questionnaire showed a list with six personal needs and six professional needs they had to classify according to their degree of importance from 1 (*most important*) to 6 (*least important*). The three most important personal needs were "take care of my health" (43%), "more balance between private and professional life" (21%), and "spend more time with family and loved ones" (17%). The three most important professional needs were "the need for more hygiene and safety in the workplace" (32%), the need to "review the time allowed by the company to telework" (26%) and the need for "autonomy" (18%).

Unsurprisingly, the Covid-19 crisis made participants' concerns with their health more salient in both their personal and professional needs. However, the experience of telework during the lockdown made time and autonomy issues more salient. Participants want more balance between their private and professional lives (to spend more time with family and loved ones) and more autonomy in their professional lives. To obtain that, they need to review the time allowed by the company for teleworking.

Concerning their physical offices, we ask all the participants: "Do you think that the physical office you had before the lockdown meets your post-lockdown needs?", and 47% believed that their physical offices did not correspond to their needs post-lockdown. The majority of the respondents justified their answer by citing problems in keeping social distancing in the office.[2]

We asked the study participants: "Post-lockdown, would you like to continue to telework?" For those who answered yes, we asked: "How often would you like to telework?" Around 69% would like to continue to telework after the end of the lockdown. Among those, only 13% would like to telework on a five-day-basis, the majority or 71% would like to telework from one to three days/week (19% one day/week, 32% two days/week, and 20% three days/week), and 12% of them would like to telework only from time to time.

Concerning the participants' wish to come back to their habitual workplaces, we ask the following questions: "Post-lockdown, would you like to return to your usual workplace? Why?" Even though the majority of the office employees would like to continue teleworking after the lockdown, 74% affirmed that they would like to come back to their physical offices! How did they explain that? For those manifesting their wish to return to their workplaces, six main reasons were identified.

Workplace agreeableness: Appreciation of the workplace and its characteristics such as comfort, functionality and location were the reasons mentioned to justify the participants' wish to return to their usual offices: "There is conviviality, a good location (golden triangle), beautiful offices (Haussmannian building, high ceilings)", "The layout has been adapted and therefore meets my professional needs", "My workplace is pleasant and functional" and "Well located, pleasant neighbourhood, fairly spacious workplace (small open space)."

Workplace attachment: Emotional ties, habitude and workplace attachment were mentioned to justify the participants' wish to return to work in their usual offices: "I love my office and my ritual", "I like my workplace", "I love my workplace", "I enjoy my usual workplace", "I appreciate my current workplace", "It's my environment", "It's a secure place and I like it", "It is a landmark", "I miss it"; "Because it meets my expectations", and "Because I feel good in my office and I'm used to it".

Workplace efficiency: Being in an environment that allows employees to work more efficiently was one of the reasons mentioned by participants to justify their wish to return to work in their usual offices: "Relatively adaptable office according to different configurations",

"Social interactions, working in a setting that allows you to work more efficiently", "Functional office with on-site documentation", "It is more convenient for accessing the functionalities of the service", "Working comfort, with adapted seat and double screen" and "Hard to work at home without dedicated office and with small children."

Trust in the employer: People who like their company justified their wish to return to work in their usual offices by the trust in their employer to take measures to protect its employees: "I feel good in my company and I have confidence in my employer to put in place all the measures necessary for our health", "I like my company" and "The office is secure and hygienic."

Social interaction: The need for face-to-face contact with colleagues and managers as a way to build team spirit, creativity, motivation and fun work environments: "For team spirit and human contact", "To find human warmth, eye contact and laughter!", "Human relations with colleagues and to share creative thoughts", "Very pleasant offices and interaction with a team, energy, and collective intelligence", "Because my motivation in my work is team spirit and human contact" and "Seeing people, discussing, joking with colleagues, that's missing!".

To separate private and professional lives: Some participants feel that telework and virtual office practices make it difficult to separate professional and personal lives. Therefore, returning to work in their usual offices allows them to better delimitate the frontiers between these worlds: "Rediscover the limit between work and personal life. Teleworking blurs the line", "Light, comfort, separation between working time and personal life", "To meet people and separate my private life from my professional life" and "Ties with my work team and greater separation from my personal space."

The 26% of participants manifesting the wish of not returning to their usual offices after the end of lockdown explain their choice by indicating four main reasons.

Workplace dissatisfaction: Participants justified their wish to avoid coming back to work in their usual office premises due to bad physical conditions (noise, temperature, office ventilation) or working in an unpleasant environment: "My workplace did not satisfy me before but it seems to be poorly suited now in terms of hygiene", "Too much noise, too much traffic, cigarette smells because I'm near the patio, no soundproofing with the other offices (ringing phone, laughter, etc.)", "Noisy office not suitable for an executive assistant" and "Very noisy office, very hot in the summer."

Workplace density: The Covid-19 crisis made office density a salient issue. The difficulty in maintaining social distance in the office made participants wish to continue to work at home: "Fear of the collectivity and the lack of serious health or hygiene of my colleagues", "Four people in an office with less than one meter of separation" and "Not to be one of four in sixteen square meters."

Hygiene and security norms: The Covid-19 crisis made issues of hygiene and security extremely important in the workplace environment, sharing computers and other office equipment (printers, telephone, etc.) is not possible anymore and became a source of worry and anxiety to some participants: "I work in a shared office so nothing will be disinfected each time. I absolutely do not believe it. Office not cleaned, not disinfected, shared with several, office supplies shared just like the computer", "To avoid risking my health", "Anxiety and mistrust about the adequacy of the measures taken by my employer", "It's scary because of the virus because we're in mainly closed premises", "Huge problem of hygiene and social distancing in an open space" and "As a person with health problems, I prefer to keep working at home."

Telework advantages: Some of the respondents affirmed that their job activities could be performed away from their office setting and others because they would avoid contact with other people in public transportation or office settings: "My work can be done remotely and no desire to use public transport and to be in a closed office with several people" and "Because of public transportation and the shared office."

2.2 Study 2 Results (Four Months After the End of the First Lockdown)

Study 2 has a sample size of 2643 white-collar employees. Among them, 70% were female and 30% male; their average age was 43 (the youngest was 18 and the oldest 67 years old, the median age is 44). Around 70% of respondents are private industry employees, 26% public servants, 2% self-employed and 2% other worker categories. Among the participants that were employees of the private industry or the public service, around 13% of them were managers and 4% directors. Regarding the office type that the participants used to work in before the lockdown, 26% worked in individual enclosed offices, 36% in shared enclosed offices (two to six people), 25% in open-plan offices, 7% in flexible offices (hot-desking), 3% performed telework and 3% worked in other types of office arrangements (co-working, etc.) most of the time.

In the study conducted four months after the end of the first lockdown, unsurprisingly, the Covid-19 crisis continues to affect the office employees' expectations about their workplaces. We asked the study participants: "Post-lockdown, what are your expectations regarding your physical workplace? Choose, in order of priority, the three items that best meet your needs."[3] Their three principal needs were "to keep the social distances between office co-workers" (26%), "the adaptation of office collective areas to the hygiene and security norms" (16%) and "to have a personalised desk" (14%). The ability to personalise office desks is important and valuable to employees since it gives them feelings of familiarity, a sense of belonging and a feeling of permanence (Inalhan & Finch, 2004). These aspects favour feelings of security that the physical office transmits to its occupants. Besides, personalisation carries potential links to employee satisfaction and productivity (Parker, 2016).

Concerning the virtual office practices, we asked the study participants: "Are you teleworking presently?", and for those who answered yes, we asked: "How often do you telework presently?" Four months after the end of the first lockdown, 37% of the study participants still pursued the telework experience (see Fig. 1), and the majority of those who telework did so on one day (22%), two days (38%) or three days (20%) a week during the post-lockdown period in September 2020 (see Fig. 2).

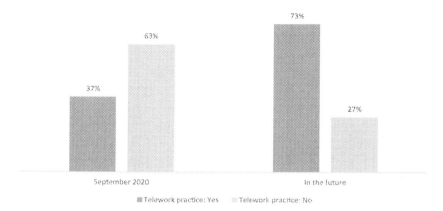

Fig. 1 The telework practice. n = 2,643

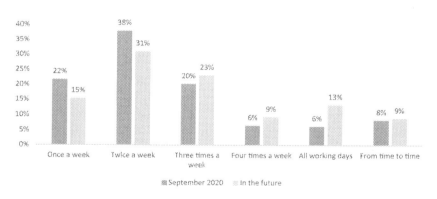

Fig. 2 The frequency of teleworking practices. n = 2,643

We also asked participants about their wish to pursue the virtual office experience in a post-pandemic world: "In the future, would you like to continue teleworking?", and for those who answered yes, we asked: "How often would you like to telework in the future?" When thinking about the future, 73% affirm that they would like to continue to telework in the future (see Fig. 1). Compared with the figures of teleworking frequency in September 2020, the proportion of respondents that would like to pursue telework one day/week (15%) or two days/week (31%) has decreased. However, the proportion of respondents that would like to pursue telework three days/week, four days/week or, even all working days, has increased (in the future) (see Fig. 2).

These days, technology allows working at any time everywhere. The Covid-19 crisis has fostered the adoption of virtual office practices, and as we saw previously, the majority of the study's participants would like to continue to pursue virtual office practices in the future.

We asked the study participants: "Today technology makes it possible to work anywhere. Ideally, how much of your working time would you like to work in the following office arrangements?[4] (Total must be 100%)." According to the study participants, ideally, 55% of their professional activities should be performed in their physical offices (company's premises), 37% at home (telework), 6% in a third place, and only 2% in other types of places (cafes, clients' premises, etc.).

We also asked the study participants which office type or new ways of working they judged most adequate to their post-lockdown needs.[5] Those arrangements with low people-density were the preferred ones. Around 40% of the participants chose individual enclosed offices, 21% chose shared offices, and 19% chose telework as their preferred format (see Table 1, column Total). These results show that the Covid-19 crisis was still present in the minds of the study participants, with around 80% having chosen traditional offices arrangements (individual or shared enclosed offices) and telework as the most adequate place to work. Open-plan offices that, in general, have higher people-density, arrived in the fourth position with 12% of preference.

As in the first study, we also asked: "Do you think that the workplace you had before March 2020 still meets your post-lockdown needs?" This time, around 75% of the study participants affirm that their physical office corresponds to their post-lockdown needs. Therefore, it seems that the measures taken by companies to protect their employees have reassured the study participants.

We used the Chi-Squared Test to evaluate if the office type the respondents had chosen as the most appropriate to their post-lockdown needs was associated with the office type they worked in before the first lockdown in March 2020. The Chi-Squared Test showed that the association between the participants' usual workplace and the one they think the most appropriated is significant ($X^2 = 2.188,98$; $df = 36$ and $p <$

Table 1 Cross-tab between the type of space or NWOW used most before the lockdown and the most adequate to needs in terms of work activities and physical space in the post-lockdown period (percentages)

Type of space or NWOW in the post-lockdown period	1(%)	2(%)	3(%)	4(%)	5(%)	6(%)	7(%)	Total (%)
1. Individual enclosed office	**79**	32	23	13	22	6	17	40
2. Shared enclosed office (< 6 people)	3	**43**	13	8	6	6	19	21
3. Open plan office	1	5	**33**	18	8	13	6	12
4. Flexible office (non-territorial office)	1	2	3	**33**	1	6	4	4
5. Teleworking	14	16	23	23	**56**	25	10	19
6. Co-working spaces	0	1	2	3	6	**44**	1	2
7. Others	2	2	2	1	1	0	**42**	3
Total	100	100	100	100	100	**100**	100	100

Note NWOW = New Ways of Working. n = 2,643

0,001) and slightly moderated according to Cramér's V coefficient ($V = 0.372$). Therefore, this result shows that people prefer what they already know, that is, when asked about what is their most appropriate office type, participants show a tendency to choose in the first place the same office type in which they had the habit of working before the first lockdown. The cross-tabulation between participants' usual office type and preferred office type illustrates this significant association (see Table 1).

For instance, among those who previously worked in individual enclosed offices, 79% have chosen this same office type as their ideal one. Among those who previously worked in shared enclosed offices, 43% choose this same office type as their ideal one. Thus, if we look at Table 1 (read diagonally), we see that those who previously worked in a specific office type are the majority (or the most important group) to choose that same office type as the ideal one. The *Cramér's V* coefficient is a number between zero and one that indicates how strongly two categorical variables (or nominals) are associated. In our study, if the association between the two variables were perfect, the values into the Table 1 diagonal would be equal to 100% (identity matrix); as the *Cramér's V* coefficient is 0.372, we have a moderate association between these two variables, that is why the majority of the diagonal values in Table 1 range between 33 and 79%.

The rapid growth of virtual office practices (due to the pandemic), and the result of Study 1 showing that the majority of the study participants desired to continue virtual office activities in the future motivate us to question Study 2 participants about their vision of the future of the physical workplace. Thus, we asked Study 2 participants the following question: "According to you, what will be the essential function of the office in the post-Covid 19 world?"[6] According to them, the three main functions of the physical office will be a place that we go to in order to participate in the company's life (27% of mentions); a place to meet people, exchange and conviviality (26% of mentions); and finally, a place to work regularly (26% of mentions).

3 Discussion and Conclusion

The COVID-19 pandemic and the lockdown have accelerated the adoption of teleworking and virtual office practices. During the 2020 Covid-19 pandemic, other categories of office employees than just managers and highly skilled employees from informatics and finance domains have experienced telework and virtual office practices for the first time on a five-days/week basis. They started to routinely use virtual office artifacts such as collaboration and conferencing tools like Zoom, Microsoft Teams and Google Meet to work and keep in contact with their managers and colleagues. This article used this period of exception as an input to evaluate office employees' work experience in the physical and virtual offices environment (RQ 1) and the idea that the virtual office could replace employee's need or desire for the physical office (RQ 2). To answer these two questions, the literature concerning the work in physical and virtual settings was examined and completed by the data of two online surveys.

In general, the experience of virtual work was positive, and the majority of the office employees participating in Study 1 and Study 2 would like to pursue this experience in the future. However, companies and real-estate actors tempted to embrace the virtual office practices and forget their physical offices should be cautious when deriving measures from these results.

Study 1 showed that the experience of telework during the first lockdown made time and autonomy issues more salient. Participants mentioned the need for more balance between their private and professional lives (to spend more time with family and loved ones), and the need for more autonomy in their professional lives. To obtain those things, they need to review the time allowed by the company for teleworking.

Study 1 also showed that the majority of the study participants are not ready to forgo their physical offices in favour of the virtual office. Participants justified their wish to return to work in their usual offices by citing feelings of workplace attachment (or emotional ties with their workplaces), the need for social interaction (need for face-to-face contact with colleagues and managers), workplace agreeableness (office characteristics such as comfort, functionality and location), workplace efficiency (right conditions to work), trust in the employer, and to better separate their private and professional lives. They want to return to their physical offices because they missed their work routine, face-to-face communication and social interaction with co-workers. These things are an essential part of their professional lives. In addition, the physical workplace delimits the bond between the participants' private and professional lives.

When people interact only virtually, projects take longer, training is harder, hiring and integrating new employees is more difficult, and their performance does not evolve at the same rate, as would be the case in the physical office where they can observe their colleagues and absorb how they perform their job activities (Cutter, 2020). In addition, many office employees forced to telework during the lockdown did not have adequate conditions at home to telework (Internet connection, a place dedicated to work, small children at home, etc.). The days they spent working in kitchens, on sofas or in small bedrooms made some of the teleworkers long for their physical offices and their colleagues and even generated feelings of loneliness.

Even though the majority of the participants of both studies expressed their wishes to return to their usual workplaces, they also expressed their wish to pursue the virtual office experience in the future. Study 2 showed that, ideally, participants would like to spend 55% of their working time working in the company premises (the physical office) and 37% of time working at their homes (the virtual office). Therefore, companies should encourage employees to balance their work activities between the physical and the virtual office. Employees could perform simple or well-learned tasks when they work in the physical office, and also profit from the colleagues' presence, face-to-face interaction and social interaction. The virtual office, or telework, could be utilised to perform complex tasks or those job activities that need great concentration. Besides, Baruch (2000) claims that the best results of virtual office practices are obtained when people work part of their time from home and part of their time at the office. Both Study 1 and Study 2 showed that the material function of the physical office is important (a place to regularly work), but this is not its essential function. A physical office is a place that allows participation in the company's life, meeting people, exchange of ideas and a place of conviviality. Therefore, the impressive growth of the virtual office did not make, and will not make, the physical workplace redundant, but rather it is likely to shrink it a little bit (Baruch, 2000).

The Covid-19 crisis and the lockdown have forced many companies to adopt the virtual office as a strategy for surviving. Our results showed that this experience was positive for the office employees participating in our two studies. However, even though some company executives could be excited by the idea of reducing real estate costs, or even becoming a virtual company, this is not the wish of our study participants. The reason for this relies on the fact that physical offices, besides their functional capabilities and physical resources, have an important social function. They are a place where work becomes meaningful through employee interaction, where friendship and networks are formed, where newcomers are integrated and where the acculturation process takes place (van Meel, 2011).

Even though the experience with the virtual office practices was positive, both studies showed the importance of the ties that the office employees have with their workplaces. During the first lockdown, 74% went on to manifest the wish to return to work in their usual workplaces (Study 1), and when asked about which office type or new ways of working were most adequate to their post-lockdown needs, they chose in the first place the same office type they had worked in before (Study 2). The physical office is more than a place where people come to work; it is a place of socialisation, collaboration and creativity. It cannot and will not disappear, but will coexist with the virtual office. The virtual office experience made the participants' need for balancing time and autonomy more salient. The design and provision of a correctly balanced infrastructure of physical and virtual workplaces will be at the heart of strategic planning for modern corporations (Then, 2012). Indeed, the two studies showed that the office employees value the autonomy and freedom obtained from virtual work practices. However, they are not ready to give up the office life and their colleagues. People need to see and interact with each other in order to perform well. The physical office will not disappear. It is essential for the life of the organisation, work will evolve with the spread of teleworking, but the office will always be a vital part of organisational culture. The physical office is the element that brings together all the dynamics and actors that build a company.

4 Limitations

Even though the present article brings important considerations to the understanding of the duality of the physical and virtual worlds of work, it is not exempt from reservations. The first reservation relates to the nature of the sample used in the research. This study examined only French office employees' experiences with physical and virtual office practices. A second reservation is the fact that in our two samples, the number of non-territorial offices is relatively small. This situation might affect the employees' wish to return to their physical office as people who work in territorial offices tend to be more attached to their offices. The third limitation is the fact that the second study was conducted only four months after the end of the first lockdown. Between the end of the first lockdown and our data collection, many employees had their summer vacation; therefore, they may not have had enough time to form attitudes towards virtual office practices.

Notes

1. In France, the first lockdown started on 17 March 2020 and finished on 11 May 2020.
2. Open-ended question.
3. Question items: More friendly places at work; Respect of safety distances between colleagues in the office; Have a personalised desk; Assigned workstation; Unassigned workstation; Adaptation of collective areas to hygiene and safety rules (hydro alcoholic gel, space between chairs, etc.); More autonomy to choose the place where you will work; and Better control of the physical environment of my workplace (temperature, light, etc.).
4. Questions items: "At the office (head office)", "In a third place", "At home" and "Other".
5. Post-confinement, in your opinion, what type of office design arrangement would be best suited to your needs in terms of work mode and physical space?
6. Question items: "A place to work regularly", "A place for meeting, exchange and conviviality", "A place of creativity", "A place to receive people, a showcase", "A place for concentration and production", "A place to participate in the company's life", "Other (text entry)".

References

Akkirman, A. D., & Harris, D. L. (2004). Organizational communication satisfaction in the virtual workplace. *Journal of Management Development, 24*, 397–409.

Albouy, V., & Legleye, S. (2020). *Conditions de vie pendant le confinement: Des écarts selon le niveau de vie et la catégorie socioprofessionnelle* (INSEE FOCUS No 197). Institut national de la statistique et des études économiques. https://www.insee.fr/fr/statistiques/4513259. Accessed 16 February 2021.

Allen, T. D., Golden, T. D., & Shockley, K. M. (2015). How effective is telecommuting? Assessing the status of our scientific findings. *Psychological Science in the Public Interest, 16*, 40–68.

Baruch, Y. (2000). Teleworking: Benefits and pitfalls as perceived by professionals and managers. *New Technology, Work and Employment, 15*, 34–49.

Baruch, Y., & Nicholson, N. (1997). Home, sweet work: Requirements for effective home-working. *Journal of General Management, 23*(2), 15–30.

Brunia, S., de Been, I., & van der Voordt, T. J. M. (2016). Accomodating new ways of working: Lessons from best practices and worst cases. *Journal of Corporate Real Estate, 18*, 30–47.

Cascio, W. F. (2000). Managing a virtual workplace. *Academy of Management Executive, 14*(3), 81–90.

Crisp, C. B., & Jarvenpaa, S. L. (2013). Swift trust in global virtual teams. Trusting beliefs and normative actions. *Journal of Personnel Psychology, 12*, 45–56.

Cutter, C. (2020, July). Companies start to think remote work isn't so great after all: Projects take longer. Collaboration is harder. And training new workers is a struggle. 'This is going to be sustainable.' *The Wall Street Journal*. https://www.wsj.com/articles/companies-start-to-think-remote-work-isnt-so-great-after-all-11595603397. Accessed 16 February 2021.

De Guinea, A. O., Webster, J., & Staples, D. S. (2012). A meta-analysis of the consequences of virtualness on team functioning. *Information & Management, 49*, 301–308.

Demerouti, E., Derks, D., ten Brummelhuis, L. L., & Bakker, A. B. (2014). New ways of working: Impact on working conditions, work–family balance, and well-being. In C. Korunka & P. Hoonakker (Eds.), *The impact of ICT on quality of working life* (pp. 123–141). Springer.

Depickere, A. (1999). Managing virtual working: Between commitment and control? In P. J. Jack (Ed.), *Virtual working: Social and organisational dynamics* (pp. 99–120). Routledge.

Dinç, P. (2010). Spatial and behavioral variables that affect "emotional attachment" of users: A multidimensional approach for private offices. *Gazi University Journal of Science, 20*(2), 41–50.

Dirks, K. T., & Ferrin, D. L. (2001). The role of trust in organizational settings. *Organization Science, 12*, 450–467.

Fried, M. (1963). Grieving for a lost home. In L. J. Duhl (Ed.), *The urban condition—People and policy in the metropolis* (pp. 151–171). Basic Books.

Golden, T. (2007). Co-workers who telework and the impact on those in the office: Understanding the implications of virtual work for co-worker satisfaction and turnover intentions. *Human Relations, 60*, 1641–1667.

Gutwin, C., & Greenberg, S. (2002). A descriptive framework of workspace awareness for real-time groupware. *Computer Supported Cooperative Work, 11*, 411–446.

Gutwin, C., Greenberg, S., & Roseman, M. (1996). Workspace awareness in real-time distributed groupware: Framework, widgets, and evaluation. *People and Computers XI*, 281–298. https://doi.org/10.1007/978-1-4471-3588-3_18

Hallépée, S., & Mauroux, A. (2019). *Quels sont les salariés concernés par le télétravail ?* (DARES Analyses No 051). https://dares.travail-emploi.gouv.fr/dares-etudes-et-statistiques/etudes-et-syntheses/dares-analyses-dares-indicateurs-dares-resultats/article/quels-sont-les-salaries-concernes-par-le-teletravail. Accessed 23 February 2021.

Harris, R. (2015). The changing nature of the workplace and the future of the office space. *Journal of Property Investment & Finance, 33*, 424–435.

Helms, M. M., & Raiszadeh, F. M. E. (2002). Virtual offices: Understanding and managing what you cannot see. *Work Study, 51*, 240–247.

Inalhan, G., & Finch, E. (2004). Place attachment and sense of belonging. *Facilities, 22*, 120–128.

Inalhan, G., & Finch, E. (2012). Change and attachment to place. In E. Finch (Ed.), *Facilities change management* (pp. 155–174). Blackwell.

Josef, B., & Back, A. (2018, April). *Coworking as a new innovation scenario from the perspective of mature organizations.* Paper presented at the Sixth International OFEL Conference on Governance, Management and Entrepreneurship: New Business Models and Institutional Entrepreneurs: Leading Disruptive Change. Dubrovnik, HR. Abstract retrieved from https://www.alexandria.unisg.ch/254939/1/Coworking%20Josef%20Back%20OFEL%202018.pdf. Accessed 16 February 2021.

Karia, N., & Asaari, M. H. A. H. (2016). Innovation capability: The impact of teleworking on sustainable competitive advantage. *International Journal of Technology, Policy and Management, 16*, 181–194.

Kelly, E. L., & Kalev, A. (2006). Managing flexible work arrangements in US organizations: Formalized discretion or 'a right to ask.' *Socio-Economic Review, 4*, 379–416.

Kessler, S. (2017). IBM, remote-work pioneer, is calling thousands of employees back to the office. *Quartz.* https://qz.com/924167/ibm-remote-work-pioneer-is-calling-thousands-of-employees-back-to-the-office/. Accessed 23 February 2021.

Koroma, J., Hyrkkänen, U., & Vartiainen, M. (2014). Looking for people, places and connections: Hindrances when working in multiple locations: A review. *New Technology, Work and Employment, 29,* 139–159.

Larsen, K. R. T., & McInerney, C. R. (2002). Preparing to work in the virtual organization. *Information & Management, 39,* 445–456.

Makarius, E. E., & Larson, B. (2017). Changing the perspective of virtual work: Building virtual intelligence at the individual level. *Academy of Management Perspectives, 31,* 159–178.

McCoy, J. M. (2002). Work environments. In R. B. Betchel & A. Churchman (Eds.), *Handbook of environmental psychology* (pp. 443–460). Wiley.

Mehrabian, A. (1972). *Nonverbal communication.* Aldine-Atherton.

Messenger, J. C., & Gschwind, L. (2016). Three generations of telework: New ICTs and the (r)evolution from home office to virtual office. *New Technology, Work and Employment, 31,* 195–208.

Moser, G., & Uzzell, D. (2003). Environmental psychology. In T. Millon & M. J. Lerner (Eds.), *Handbook of Psychology* (Vol. 5, personality and social psychology, pp. 419–445). Wiley.

Nappi, I., & de Campos Ribeiro, G. (2020). Internet of Things technology applications in the workplace environment: A critical review. *Journal of Corporate Real Estate, 22,* 71–90. https://doi.org/10.1108/JCRE-06-2019-0028

Myers, D., Abell, J., & Sani, F. (2014). *Social psychology* (2nd ed.). McGraw Hill.

Parker, L. D. (2016). From scientific to activity based office management: A mirage of change. *Journal of Accounting & Organizational Change, 12,* 177–202.

Pearson, C. M., & Clair, J. A. (1998). Reframing crisis management. *Academy of Management Review, 23,* 59–76.

Pentland, A. S. (2012). The new science of building great teams. *Harvard Business Review, 91*(2), 3–11.

Pérez, M. P., Sanchez, A. M., de-Luis Carnicer, M., & Jiménez, M. J. V. (2004). The environmental impacts of teleworking: A model of urban analysis and a case study. *Management of Environmental Quality, 15,* 656–671.

Raghuram, S., Garud, R., Wiesenfeld, B., & Gupta, V. (2001). Factors contributing to virtual work adjustment. *Journal of Management, 27*, 383–405.

Rioux, L. (2006). Construction d'une échelle d'attachement au lieu de travail: Une démarche exploratoire. *Canadian Journal of Behavioural Science/revue Canadienne Des Sciences Du Comportement, 38*, 325–336.

Rousseau, D. M., Sitkin, S. B., Burt, R. S., & Camerer, C. (1998). Not so different after all: A cross-discipline view of trust. *Academy of Management Review, 23*, 393–404.

Roux-Dufort, C. (2007). Is crisis management (only) a management of exceptions? *Journal of Contingences and Crisis Management, 15*, 105–114.

Scannell, L., & Gifford, R. (2010). Defining place attachment: A tripartite organizing framework. *Journal of Environmental Psychology, 30*, 1–10.

Schweitzer, L., & Duxbury, L. (2010). Conceptualizing and measuring the virtuality of teams. *Information Systems Journal, 20*, 267–295.

Secunda, P. M. (2019). The employee right to disconnect. *Notre Dame Journal of International & Comparative Law, 9*(1), article 3. https://scholarship.law.nd.edu/ndjicl/vol9/iss1/3. Accessed 23 February 2021.

Simola, S. K. (2005). Organizational crisis management: Overview and opportunities. *Consulting Psychology Journal: Practice and Research, 57*, 180–192.

Simons, J. (2017, May 18). IBM, a pioneer of remote work, calls workers back to the office. *The Wall Street Journal*. https://www.wsj.com/articles/ibm-a-pioneer-of-remote-work-calls-workers-back-to-the-office-1495108802. Accessed 16 February 2021.

Stokols, D., & Shumaker, S. A. (1981). People in places: A transactional view of settings. In J. Harvey (Ed.), *Cognition, social behavior and environment* (pp. 441–488). Erlbaum.

Strengers, Y. (2015). Meeting in the global workplace: Air travel, telepresence and the body. *Mobilities, 10*, 592–608.

Suh, A., & Shin, K. (2010). Exploring the effects of online social ties on knowledge sharing: A comparative analysis of collocated vs dispersed teams. *Journal of Information Science, 36*, 443–463.

Then, D. S. S. (2012). The business of space. In E. Finch (Ed.), *Facilities change management* (pp. 57–75). Blackwell.

U.S. Bureau of Labor Statistics. (2019). *National Compensation Survey (NCS)*. https://www.bls.gov/ncs/ncspubs.htm. Accessed 23 February 2021.

Van Meel, J. (2011). The origins of news ways of working: Office concepts in the 1970s. *Facilities, 29*, 357–367.

Zajonc, R. B. (1965). Social facilitation. *Science, 149*(3681), 269–274.

Part IV

Synopsis

11

Synopsis: How Space and Place Matter in the Context of Digital Work

Caroline Roth-Ebner and Mascha Will-Zocholl

As already mentioned in the Introduction, the debate about the *spatial turn* placed emphasis on the confrontation with changing spatial conditions. This was preceded by the expansion of the previous understanding of space, away from the "container space" or a purely geographical space to a system of references that is socially constructed and emerges through interaction by means of social practices (Lefebvre, 1974, 1991). With the development of modern information and communication technologies, the understanding of space once again came into sharper focus: What should the consequences of these technologies be? This question was first dealt with in the context of science fiction in literature and film.

C. Roth-Ebner (✉)
University of Klagenfurt, Klagenfurt, Austria
e-mail: Caroline.Roth@aau.at

M. Will-Zocholl
Hessian University of Police and Administration, Wiesbaden, Germany
e-mail: Mascha.Will-Zocholl@hfpv-hessen.de

The focus lay on the emergence of computer-generated virtual worlds. This was the hour of Gibson's (1984) "cyberspace". The term drew attention to the description of technologically enabled spaces. Based on his literary intention of unfolding a space of action in his novel that was neither place, nor space, but "notional space" (Gibson, 1989, n.p.), arising from a common shared spatial imagination, everything that had anything to do with virtual worlds was soon called cyberspace, including the World Wide Web. The talk of immaterial, virtual worlds or realities, which exist detached from places and time restrictions, became established. These developments promoted the idea that due to the fact that the material basis of these technologies plays less of a role, a "death of distance" (Cairncross, 2001) would be imminent, which would make places interchangeable and distances irrelevant.

The following years were marked by a further technological leap in development allowing many of the hitherto theoretical considerations and developments that were still in their infancy to become reality. The anyplace-anytime paradigm prevailed, supported by the technical sciences, business associations and companies. In fact, this was also reflected in scientific debates. In sociology, the theory of the "network society" (Castells, 1996) was introduced in order to describe society, and as part of it, the world of work, as constituted by networks based on using modern information technology. Following Castells, we are dealing with a "hybrid space, made up of places and flows" (Castells, 2001, p. 235). He differentiates between the conventional "space of places", which is bound to territories and a "space of flows" that is created by information and communication technologies (ICTs) (Castells, 1996). Castells emphasises that new geographies evolve based on information flows that are not "placeless" but networked places.

In fact, this conceptualisation corresponds with the theory of the "information space" (Baukrowitz & Boes, 1996) as already elaborated in the Introduction, that combines Castells' thoughts and Lefebvre's concept of socially constructed spaces with the theory of informatisation (Schmiede, 2006). Digitisation and a worldwide ICT infrastructure in the form of the Internet provide the basis for new spatial dimensions of informatisation, the "information space" (Boes & Kämpf, 2007). With the transformation of more and more working objects to information objects, it is potentially possible to work from anywhere at any time. This development has gained in importance in recent years and is reflected in concepts such as crowd or platform work or other outsourcing activities in the field of knowledge work. The current phase in this process has been identified as "informational capitalism" (Castells, 1996), with reference to the increasing importance of information within capitalism accompanied by digitalisation and globalisation processes.

Recent research shows that this development does not include a detachment from places or a unilateral delocalisation (e.g., contributions in Flecker, 2016 or Boes et al., 2017). Digitised or virtual work is absolutely not detached from spatial ties, rather, as Will-Zocholl et al., (2019, p. 50) state, it shifts in spatial references. As Roth-Ebner (2016, p. 244) has shown with her study on the mediatisation of work, in many cases several virtual and physical spaces are used in parallel or superimposed with each other, since they are just a click away. The results can also be linked to Doreen Massey's (2005, p. 9ff.) conceptualisation of space, in the sense that space is constituted through relations and interactions, which, by using digital media, produce a virtual working space. As emphasised in the Introduction, everything that is done in this working space has real consequences.

Taking these developments into account, it can be said that the evolution of digital information and communication technologies has had a large impact on the topologies of work, the way work is organised, performed, evaluated and perceived. This transformation is an interdisciplinary topic and can be discussed using multiple perspectives. What "informatisation" and "information space" describe from a sociological view, media and communications tend to introduce with the term "mediatisation of work" (Roth-Ebner, 2016) in order to grasp the interrelation between the medial-communicative transformation and the changes in the world of work. Since space and time are particularly influenced by mediatisation processes (Krotz, 2007, p. 39), the concept of mediatisation of work specifically refers to spatial dimensions and new topologies of work.

The contributions in this volume represent additional perspectives on the interrelation of work, space and digital media resp. ICTs and the question of how places and spaces are shaped by the ongoing digitalisation of work. It includes approaches from sociology, media and communications, political economy, working life science, management sciences, environmental psychology, and communication history. Each of the three Parts of the book deal with different scales of spatial reorganisation:

- geographies of digital work;
- places of work (and their conditions); and
- virtual working spaces.

In the upcoming chapter, we reflect on the authors' contributions to the general aim of this anthology.

1 Geographies of Digital Work: Context Matters

The contributions reveal that the geographical location still matters in the globalised and digitised world of work. As put forward in the contribution by Andrey Shevchuk, Denis Strebkov and Alexey Tyulyupo, proclamations of the "death of distance" (Cairncross, 2001), or of a "flat world" (Friedman, 2007) are not irrefutable, since new hierarchies between regions are appearing ("geographic stereotyping"), and geographical factors still mould the way work is being distributed, organised and performed. Anna Ozimek emphasises the significance of the local embeddedness for the digital game production. She demonstrates that the establishment of Poland and Estonia as places for subcontracted work are "based on political, economic and technological power asymmetries in the development of game production between 'Eastern' and 'Western' countries" (see the contribution by Anna Ozimek in this volume). In their chapter, Brett Neilson and Ned Rossiter demonstrate that data centre environments also depend on national regulatory frames as well as on infrastructural and natural environments that supply grids, cable networks, energy, water resources and—to a certain extent—people.

Concerning the reorganisation of space along with the emergence of the information space, Andrey Shevchuk, Denis Strebkov and Alexey Tyulyupo identify a strong trend of spatial decentralisation in the Russian online labour market in their chapter, diffusing from economically developed centres to less developed regions. Jian Lin also shows this effect—albeit more pronounced—concerning China's wanghong economy. Its networks span from the urban centres to rural regions and populations, where individuals gain a chance of employment that they are less likely to obtain in the traditional local-social settings. Keita Matsushita points to a further aspect of—in his words "delocalisation" (which could also be described as a relocalisation of work): the trend of equipping rural areas with working infrastructure in order to relieve crowded cities. Under current conditions of the Covid-19 pandemic, this trend could increase as we observe similar developments in Silicon Valley, where tech firms are leaving crowded Californian urban areas and heading towards more affordable regions of the USA like Arizona and Texas.[1]

The contributions to this volume disclose a regional embeddedness of work that is linked to language and a common understanding of qualifications, as elaborated by Anna Ozimek using the example of the outsourcing practices of the digital games industry. Similarly, Andrey Shevchuk, Denis Strebkov and Alexey Tyulyupo demonstrate that language and the socio-economic situation of a country or region may contribute to the establishment of distinct online labour markets presenting the example of the digital freelance economy in Russia and beyond. The numbers of registered users and customers of the platform studied show that the Russian-speaking area is still closely linked to the territories of the states that formerly belonged to the Soviet Union. In this way, the platform facilitates an information space for Russian-language orders and offers. This corresponds to the results of other platform work studies that showed a concentration of online labour in specific countries, for example in urban English-speaking areas (Lehdonvirta, 2017; Lehdonvirta et al., 2019).[2]

Moreover, in their study, Andrey Shevchuk, Denis Strebkov and Alexey Tyulyupo were able to determine that clients in the sphere of crowd working tend to prefer contracting with freelancers from the same country or geographical region. Although the researched platform

(FL.ru) is transnationally dispersed, they report a "geographical clustering of economic activity" (see their contribution in this volume), that has arisen with the emergence of the political conflict between Russia and the Ukraine. Thus, topologies of work also have to be seen in terms of political conditions and developments. Other contributions to this volume serve as an example as well: Anna Ozimek shows that outsourcing practices that centred on Central and Eastern European countries, as in her example, Poland and Estonia, were fostered by the collapse of the Soviet Union. Jian Lin demonstrates how the Chinese government initiatives which aimed at upgrading the Internet infrastructure, on the one hand, and fostering mass entrepreneurship, on the other hand, propelled the establishment of the Chinese wanghong economy. (However, Chinese Internet censorship is also a threat to the careers of wanghong creators.) Similarly, Keita Matsushita points out that local governmental initiatives with the goal of community revitalisation are the drivers for the establishment of workationing facilities in rural areas of Japan. These findings fit seamlessly with the analysis of other authors, such as Noronha and D'Cruz (2016), who traced for India how policies fostered the emergence of the Indian IT success model, or Wolff (2016), who uncovered the impact of regional policies on the emergence of a local IT market in Brazil. Hence, policy influences the establishment and distribution of digital work, and digital work and its consequences have an impact on policy regulations (Meil & Kirov, 2017).

Brett Neilson and Ned Rossiter go even further, interpreting data centres "as political institutions, which shift power relations across wide spatial vistas and contribute to changing patterns of geopolitics and governance across diverse geographical scales" (see their contribution in this volume). As an example, Singapore's future as a data centre hub depends on the race between China and the US to establish standards for data transfer and artificial intelligence. The influence of political decisions on the location of certain industries, such as the data centres, should not be underestimated; it also strengthens the negotiating position in the global market structure, which functions on the basis of data. At the same time, the companies that are active there also influence geopolitics.

Finally, one has to consider the socio-geographical context by emphasising that the conditions of and changes wrought by a digitised world of work are not a general global phenomenon concerning all areas of work and all forms of occupation. As Christian Oggolder states, "hundreds of thousands of employees have to deal with working conditions that are no different from those of the modern era of factories, or even worse" (see his contribution in this volume). This is true above all for blue collar work (in mines, in the textile industry, etc.) but also for an increasing number of digital workers. Huws (2003) describes this development of worsening conditions in terms of insecurity, control and payment around the globe, as the rise of a "cybertariat".

This is especially pronounced in the case of workers in data centres who are confronted with the fact that their work contributes to training and optimising the algorithms and artificial intelligence so that their own work can be automated. As Brett Neilson and Ned Rossiter argue, the workers actively contribute to rationalising and abolishing their work. Some forms of platform work tend to show similar developments, especially in "microwork" (Lehdonvirta, 2016). Other forms of digital work are additionally emotionally and ethically demanding like the work of content moderators in social media (Roberts, 2019).

To sum up briefly, the contributions reveal that the construction of spatial relations in interaction with working or production environments cannot be understood without referring to the geographical embeddedness including historical, political, social and economic contexts. Altogether, they mould the distribution and division of economic activities, labour and of working conditions.

2 Places of Work: About Changing Workplaces and Locations of Work

As was claimed for the geographies of work, concrete locations and places of work also matter. In her research on the digital games industry and its outsourcing to Poland and Estonia, Anna Ozimek shows that the workforce is "influenced by the available infrastructure, resources and regulations" (see her contribution in this volume). Keita Matsushita reveals movements of mobile work in his contribution that transform urban spaces into working places, for example, cafés, train stations and airports, which Dominik Klaus and Jörg Flecker call "intermediate places" (see their contribution in this volume). Thus, a working place in a digitised world of work can be defined simply as a place where people work, notwithstanding the original intention of the space. This has consequences for the experience of work. Keita Matsushita interprets this as the emergence of style-based workplaces, "where an individual's workstyle renders their workplace to be possible anytime, anywhere" (see his contribution in this volume). He sees a shift in the perception of workplaces from "'what workstyles are possible at this place' to 'how will I use spaces […] to suit my workstyle?'" and explores this transformation using the example of co-working spaces in Tokyo's business centre Shibuya and workationing at the seaside in Shirahama (Japan). The negotiation of workstyles and workplaces shows that the identity of the workers plays a role as well. This is also true for China's wanghong economy actors, where local places and identities still matter. However, they are reduced to the "surface level that can add to the performative authenticity creators attempt to claim and monetize", as put forward by Jian Lin (in this volume). In their contribution, Ingrid Nappi and Gisele de Campos Ribeiro also point to the material function of the physical office, which is reflected in the theory of place attachment (Fried, 1963). In fact, the feeling of being attached to a certain place is not fundamentally changed by the experience of telework. The majority (75 per cent) of respondents in Ingrid Nappi and Gisele de Campos Ribeiro's study on workplaces before and after the first lockdown during the 2020 Covid-19 crisis continue to find the physical office at the company's premises adequate for their work tasks. The results of the survey showed that the location for working in the information space does not become arbitrary, and that the social embedding in the office is still highly valued—some aspects even more than before (see their contribution in this volume).

Yet, workplaces have to be seen in their relation to the information space. Anna Ozimek shows for the digital games industry that the production takes place in the information space locally based in "fragmented and decentralised production networks" (see her contribution in this volume). The same is true for Andrey Shevchuk, Denis Strebkov and

Alexey Tyulyupo's example of the digital freelance economy in Russian-speaking countries as well as Jian Lin's description of wanghong network effects which "transform the local space of place into 'the space of flows'" (in this volume), where individuals participate in the seeming "placeness" of Chinese social media communities or, in other words, create information space(s).

In conclusion, concrete places of work have not become meaningless, yet they are extended through virtual workspaces and networks as part of the information space.

3   Virtual Working Spaces: Identity, Subjectivity and Individual Preferences

Today, "business, politics, culture, and communication are shifting from physical places to virtual spaces", as Christian Oggolder (in this volume) argues. Those virtual spaces and their impact constitute Part III. Several contributions in this volume highlight the constructive aspect of space(s), as discussed in the Introduction with reference to Brenneis et al. (2018), Lefebvre (1974/1991) and Massey (2005). As Calle Rosengren, Ann Bergman and Kristina Palm maintain in their contribution, working spaces are constructed through the use of ICT and "can thus not be seen as separate from human action and interaction" (in this volume). The multiplication of work and non-workplaces in the virtual space leads to the demand to be simultaneously available in different work settings and "spheres of life" (ibid.). Consequently, formerly separated spaces are blurring, especially in the concept of "home office work" where private spaces and workspaces increasingly overlap, as described by Calle Rosengren, Ann Bergman, Kristina Palm, Dominik Klaus, Jörg Flecker as well as Christian Oggolder in this volume (and others, e.g., Koslowski, 2016; Roth-Ebner, 2016). This is also associated with a temporal delimitation, leading to all-day accessibility which is controlled socially and technically. This overlapping was already a common concept in the early modern period, where work and family life were combined in the house which served as place of work and living, as Christian Oggolder reminds us in his contribution.

The blurring of boundaries is not the only challenge for people who work. Increased density of work, flexible structures and precarious working conditions have consequences for subjectivity. Thus, new competencies are required in order to deal with the affordances of a digitised world of work (Diehl et al., 2013). Some of the contributions clearly set out that different practices are becoming established, which are related to diverse framing conditions. Calle Rosengren, Ann Bergman and Kristina Palm define the practices of "separating or integrating work and non-work to different times and places" as "boundary work" (in this volume). They demonstrate that ICTs are used to manage one's availability for different life spheres, yet in different ways, depending on subjective dispositions. How a person handles their boundary work is a subjective and a dynamic process and depends on personal preferences, technological infrastructure as well as on contextual variables (workload, expectations of colleagues and family). Consequently, the authors speak of ICT as a "double edged sword" (in this volume). For example, the spatial flexibility due to the use of Internet-based work applications can be seen as a blessing that enables more freedom and autonomy for the individual. However, it is also a burden, as it requires increased personal responsibility and boundary management effort. Dominik Klaus and Jörg Flecker also conclude their research on the interrelation between boundaryless work and identity work in a similar way: "What may be experienced as a pillar of identity for some, poses a threat to others" (in this volume). Anna Ozimek's study of game industry workers provides yet more evidence of these ambivalences. She outlines that even the skilled subcontractor's work is often precarious in terms of uncertain employment status and low salary and, as a consequence, their work is not valued as socially prestigious. Finally, referring to the example of the wanghong economy, Jian Lin shows that the creative protagonists are subject to the logics of platform capitalism and state surveillance and are thus limited in their creativity. Other ambivalences were also addressed in the contributions to this volume: from delocalisation versus localisation, decentralisation versus centralisation, autonomy versus control, physical versus virtual office to empowerment versus burden. This underlines the notion that technological innovations always depend on the social use they are put to (Matuschek et al., 2003, p. 139) and "that the transformative potential of digital media is just a potential one that does not guarantee any unequivocal effect" (Roth-Ebner, in press).

Some of the contributions in this volume refer to the fact that spatial aspects are interrelated with identity work. With their research on highly mobile knowledge workers, Dominik Klaus and Jörg Flecker stress the importance of spatial identity resources, like owning a desk, being part of an office peer group and having access to infrastructure. These resources can be lost in cases of freelancing or teleworking. For home office work, Ingrid Nappi and Gisele de Campos Ribeiro come to the same conclusion in their study conducted during the Covid-19 pandemic, which is why they emphasise the physical office as an essential part of an organisation. The organisational affiliation (occupational identity) or the affiliation to an employee group or social group ("class") is at stake under these conditions (e.g., Huws & Dahlmann, 2010).

Further, the blurring of professional and private boundaries is relevant for the workers' identities. The "way people relate to their jobs affects their boundary management" (see the contribution by Dominik Klaus and Jörg Flecker in this volume). They identify an increased demand for self-governance or self-control regarding boundaryless telework. Calle Rosengren, Ann Bergman and Kristina Palm take the same line when they underscore the relevance of the feeling of being in control with regard to boundary work. However, the interrelation between identity and digitised worlds of work or working in the information space goes beyond boundary work or boundary management. Jian Lin emphasises the relevance of "a continuous self-governance that incorporates self-censorship, continuous learning and emotional management" (see his contribution in this volume) regarding employment in the digital economy.

4   The Covid-19 Crisis as Laboratory for Future Work

During the time the contributions were being written, the Covid-19 crisis, starting in late 2019 and spreading all over the world in 2020, caused a caesura in the world of work. Due to more or less strict lockdowns, companies were forced to facilitate home office arrangements for their employees where applicable in order to prevent the spread of infection. Meetings, even whole conferences, were organised on a virtual basis. Some of the employees' homes were crowded with both home workers and children who performed their distance learning from home, because in some countries even schools closed due to strict lockdown rules. This situation served as a laboratory where the effects of virtual work were all condensed in a short period of time: from the benefit of keeping work processes and communication going in times of social distancing and reduced commuting times to the downsides of distraction due to family affairs, technological problems and IT security as well as difficulties in team communication and with the flow of information.

The contribution by Ingrid Nappi and Gisele de Campos Ribeiro explicitly discusses the relationship between the Covid-19 crisis in 2020 and the attitude towards home office and altered working practices. Their study reveals that most of the surveyed employees wanted to continue with home office practices after the crisis, alternating this with working at the company's premises. In fact, their results are relevant for post-crisis times as well and the general question of virtual work settings replacing physical ones. As the authors emphasise, "virtual office arrangements still do not replace some essential functions of the physical office such as workspace awareness, the positive dynamics of employee face-to-face interactions, and employees' feelings of workplace attachment" (Ingrid Nappi and Gisele de Campos Ribeiro in this volume). Thus, they conclude that the physical office will continue to persist in post-crisis times, yet it will co-exist with virtual offices. This is again evidence for the central statement of the volume that place matters and that, with the emergence of the information space, place does not become arbitrary.

Today, due to the ubiquitous use of the Internet and the transformation of social action into the information space, the proportion and variety of spatial references has increased, regardless of the actual location from which work is performed. This has consequences for the work of the future, that is, it must also be spatially possible to work in a concentrated manner at home. But if more work is done at home, it may also be important to ensure that there is a community within reach. In this context, co-working spaces, like satellite offices, can also be considered for ordinary employees (beyond the digital bohemians). And ultimately, the question of where one chooses to live may also come to hinge on the fact that one no longer has to travel to the place of work every day, but is on the road less frequently.

All in all, instead of placelessness, a multiplication of places could be the new normal of work not limited to knowledge work. The further digitalisation in many different occupations could lead to an individualisation of workplaces (home office, corporation, mobile, etc.).

One of the big questions will be how the recognition of and attachment to organisations will be realised. Corporality will still play an important role. Being somewhere physically creates a feeling of belonging and connectedness, as highlighted by Ingrid Nappi and Gisele de Campos Ribeiro in this volume.

5 Full Circle: A Return to Our Research Questions

After reflecting the essence of the contributions to the book, we now return to the guiding questions first raised in the Introduction. These can be tentatively answered as follows:

1. "How relevant is the local embeddedness of work? To what extent does place matter in the context of a digitised world of work, and what does this mean for the division of labour (national–international, but also urban–rural)?"

Even though industries act on a global basis and work is globally distributed, the contributions give credence to the fact that work is still locally embedded. Anna Ozimek has demonstrated this using the example of Polish and Estonian subcontractors working for the digital games industry. The political and economic history of the Central and Eastern Europe (CEE) region has established asymmetrical power relations that persist in the globally distributed workforce. Andrey Shevchuk, Denis Strebkov and Alexey Tyulyupo have shown that even in crowd working, contracting tends to be based on geographical proximity. According to Dominik Klaus and Jörg Flecker, whether there is a place to work at the company's premises or not has consequences for the workers' identity. The question of whether they are positive resources for identities or a threat to them, varies individually. Also, Ingrid Nappi and Gisele de Campos Ribeiro emphasise the importance of communal space in the organisation.

Work in the information space can potentially be distributed globally. Hence, Anna Ozimek as well as Andrey Shevchuk, Denis Strebkov and Alexey Tyulyupo demonstrated that this distribution is shaped by geographical factors. Jian Lin and Keita Matsushita described the decentralisation of work from urban to rural areas. Brett Neilson and Ned Rossiter even showed "how labour transitions to a society of automation" with their analysis of Singapore's data centres (see their contribution in this volume).

The contributions in this volume provide a panorama of a development that includes many other aspects. What is very clear from the different angles taken, however, is that the emergence of a global continuous information space has to be put into perspective. The information space is not as frictionless as its perception as a space of possibilities suggests. Entrance barriers, control intentions, censorship or filters contribute to the determination that no global information space has yet emerged in which everyone can participate equally and without restriction. Political tensions and regimes can also lead to closure processes. As a matter of fact, information spaces are not power-free spaces. Thus, talking about information spaces instead of an information space seems more appropriate at the moment. Even if it is possible in principle for a global information space to emerge, it is more likely that smaller spatial structures will emanate, as the examples in our anthology show.

2. "What are the consequences of the digitalisation of work for previous concepts of geographical places, workplaces and workspaces?"

The contributions reveal that a transformation of communication leads to the transformation of space as well as to the transformation of culture and society. In the virtual sphere, (working) spaces can easily be constructed with a single click (that e.g., opens a video conference room or a data base). Thus, (virtual) space emerges through (ICT-based) action. Contrary to popular belief, this does not lead to work becoming placeless. Places are used more flexibly, and the geographical, political, cultural or knowledge aspects inscribed upon them remain effective. In addition, new places for working are emerging (e.g., co-working spaces or the trend of workationing as described by Keita Matsushita).

This has consequences for the labour market. New markets (like the Chinese wanghong economy as focused on by Jian Lin) and global production networks are established based on the availability of infrastructure and workforce. These labour markets are less globalised than one might think, as language and cultural approaches still seem to be crucial. Moreover, some of the industries addressed have a geopolitical impact, as Brett Neilson and Ned Rossiter's example of data centres as critical infrastructure in a global competitive market indicates.

These spatial transformations also affect the boundaries between the private and the working space, as emphasised by Dominik Klaus and Jörg Flecker, Christian Oggolder as well as Calle Rosengren, Ann Bergman and Kristina Palm in their respective contributions. The contributions have also shown that "old" or traditional structures are retained in part, for example, as put forward by Christian Oggolder, when stating that the dissolving barriers between the home and work that we observe today were already a model of life in the early modern period.

Concerning the conceptual differentiation of place and space, as put forward in the Introduction, it has become increasingly apparent over the course of this volume that a strict separation cannot be maintained in all contexts. However, against the background of greater analytical acuity, we nonetheless plead for this differentiation to be taken seriously. It helps to describe relationships between people, organisations and technology as well as between structure and subjects. Consequently, *place* refers to a geographically localisable location, also in connection with work as a workplace (material equipment), whereas *space* is considered as a spatial reference level (independent of built space), including virtual spaces such as the information space respectively information spaces.

To sum up: Geographical places, workplaces and workspaces do not dissolve, but the relations among them are reconfigured through the information space.

3. "How are those who work located in the digitised world of work? What subjective capacities do they need to cope with these changing working conditions?"

The contributions demonstrate that the workers are of course located in a certain place, be it in a traditional office, at the kitchen table, at a desk in a co-working space or on vacation. Yet, they are also co-present in virtual spaces; even multiple spaces can be used simultaneously or in superimposition.

Regarding the subjective capacities, the contributions serve to manifest that boundary management is a central competency in digitised worlds of work, in order to cope with the blurring of private and professional life spheres due to the availability of digital media independently of time and space, and boundaryless work (as pointed out by Calle Rosengren, Ann Bergman and Kristina Palm as well as by Dominik Klaus and Jörg Flecker). Moreover, people engaged in digitised worlds of work may have to cope with insecure and precarious labour conditions, as stated by Anna Ozimek regarding digital game outsourcing and Jian Lin concerning China's wanghong economy as well as other examples of platform work or the workforce in data centres, as Brett Neilson and Ned Rossiter emphasised. Another field of activity for those working in these new topologies of work is the continuous emergence of new challenges. Whether it is keeping up with technical developments, identifying and acquiring necessary skills independently (how do I even shoot a wanghong video?), or organising and maintaining contact with colleagues and or customers. Providing visibility without having personal contact and making sure that one's professional development continues are further challenges that workers have to cope with.

Of course, this book cannot provide ready-made, all-encompassing answers, but has to be understood as an open panorama of the multiple facets of the relationship between work, space, place and digitalisation, that has to be constantly revised and complemented by further research.

One of the desiderata derived from this volume is the elaboration of a concept that refers to the power structures that are evident in the information space, taking into account new technological and social developments. Another major issue concerns the regulation of those new forms of work, described in this volume using the example of platform work and the wanghong industry. How can workers be protected, income secured and so forth? Is that even intended? How can occupational relationships and labour relations be organised in such distributed forms of organisation? And how can persisting hierarchies be overcome in order to create fairer chances for everyone participating in the global labour market? As a matter of fact, research will not provide prefabricated answers to these questions. In addition to science, the sphere of politics is called upon to construct framework conditions that are valid not merely for nations, but for the global labour market.

Acknowledgements The Authors acknowledge the financial support by the University of Klagenfurt.

Notes

1. Examples that are mentioned in press: Hewlett Packard, Oracle, Apple and Tesla: https://www.technologytimes.pk/2020/12/14/silicon-valley-loses-grip-on-tech-firms/. Accessed 23 Feb 2021.
2. The explanations here show that we are not dealing with a global market, but with linguistically delimited markets. This also has consequences for previous research on the platform economy, in which the English-speaking market is overrepresented (as Andrey Shevchuk, Denis Strebkov and Alexey Tyulyupo note).

References

Baukrowitz, A., & Boes, A. (1996). Arbeit in der "Informationsgesellschaft": Einige Überlegungen aus einer (fast schon) ungewohnten Perspektive. In R. Schmiede (Ed.), *Virtuelle Arbeitswelten. Arbeit, Produktion und Subjekt in der "Informationsgesellschaft"* (pp. 129–158). Edition sigma.

Boes, A., & Kämpf, T. (2007). The nexus of informatization and internationalisation—A new stage in the internationalisation of labour in globalised working environments. *Work Organisation, Labour and Globalisation, 1*(2), 193–208.

Boes, A., Kämpf, T., Langes, B., & Lühr, T. (2017). The disruptive power of digital transformation. In K. Briken, S., Chillas, M. Krzywdzinski, & A. Marks (Eds.), *The new digital workplace: How new technologies revolutionise work* (Critical perspective on work and employment, pp. 153–175). Palgrave Macmillan.

Brenneis, A., Honer, O., Keesser, S., Ripper, A., & Vetter-Schultheiß, S. (2018). Topologie der Technik: Manifestation eines interdisziplinären Forschungsprogramms. In A. Brenneis, O. Honer, S. Keesser, A. Ripper, & S. Vetter-Schultheiß (Eds.), *Technik – Macht – Raum: Das topologische Manifest im Kontext interdisziplinärer Studien* (pp. 1–35). Wiesbaden, DE: Springer VS.

Cairncross, F. (2001). *The death of distance: How the communications revolution is changing our lives.* HBS.

Castells, M. (1996). *The rise of the network society: The information age: Economy, Society, and Culture* (Vol. 1, 2nd ed.). Blackwell.

Castells, M. (2001). *The internet galaxy: Reflections on the internet, business, and society.* OUP.

Diehl, S., Karmasin, M., Leopold, A., & Koinig, I. (2013). New competencies for the future: How changes and trends in media convergence demand new skills from the workforce. In S. Diehl & M. Karmasin (Eds.), *Media and convergence management* (pp. 353–376). Springer.

Flecker, J. (Ed.). (2016). *Space, place and global digital work.* Palgrave Macmillan.

Fried, M. (1963). Grieving for a lost home. In L. J. Duhl (Ed.), *The urban condition—People and policy in the metropolis* (pp. 151–171). Basic Books.

Friedman, T. L. (2007). *The world is flat 3.0: A brief history of the twenty-first century.* Picador.

Gibson, W. (1984). *Neuromancer*. Ace.
Gibson, W. (1989). High tech high life: William Gibson & Timothy Leary in conversation/Interviewer: T. Leary. Mondo 2000. https://www.mondo2 000.com/2017/11/29/high-tech-high-life-william-gibson-timothy-leary-con versation-1989/. Accessed 23 February 2021.
Huws, U. (2003). *The making of a cybertariat: Virtual work in a real world*. Monthly Review.
Huws, U., & Dahlmann, S. (2010). Global restructuring of value chains and class issues. In N. J. Pupo, & M. P. Thomas (Eds.), *Interrogating the new economy: Restructuring work in the 21st century* (pp. 65–92). UTP.
Koslowski, N. C. (2016). 'My company is invisible'—Generating trust in the context of placelessness, precarity and invisibility in virtual work. In J. Flecker (Ed.), *Space, place and global digital work* (pp. 171–199). Palgrave Macmillan.
Krotz, F. (2007). *Mediatisierung: Fallstudien zum Wandel von Kommunikation*. VS Verlag für Sozialwissenschaften.
Lefebvre, H. (1974). *La production de l'espace*. Paris, F: Anthropos. English edition: Lefebvre, H. (1991). *The production of space*, translated by D. Nicholson-Smith. Blackwell.
Lehdonvirta, V. (2016). Algorithms that divide and unite: Delocalisation, identity and collective action in 'microwork.' In J. Flecker (Ed.), *Space, place and global digital work* (pp. 53–80). Palgrave Macmillan.
Lehdonvirta, V. (2017). Where are online workers located? The international division of digital gig work. Oxford Internet Institute. https://ilabour.oii. ox.ac.uk/where-are-online-workers-located-the-international-division-of-dig ital-gig-work/. Accessed 23 Feb 2021.
Lehdonvirta, V., Kässi, O., Hjorth, I., Barnard, H., & Graham, M. (2019). The global platform economy: A new offshoring institution enabling emerging-economy microproviders. *Journal of Management, 45*, 567–599. https://doi. org/10.1177/0149206318786781
Massey, D. (2005). *For space*. Sage.
Matuschek, I., Kleemann, F., & Voß, G. G. (2003). Neue Medien – Neue Arbeit? Informatisierung der Arbeit und personale Stile medienvermittelten Arbeitens. In E. Keitel, K. Boehnke, & K. Wenz (Eds.), *Neue Medien im Alltag: Nutzung, Vernetzung, Interaktion* (Vol. 3, pp. 138–157). Pabst Science.
Meil, P., & Kirov, V. (Eds.). (2017). *Policy implications of virtual work*. Palgrave Macmillan.

Noronha, E., & D'Cruz, P. (2016). Creating space: The role of the state in the Indian IT-related offshoring sector. In J. Flecker (Ed.), *Space, place and global digital work* (pp. 151–168). Palgrave Macmillan.

Roberts, S. (2019). *Behind the screen: Content moderation in the shadows of social media*. YUP.

Roth-Ebner, C. (2016). Spatial phenomena of mediatised work. In J. Flecker (Ed.), *Space, place and global digital work* (pp. 227–245). Palgrave Macmillan.

Roth-Ebner, C. (in press). Work in transition: Digital media and its transformative potential for work. In M. Karmasin, S. Diehl, & I. Koinig (Eds.), *Creating a path for new content formats, business models, consumer roles, and business responsibility*. Springer.

Schmiede, R. (2006). Knowledge, work and subject in informational capitalism. In J. Berleur, M. I. Nurminen, & J. Impagliazzo (Eds.), *Social informatics: An information society for all? In remembrance of Rob Kling: Proceedings of the Seventh International Conference Human Choice and Computers (HCC7), IFIP TC 9, Maribor, Slovenia, September 21–23* (pp. 333–354). Springer Science and Business Media.

Will-Zocholl, M., Flecker, J., & Schörpf, P. (2019). Zur realen Virtualität von Arbeit: Raumbezüge digitalisierter Wissensarbeit. *AIS-Studien, 12*(1), 36–54.

Wolff, S. (2016). Local development policies, the labour market and the dynamics of virtual value chains: The case of the IT sector in the municipality of Londrina, Brazil. In J. Flecker (Ed.), *Space, place and global digital work* (pp. 127–149). Palgrave Macmillan.

Open Access This chapter is licensed under the terms of the Creative Commons Attribution 4.0 International License (http://creativecommons.org/licenses/by/4.0/), which permits use, sharing, adaptation, distribution and reproduction in any medium or format, as long as you give appropriate credit to the original author(s) and the source, provide a link to the Creative Commons license and indicate if changes were made.

The images or other third party material in this chapter are included in the chapter's Creative Commons license, unless indicated otherwise in a credit line to the material. If material is not included in the chapter's Creative Commons license and your intended use is not permitted by statutory regulation or exceeds the permitted use, you will need to obtain permission directly from the copyright holder.

Index

A
adaptability to virtual work 236
Amazon 92
artificial intelligence 77
assistance 211
automation 78
availability 174, 211

B
better self 139, 143
blurring of boundaries 197
borders 88
boundary control 175
boundary management 189, 203
boundary theory 175
boundary work 175
business competitiveness 226
business consulting 207

C
capitalist world system 88
CEE region 53
China 92
city(ies) 108–113, 115
clients 66
communities of style 150, 156, 166
Covid-19 5
Covid-19 crisis 241
creative workforce 52
creator 122, 123, 125, 128–138, 141–144
crowd work 20

D
data sovereignty 95
decentralised production networks 54
delocalisation 165

delocalisation/localisation 164
deofficisation 165
deofficisation/officisation 164
deterritorialise 142, 143
digital 106, 113, 114
digital games industry 54
digitalisation 3, 23, 105, 108, 111, 113–115, 173
digital labour 20
digital labour platforms 20
digitally 115
digital media 2
digital nomads 212
digital traces 28
digitised work 3
domestic sphere. 184
Douyin 121, 131, 132, 140, 141
Douyin (Chinese version of TikTok) 127

E

early modern period 107–109
Eastern European 68
employee well-being 175
environmental psychology 228
experience of work 198
extraction 79

F

face-to-face communications 228
flexibility through empowerment 198
flexible contracts 66
freelancers 20
fully mobile 233

G

geopolitics 79
gig economy 20
globalisation 23
Google 92

H

historical 105, 106
history 106, 109, 112
home office 232
homework 114, 115
homeworkers 233
hotelling virtual arrangement 233
house 108–111, 115, 116
hybrid companies 69

I

ICT boundary work 175
ICT-enabled telework 204
identity work 198
indirect control 209
information and communication technologies (ICTs) 2, 56, 173, 197, 231
information space 4
informatisation 3
infrastructure 79
integration 176
intermediate places 202
Internet 105, 112, 113
Internet + 125, 126
Internet of Things (IoT) 229

K

Kuaishou 126, 127, 131, 135–137, 139–141

Index

L
labour 79, 122–124, 129, 132, 137, 139–141, 143
labour agency 198
labour relations 134
leisure 105, 113, 115
livestream 141
livestreaming 121, 126, 128, 131, 132, 136–138, 140
localisation 165
lockdown 241
logistics 80

M
machine learning 77
mass entrepreneurship 125, 126
meaningful work 201
media 79
mediaspaces 123
mediatisation 3
Microsoft 92
mobile office 232
modern 105, 106, 109, 111, 112
modernity 106, 108, 113

N
networks 108, 112–114
new ways of working 226

O
occupancy costs 226
occupations 200
officisation 152, 165
offshoring 20
on-demand work 20
online labour markets 20
Organisational Crisis Management Plan 240
organisational membership 200
outsourcing 20, 52

P
permeability 189
perpetually under construction 160
physical workplace 228
places 4
places of work 108, 109, 111, 113, 114, 116
platform 121–124, 126–137, 140–143
platformisation 125
Poland and Estonia 53
political economy 123, 129
poverty alleviation 123, 128
practice-based approach 175
premodern 106, 109, 112, 115
presenteeism 210
private 105, 111–113, 116
public 105, 111, 113, 116

Q
qualitative methodology 180
quality assurance 66

R
remote work 19
robotics 77

S
sedentarisation 177
segmentation 176

self-employment 214
service providers 65
short video 126, 127, 131, 132, 135, 136
Singapore 92
social facilitation theory 230
social interaction 201
social media entertainment 121, 124, 130, 134
society(ies) 107, 108, 110–112, 114
sociomaterial practice 175
space 1, 105, 111–114, 128, 129, 133, 135–138, 142, 143
space of flows 124, 141, 143
space of places 142, 143
spatial division of labour 9, 20
spatialisation 55
spatial relations 8
spatial relationships 142
spatial turn 1, 13, 263
standards 79
stress 178
style-based workplaces 164
subcontracted work 69
subjectivation of work 206

tamatama 160
telecommuting 233
telework 19
teleworking 226, 232
territorialise 141
territory 79
theory of place attachment 230
time diary method 181
topologies 2

trust 238

United States (US) 92, 95
unlikely creativity 139, 144
urban 105, 107, 110–113
urban societies 107
use of technology 192

vernacular creativity 141
virtual 105, 113
virtualisation 3
virtual migration 20
virtual office 226, 232
virtual spaces 202
virtual teams 237
virtual work 4, 19
virtual work arrangements 233
vlogging 131

wanghong 121–125, 128–139, 141–143
wanghong culture 123, 128, 129, 139, 140, 142–144
wanghong economy 122–124, 128, 129, 133–135, 139–143
wanghong industry 123–125, 127, 129, 134, 142, 143
wazawaza 160
workation 160, 163, 165
workationing 149, 161
work experience 215

working 129
work–life balance 174, 178
workplace attachment 231
workplaces 106, 109, 111, 113–115

work-related identities 199
workspace awareness 229
workstyle reform 160

Printed in the United States
by Baker & Taylor Publisher Services